Women Aren't Supposed to Fly

Women Aren't Supposed to Fly

to Fly

✦

The Memoirs of a Female Flight Surgeon

Harriet A. Hall, MD

iUniverse, Inc.
New York Lincoln Shanghai

Women Aren't Supposed to Fly
The Memoirs of a Female Flight Surgeon

iUniverse books may be ordered through booksellers or by contacting:

iUniverse
2021 Pine Lake Road, Suite 100
Lincoln, NE 68512
www.iuniverse.com
1-800-Authors (1-800-288-4677)

Because of the dynamic nature of the Internet, any Web addresses or links contained in this book may have changed since publication and may no longer be valid.

The views expressed in this work are solely those of the author and do not necessarily reflect the views of the publisher, and the publisher hereby disclaims any responsibility for them.

Everything in this book is true as I remember it. Memory is fallible, so no guarantees. Some names were changed to disguise the guilty.

ISBN: 978-0-595-49958-8 (pbk)
ISBN: 978-0-595-61320-5 (ebk)

Printed in the United States of America

Contents

A Note on the Language ix

Preface xi

CHAPTER 1   Growing Up and Deciding What to Be 1

- *A Plain Vanilla Childhood* *1*
- *My Father* *6*
- *My Ancestors* *8*
- *Is Heredity Important?* *11*

CHAPTER 2   College 13

- *Pre-Med* *13*
- *Junior Year in Spain* *15*
- *Back in Seattle* *20*

CHAPTER 3   Medical School 21

- *First Year Med Student* *22*
- *On the Wards* *26*
- *Internal Medicine* *27*
- *Pediatrics* *28*
- *Radiology—In the Shadows* *30*
- *The County Hospital* *31*
- *Miscellaneous Medical Aberrations* *35*
- *Marriage* *37*
- *Vacation* *42*

CHAPTER 4   Internship 46

- *Orientation* *46*
- *Call Rooms* *48*

- *Yes, I Really Am a Doctor* *49*
- *Emergency Room Duty* *50*
- *On the Wards*. *53*
- *Z Service* *56*
- *Husbands Can't Be Dependents*. *57*
- *Nursing Notes*. *59*
- *Surgery*. *61*
- *Little Old Lady with Jokes*. *64*
- *Women Aren't Retainable* *65*

CHAPTER 5   A General Medical Officer in Spain *67*
- *The Base at Morón*. *70*
- *A Villa in Spain*. *71*
- *Spanish Telephones*. *73*
- *Seeing Patients* *74*
- *Base Housing* *78*
- *No More Dispensary*. *79*
- *Watergate*. *83*
- *A Digression on Food* *84*
- *IG Inspection* *86*
- *Human Relations* *87*
- *Drugs*. *89*
- *The Attractions of Seville*. *91*
- *My Staff*. *92*
- *Cultural Differences* *94*
- *Wiesbaden* *95*
- *More Money!* *95*

CHAPTER 6   Torrejón—Working in a Hospital Again *97*
- *Living in Madrid* *98*
- *Emergency Room Antics*. *99*
- *ATH—6 Tents, 4 Days* *101*
- *Disaster Exercises* *103*
- *Plane Crash* *105*

- *Dr. Muddle* *107*
- *Miscellaneous Annoyances* *108*
- *Spanish Medicine* *110*
- *TDYs to Zaragoza, the Netherlands, and Lisbon* *113*
- *Aerobics Testing* *115*
- *Dermatology and Other Specialties* *116*
- *The End of an Era* *121*

CHAPTER 7 Family Practice Residency/Learning to Fly *123*
- *Playing Stork* *125*
- *My First Vasectomy and Other Memorable Patients* *127*
- *Who's Nuts?* *128*
- *Working Conditions* *131*
- *Misunderstandings* *133*
- *Learning to Fly* *134*
- *Divorce and a Vacation in Alaska* *140*
- *Graduation* *141*

CHAPTER 8 Flight Surgeon Training *143*
- *Ducks, Owls and Crispy Critters* *144*
- *Survival Training* *145*
- *Weekend Adventures* *146*
- *Off to Work We Go* *146*

CHAPTER 9 Flight Surgeon at a Missile Base *148*
- *Helicopters* *150*
- *Launch Control Facility Visit* *152*
- *Flight Physicals and Shop Visits* *155*
- *Bringing Family Practice to the Flight Surgeon's Office* *157*
- *OB* *158*
- *Supplanted by Dr. Quack* *160*
- *Dr Mushroom* *163*
- *Mushing, MASHing, and Miscellaneous Memories* *164*
- *Flying High* *167*

- *Marriage—Better the Second Time Around* 169
- *Guns* 172
- *Pregnant!* 173
- *Combat Casualty Care Course* 176
- *ER Patients* 177
- *An Unwelcome Transfer* 179

CHAPTER 10   Plattsburgh, New York 181
- *Living in Peru* 182
- *Promotion to Colonel* 183
- *OERs* 185
- *Baby Stuff* 189
- *Back on Flying Status* 191
- *Male Strippers and All-Female Ambulances* 194
- *ER* 195
- *We Call It the Box Office* 198
- *Home Sweet Tent* 199

CHAPTER 11   Chief of Clinic Services 201
- *Administrative Duties* 203
- *The Fat Boy Program* 205
- *Cholesterol, Smoking, Alcohol, and AIDS* 206
- *An Eagle with a Warped Sense of Humor* 208
- *I'm a Mommy, Too* 209

CHAPTER 12   Retirement 211

APPENDIX A   Little Old Lady's One-Liners 215

APPENDIX B   Captions without Cartoons 219

A Note on the Language

I have chosen not to use politically correct pronouns. I was educated before political correctness infected our language. When I read "One small step for man" I hear "mankind" and I know half of mankind is female. When I read "A doctor is responsible for his patients" I know "his" refers to both his and hers. I give my readers some credit: I trust them to remember that some of us are women without having to be constantly reminded. I knew political correctness had gone too far when a letter I wrote to a missile squadron was kicked back because I used the word "he." All our missile officers were in fact men, and at the time it was impossible for a woman to be a missile officer; so "he" was precisely and unassailably correct, but they wouldn't let me use it! Enough is enough!

I also refuse to bowdlerize or euphemize. If you don't like it, hide the book from the kids.

Preface

It was "a dark and stormy night" somewhere, but a sunny Saturday morning in the Florida Panhandle where I was. I had been taking flying lessons and I was on my first cross-country solo flight. I did everything right. I navigated precisely, found my destination airport, made the appropriate radio calls, landed smoothly, taxied in, and parked the plane. Feeling rather proud of myself, I walked over to the flight service station to close out my flight plan. The man behind the counter leaned forward, narrowed his eyes, glared at me, and barked, "Didn't anybody ever tell you women aren't supposed to fly?"

That was the story of my life. I would blithely accomplish something in pursuit of my goals, I would be flying high, and someone would abruptly jerk me back down to earth by reminding me that I was defective. Just because I lacked certain dangly bits between my legs.

I was born in 1945, before Women's Lib, before integration, before legal abortion, before effective birth control, before Gay Rights, before equal opportunity, and before affirmative action. As the cigarette commercial said, "You've come a long way, baby!" It's easy to forget how much the world changed during the second half of the 20th century. When I was young, there were very few women doctors, few women in the military, few women pilots, and even fewer women flight surgeons. I was one of the few.

I stuck out like a kitten in a litter of warthogs. The only way to survive was to have a tough skin, wear blinders, fight my way to a teat at the milk bar, and hold on for dear life.

I wished just once someone would judge me on my performance rather than on my testosterone level. I wondered how different my life might have been if I'd gone to Denmark like Christine Jorgenson. What if I had bound my breasts flat, stuffed a jock strap with two rubber balls and a sausage, gotten a crew cut and changed my name from Harriet to Harry? Life would surely have been easier. But why should I have to go through contortions like that just to be accepted? Life wasn't fair.

There's an old curse "may you live in interesting times." I lived in an era when society was starting to *allow* women to enter male-dominated fields, but didn't yet entirely *approve*. Someone said, "Whatever women do they must do twice as well as men to be thought half as good. Luckily this is not difficult." Actually it was difficult. It was frequently frustrating, sometimes painful, often ridiculously funny, and always interesting. Come with me on a ramble through my education and career and let me tell you what it was like.

1

Growing Up and Deciding What to Be

o o o o o o o o o o o o o o o o o o o o o o o o o o o o o o o o o o
I didn't raise my daughter to be a soldier.

—my father, Albert L. Hoag

Here's where I'm supposed to tell you about my family background and my childhood so you can speculate about why I turned out the way I did—so you can decide whether you want to blame heredity, environment, or alien abduction. I'm afraid I can't give you many clues.

A PLAIN VANILLA CHILDHOOD

I had a plain vanilla childhood in Seattle, Washington. Middle class, secure, conventional, uneventful. Dad taught engineering at the University of Washington, Mom was a traditional stay-at-home housewife who told us to "Eat everything on your plate because there are starving children in Africa." I suppose you could hypothesize something stimulating in the water in our View Ridge neighborhood, since Bill Gates grew up just over the hill (my mother knew his mother and he went to the same grade school I did), and our paperboy grew up to be Washington State Governor.

I was the oldest of four children; so if you want, you can try to apply some of those theories about firstborns. I was supposed to be a boy named Steven Michael, but the name had to wait until my brother was born. Instead, I was named Harriet Anne Hoag (which made my initials a laugh). I was named after Harriet Beecher Stowe, who was a distant relative by marriage. Actually my father used to insist I was named after George Washington—about two centuries after![1] Twins were born 7 years after me (a boy and a girl, Steven Michael and Stephanie Michelle) and my youngest sister Andrea came along 5 years later. My parents had a solid marriage; they claimed that their secret was an agreement that whoever filed for divorce had to take the kids.

My earliest ambition was to be a cowgirl like Day Levens—you remember, Roy Rogers' sidekick?[2] Well, that's the way her name sounded to me at age 6, anyway. Having no access whatsoever to horses, cows, six-shooters, or rustlers in black hats, I soon gave up that plan as a bad idea.

An Early Career Plan Was Discarded. Harriet, age 6, wearing her Day Levens outfit, with Billy the Kid. Really: he was a kid from the neighborhood and his name was Billy.

For a long time, I assumed I would be a housewife and mother. In the 6th grade I went to a party where you were supposed to dress as what you wanted to be when

1.   Some people don't get this joke—my own daughter didn't—so I'd better explain. George Washington was born (and named) in 1732. I was born and named in 1945. 1945 is after 1732. I was named after George Washington was named.
2.   In case you're too young to remember, Roy Rogers' wife was Dale Evans.

you grew up. I went as a farmer's wife. My highest ambition was to can things, sew, weed the garden, wipe runny noses, and put hot meals on the table for an appreciative, ruggedly handsome superior male being, my H*U*S*B*A*N*D. Cultural brainwashing had kicked in.

I read about the discovery of King Tut's tomb and for a while I thought it would be great fun to be an archaeologist and work outdoors in exotic places and get dirty and do strong, heroic things. Then a junior high school science teacher turned me on to physics; he made it sound fascinating to study how the world works. But as I progressed into high school, I noticed that whenever I opened a magazine, I would automatically turn to the articles on medicine and read them first. Then I read about Dr. Tom Dooley saving lives in Southeast Asia, and I was hooked. It was going to be medicine for me.

Maybe part of the reason I was interested in medicine was to master my fear of blood and emergencies. I used to be squeamish. When I skinned my knee I wanted to keep it entirely covered up until it healed. I didn't like the look of it, and I thought if a watched pot doesn't boil, a watched wound might not heal. When my sister cut the tip of her finger off in a door hinge, my mother left me holding pressure on the wound with a washcloth over the sink while she called the doctor, and I was shaking like Don Knotts on caffeine. I used to flinch when my orthodontist just started walking across the room towards me. He said that doctors usually don't make good patients, and if that was any indication, I ought to make a really good doctor!

My mother had trained as a nurse and a medical records librarian but stopped working before I was born and never held another job. Part of my brain assumed I would be a traditional housewife and mother like her; but another part of my brain (Lord knows how!) developed the confidence that I could be anything I wanted to be. It never occurred to me that certain things might be harder for a girl. Once I decided on medicine, I don't remember having the slightest doubt that I *could* and *would* succeed. Take your pick: stubbornness or lack of contact with reality.

I was intelligent, but I wasn't very smart. I came home from kindergarten and told my Mom the Penguins invented Thanksgiving. When a man told me to get lost, I very seriously informed him that my Mommy wouldn't like it if I got lost. I thought you got pregnant by taking a pill. I thought Kotex pads were big Band-Aids. I learned that it was safe to cross when the light was green, but I didn't understand that cars were supposed to stop when they could see a red light from their direction. The first time I tried to cross the street on my own, I could see two sides of the traffic light and I couldn't figure out which one was supposed to be green and I almost got run over.

When I was 7 I had a bad case of scarlet fever and missed a couple of weeks of school. My mother was afraid it would put me behind; but instead they promoted me from 2nd to 3rd grade in mid-year. The first day in the 3rd grade, the boy behind me made fun of me for not knowing how to write in cursive yet. You would think I would realize I must have been intelligent to skip a grade, but instead I got the idea that I was barely competent. In junior high, I was among those selected for honors classes, which was my first inkling that I might have a brain. On a math achievement test at the beginning of the 7th grade I scored average for my grade level. A really mean teacher in our honors class made us write out the multiplication tables over and over until they were engraved in our memory, and apparently that made a difference, because by the next year I scored the second highest in the whole school.

I must have been a strange duck—intellectually advanced and socially retarded. I didn't date in high school. It wasn't that I didn't find boys attractive; it was just that the particular specimens I met didn't measure up to my idea of masculine perfection. The cute ones were dumb and the smart ones were underdeveloped nerds. The most intelligent ones hadn't gone through puberty yet. I could wait for a wider selection at college; after all, I was still only 16 when I graduated. My girlfriends would prattle on about which boy looked at them and who said what to whom, but all I cared about was reading everything I could get my hands on, from Shakespeare to the backs of cereal boxes. I practically inhaled anything in print. One day I started reading the book *1984* by George Orwell in the morning. I read between classes, during classes, during lunch and during study hall, and finished it on the bus on the way home that afternoon.

I started taking Spanish in the 7th grade because that was the only language offered. My first Spanish teacher had a Southern accent (hasta luego, y'all), but then I got a real Mexican teacher whose name (we all had to memorize it) was Señor San Luís Gonzaga de los Tres Reyes Valadez de Uranga. He let us talk in class as much as we wanted as long as it was in Spanish; so of course the smart-ass boys took advantage by saying-o stuff-o like-o this-o. One day he told us a ghost story in Spanish, a long yarn involving himself, Frankenstein and Dracula. He had pulled down all the shades and turned the lights off and was stalking between the desks making scary sounds when a messenger from the office walked in. The messenger's reaction was *muy interesante*.

When other languages were offered in the 9th grade, I decided I might as well learn one language well, so I stuck with Spanish and took it through most of high school. I got so advanced there wasn't a class for me, so I got to sit in with a lower level class and read independently and give reports to them. I loved Spanish because it was like a secret code—I could talk with other Spanish students on the telephone and in front of people who couldn't understand us. I remember standing in line at the public pool one day with my girlfriend and insulting all the boys in sight (Isn't he ugly? Gee that one looks stupid!).

A girlfriend took Latin and kept telling me I should study Latin because it was so important in English vocabulary and I would need it for medical school. One day she asked me what a word meant and I said I didn't know, but it sounded like it came from the Latin roots for ___ and ___ so I would guess it meant _____. We looked it up, and I was right. She hadn't learned those words in Latin yet, but I had picked them up from my English vocabulary. After that, she stopped nagging me about studying Latin.

Most students who know they are headed to medical school take biology in high school. I had the opposite idea. I knew I would learn enough biology later, so instead I took extra physics, chemistry, and a statistics and probability class. The statistics and probability teacher gave us a take-home open-book exam with hints, and I could tell from one hint that he had misunderstood how to solve the problem. I explained it to him, had some trouble convincing him I was right, and then the next day he announced to the class, "*I* have noticed that the hint in problem 5 was printed incorrectly. Please change it to read...." He took all the credit. I lost any respect I had for him right then and there.

Most of my high school teachers were excellent. We had honors classes, and they pushed us to excel. My Contemporary Problems teacher once gave me what he called "a stinging B" for a mid-term grade: he explained that I had done "A level" work, but he knew I hadn't done the best I was capable of. I worked harder for the rest of the semester and got a well-deserved A. My Senior Reading class was more challenging than my freshman Honors English class in college would be the following year. We read as many books as possible outside class, kept a list categorizing them by subject, took notes on what we read, collected quotations, and had to present an extensive notebook for periodic review. They taught us to analyze and question what we read. We did creative things like writing parodies of famous authors. One boy wrote this parody of Ogden Nash: "Ish squish. I hate Ogden Nish."

I knew you were supposed to join things and do extracurricular activities to look good for college applications, but I hated that kind of thing. I figured the University of Washington would accept me anyway, and I'd much rather spend most of my spare time reading. I belonged briefly to a couple of clubs, but didn't enjoy them.

As for athletics, my only claim to fame was that I was on an undefeated football team. I must explain. Some of the boys met with a few of us girls in a neighborhood park and taught us the rudiments of flag football. We set up a match with another girls' team, and they didn't show up, so we won by default. About that time, the school administration discovered what we'd been doing and put an abrupt stop to it. Football is too dangerous for girls, you see. Remember, this was 1962. We had to wear skirts to school and were supposed to be delicate flowers. Hah!

Grades were harder to come by in 1962. Only three of us graduated with a 4.0 average—straight A's—out of a graduating class of nearly 800. One was a girl who was one of my best friends, and the other was a boy who had also skipped a grade; he signed my yearbook saying he hated me because I was the only one he couldn't beat. I wasn't valedictorian though. Heck, I don't even know if there *was* a valedictorian! I didn't even go to my graduation. We were out of town on a family trip at the time, and I was glad of the excuse not to go, because I always hated silly formal ceremonies. I didn't want to go to my college graduation either, because it was only a stepping stone on my path to an MD, but my grandmother came all the way from New York to see me graduate so my mother made me go.

MY FATHER

Grandmother had come to Seattle when my father graduated, too. She had no trouble spotting him in the crowd, because he was the only one with white buck shoes under his black academic robes. Dad ended up at the University of Washington because he couldn't swim. He had started out at Syracuse studying forestry, but in order to graduate from Syracuse, forestry students had to spend a summer at a forestry camp, and to get to camp you had to travel by canoe, and before you could get in the canoe you had to pass a swimming test. Dad was tall and skinny, and his body density was such that he didn't float. No one could teach him to swim. One instructor was convinced that everyone floats. He told my Dad exactly what to do to float; Dad followed his instructions to the letter. He slowly sank to the bottom of the pool. After a while, he let out a little air. After a while, he let out a little more air. When he had emptied his lungs, he stood up to get another lungful—just in time to see the instructor diving in fully clothed to save his life. That was the end of his swimming instruction. So he ended up at the University of Washington studying engineering.

One of Dad's college classes was a Qualitative Analysis lab. The final exam consisted of identifying 5 unknowns. They gave him the first unknown. It looked like salt. It had an orange flame in the Bunsen burner like salt should. He took a chance and tasted it. It tasted like salt. He wrote down "sodium chloride" and went to the stockroom for unknown number two. The stockroom guy wasn't expecting anyone to finish so quickly, and he hadn't made up unknown number two yet. Dad, who had better than 20/20 vision, stood at the stockroom door and read the label on the stock bottle as the clerk took it down from the shelf. He went back to his desk and wrote down what the label said. He repeated the process for unknowns 3 through 5. He gathered his belongings and started out the door. The professor stopped him, "Where do you think you're going?" He said he thought he would go study for his next final. The professor said he had to finish this final first. Dad said he was finished. The professor checked his answers, which were all correct, and had to let him go. He had done exactly what the exam required: he had *identified* the unknowns.

At least Dad wasn't as dangerous in a chemistry lab as my grandfather. HE created nitroglycerine in a beaker in a high school chemistry lab and managed to explode it straight up and destroy a skylight—without even breaking the beaker!

With the influx of GI Bill students after WWII, the University of Washington was desperate for instructors, and my father was hired as a professor with only a bachelor's degree. For many years, he taught General Engineering classes, and even co-authored two textbooks, one on Descriptive Geometry. I got to type the manuscript when I was in high school. That was before computers, so you had to do three copies with carbon paper, and you had to correct the mistakes on all three copies with little strips of white correction paper. It was tedious and demanding, but it made an accurate typist of me, and it taught me how to spell words like "hyperbolic paraboloid"—whatever that is! I had taught myself to touch-type from a book when I was 13. I never did learn to touch-type the numbers ... but just last year I met a woman who resolved any guilt I might have felt about that. She had spent her whole career teaching typing in high school and she told me she had never learned the numbers either!

Towards the end of his career, Dad finally took a sabbatical year and went to Stanford to get a Master's in Construction Engineering. He bought one of very first Hewlett-Packard hand-held calculators at a cost of $400. Nobody else had one yet. In his classes at Stanford, the instructor would put a problem on the board, and the rest of the class would work along on their "slip sticks" (slide rules) and come up with an answer not quite accurate to 3 places. They would say, "The answer is 3.42 or 3.43" and then Dad would amaze them by saying, "The answer is approximately 3.426930695." With his new MS degree, he eventually supervised graduate students in the Civil Engineering department. He was a natural teacher, who used to help me with my math homework by asking *me* questions until I figured it out for myself.

My father loved to tease, and admired my new hair style with bangs because "it covered up part of my face." He said it was a good thing I chose medicine, because I didn't have enough common sense to be an engineer. Whenever I told him I had changed my mind about something, he said if he had a mind like mine he would change it too.

Once after church, a lady complimented Dad because she had seen my name in the paper for some scholastic achievement. He told her he didn't deserve any of the credit, because I was the one who did all the work. She insisted that he deserved credit because I got my brains from him. He said, "Oh, no! She didn't get her brains from me; she got them from her mother." The lady was amazed, and called some of her friends over. "Listen to this! Listen to the modesty of this man! Say it again, Al." He complied. "She didn't get her brains from me; she got them from her mother. She must have, because I still *have* mine!"

MY ANCESTORS

My mother grew up on a tobacco farm in Coats, North Carolina, my father on a dairy farm in Poughquag, New York. Mom claims she never knew "damn" and "Yankee" were separate words until she met my father. I don't know much about my mother's family, but my father's family included some unique specimens.

Dad was the third of six children; his mother taught in a one-room school. The old part of the house they lived in was stone, dating back to the late 1700s; the new part dated to the 1850s. My family moved there when my great grandfather was a teenage boy. He had to make 18 trips of 18 miles walking with an oxcart during the move, and he decided that was quite enough moving for a lifetime and he was never going to move again. He never did. When they moved in, the house featured a huge, ugly stone fireplace that sloped several ways at once, and eventually it was covered up and wallpapered over as an eyesore. My great grandfather protested that the best meal he ever ate was cooked on that fireplace the day they moved in; it tasted good because he was so tired of walking.

He married late in life; he had been courting for a while and decided it was easier to get married than to spend another winter walking up that hill to his sweetheart's house. They had two daughters, and when the older daughter, my grandmother, married, he gave the house and farm to her and her husband with the provision that they take care of him in his old age. Of all my ancestors, he is the one I would most like to have known. He was a philosopher who asked questions like, "Is the anticipation better than the event itself?" He never got angry or upset: he said it wasn't worth the trouble, because you just had to get over it. He would refuse second helpings, saying, "I ate too much once, and I was mighty uncomfortable for a couple of hours, so I don't think I'll do that again." He was patient with his grandchildren and would tell them stories and entertain them as a sort of live-in babysitter. My father especially remembered a song he used to sing them. The chorus went:

> Boys I say from the girls keep away
> Give them lots of room
> When you're wed they will hit you on the head
> With the bald-headed end of the broom.

Although Dad "sang" this song for me several times, I still don't know the tune. He claimed he could only recognize two songs: one was the "Star Spangled Banner" and the other wasn't, and he could only tell which was which because people stood up for the first one. His musical ability ranked less than 0 on a scale of 10; and yet his youngest child is now a professional musician and Grammy nominee. Heredity obviously isn't everything!

In his old age, my great grandfather was practically blind, but still worked in his woodshop by feel. One day he needed a saw sharpened, and asked my grandmother to do it. She didn't know how, but he told her she wasn't going to learn any younger and explained the procedure to her. It worked. The kids grew up with the idea that they could learn to do anything. They spent alternate weeks helping their mother in the house and their father on the farm. They made everything from hay to maple sugar. When one of my uncles was away at college and needed a pair of socks, he managed to knit himself a pair using pencils for knitting needles.

One day in his old age, my great grandfather happened to go into the barn where his grandsons were playing basketball. They tossed him the ball as a joke, knowing he couldn't even see the far wall of the barn, much less the basket; but he threw it and it went right through the hoop! They were all excited and wanted him to try again, but he said, "Nope. Don't want to break a perfect record."

He lived well into his 90s, leading my father to develop a theory that his longevity might be attributed to his laid-back personality. Then Dad's own father, my grandfather, lived into his 90s too. I'll be polite and just say my grandfather's personality was quite the opposite of my great-grandfather's. Another theory down the drain!

Big Ben. The author with her grandmother and aunt, holding Benjamin Hoag's dress shirt

Another ancestor I would have liked to meet was Benjamin Hoag, born in 1751. There was an old handmade shirt in Grandmother's attic that had belonged to him, and my 6'2" father could barely reach the top of the cuffs with his fingertips. Ben was a *big* man.

One Sunday he went to a new church. Everywhere he tried to sit down, they told him he couldn't sit there because it was someone else's family pew. So he went out of the church, found the biggest rock he could lift, brought it into the church, plunked it down in the aisle, and sat on it, declaring "*This* is *Ben Hoag's* pew!" It took four strong men to remove the stone after the service.

My grandmother used to point to a little room next to the kitchen, now a sewing room, formerly the "birthing and dying" room, and tell us, "I was born in that room. My mother was born in that room. My grandmother died in that room. My mother died in that room...." She spent her whole life in the same house and she died there too, although in a different room. Once when she and my grandfather flew out to Seattle to visit us, they couldn't find the key to the front door because it had been decades since anyone had thought of trying to lock it. The mailman would walk right in, drop the mail on the kitchen table, and help himself to a cup of coffee. (The mailman was my uncle).

Grandmother's house was fascinating to me. No one ever threw anything away. It was like a museum, with everything a working farm of the late 1800s would have had. There were spinning wheels and a side saddle up attic, a one-horse open sleigh stored in the rafters of the horse barn, candle frames, bullet molds, feather beds, a military uniform from the War of 1812, old raccoon coats, linen dusters from the early days of automobiles, a straitjacket, chamber pots, several sets of old china, and just about everything else you can think of plus a few you can't. I was most attracted to the books, some dating back to when the s's were printed like f's. One old Bible had what looked like a pencil rubbing of a coin on the flyleaf; I was puzzled because it said one cent but was far too big to be a penny. My grandmother promptly went into her bedroom and came back with an old US penny that was identical to the rubbing.

Is Heredity Important?

Was there anything in my heredity that pointed me towards a career in Air Force medicine? There were no role models in my family for postgraduate education, medicine, flying or military service (beyond the draft). In fact, my father's family had pacifist Quaker roots which one of my uncles used to claim conscientious objector status.

There were plenty of independent, capable people on both sides of the family. There were some stubborn ones, too. One elderly female didn't like sardines and wouldn't eat them. She came into the kitchen once when my grandmother was frying some fresh sardines. She said they smelled good. She ate some, enjoyed them, and then asked, "Mary, what kind of fish were those?" My grandmother said, "Sardines." She retorted, "No they weren't; *I don't eat sardines.*" I think she was the same one who was convinced that hot water would freeze faster than cold water.

On a darker note, there were two suicides and a schizophrenic in my mother's immediate family. And someone in my father's family had required the straitjacket they still kept in the attic. Come to think of it, maybe my career choice was a manifestation of mental illness! When people asked me why I went into medicine or the Air Force, I used to answer, "Temporary insanity."

2

College

If you think you can do a thing or think you can't do a thing, in either case you are right.

—*Henry Ford*

Besides my straight-A grades, I also got a perfect 800 on the English part of the SAT, and 776 on the math. The high school counselor tried to talk me into applying to an Ivy League school, but I was having no part of that. Ivy League schools cost money, even if you got scholarships. My Dad drove to the University of Washington campus every day to teach engineering, and I could live at home, ride in with him, and attend the UW for $300 tuition a year. Such a deal! He even had a parking spot in the middle of campus, so I could use his car as a study hall between classes. I would sit there with a textbook and watch the squirrels cavort in the big trees in front of the car.

PRE-MED

I enrolled at the UW as a pre-med student. The pre-med advisor was supposed to help me plan my curriculum. She was less than helpful. She talked me into taking a year of calculus that was never of any practical use to me except in working physics problems that I could have done just as well without calculus. I did enjoy the class, because I liked math—it was like doing puzzles. Once I got the second highest grade in the class on a quiz, but didn't get a single answer right; I had made some silly little arithmetic mistakes, but they gave me credit for getting the method right. As an engineer, my father was appalled—he insisted you had to get the numbers right or the bridge would fall down!

13

Every time I met with the pre-med advisor, she asked what I planned to do if I didn't get accepted to medical school. She said with my grades, if I were a boy I would be sure to get in; but since I was a girl I couldn't count on it, so I should have a back-up plan to become a lab technician or microbiologist or something. I said phooey on that; I had no desire to become a lab technician or a microbiologist. She kept harping on a back-up plan. I finally told her I was *going* to study medicine one way or another. There was a medical school in Mexico City that accepted all comers, and my Spanish was good enough to go there. *That* was my back-up plan.

I started out as a chemistry major, but didn't like the way my first college chemistry course was taught. I took a Spanish elective to fill in a hole in my schedule, and found it fun and easy. Then I discovered if I switched my major to Spanish, I could spend my junior year in Spain. Chemistry couldn't compete with *that!* My mind was made up.

When I told the pre-med advisor I was going to get a BA in Spanish instead of a BS in Chemistry, she said, "*That* won't help your chances of getting into medical school," but as a matter of fact, it probably did. They were looking for students with a broad background instead of science nerds, and the year I was accepted they also accepted a music major, a classics major, an English major, and a lawyer, among others.

Goodbye, useless discouraging sourpuss pre-med lady! From then on, I got to deal with an advisor in the Romance Languages Department. Of course, he was totally useless except to put the required rubber stamp on my plans. I would show him my proposed schedule with the required pre-med courses like comparative anatomy and qualitative analysis, and he would sigh and sign off on it, saying "I've never even *heard* of those courses!"

I took my first biology class in college. I was too squeamish to pith my own frog for the required dissection, but got a classmate to do it for me. The fetal pig was already conveniently dead. I preferred dissections that couldn't fight back; in Comparative Anatomy I rather enjoyed disassembling a lizard, a dogfish shark and a cat.

I found a part-time job as a receptionist for a surgeon downtown whose office hours were only in the afternoon. I had to arrange my classes so they were all in the mornings. One quarter I managed to schedule a physics lab in the morning but the corresponding class itself met in the afternoon. I got permission from the instructor to skip the classes and only take the exams. It worked pretty well, since the professor had written the textbook himself and followed it closely; my grade only dropped from A to B that quarter.

Sometimes I ran into complications with the final exams, because they were scheduled at odd times. I asked a Spanish professor if I could take his exam with another class that was scheduled for a morning, and he told me I didn't need to take a final exam at all because he was going to give me an A no matter what!

Apparently I excelled at Spanish language and literature. In my first college Spanish class, the professor (jokingly) asked me if I was from Madrid! When I turned in a book report to another Spanish professor, he called me into his office because, from both the content and the language of my paper, he assumed I had plagiarized it from a graduate student. He asked me a few questions about the book and quickly realized his suspicions were wrong and he apologized to me. I put minimal effort into my Spanish classes but couldn't seem to get anything less than an A on any assignment or test. This made me start to wonder about my career choice. My science classes were harder for me. Maybe I should follow my aptitude and do what I was best at rather than what I thought I wanted to do. Then I thought, if I got a PhD in Spanish I would never be able to practice medicine, but if I got an MD I could read all the Spanish literature I wanted to. So I stuck with medicine. After you finish reading this book, you can judge for yourself whether that was the wise choice.

JUNIOR YEAR IN SPAIN

The big advantage of being a Spanish major was that I got to spend my junior year in Spain. I crossed the US by Greyhound bus, visited my relatives in New York, and crossed the Atlantic on an Italian ocean liner. Several other students traveled on the same ship; one girl got a marriage proposal from the ship's doctor. We had great fun with the young Italian waiters at dinner; their English wasn't too good, and I don't think they ever got an order straight. If you ordered beef, you'd be sure to get chicken. The ship was fun, but after a week I was tired of it. We debarked in Lisbon to catch a train to Madrid.

Before we got on the train, I did a daring thing. I had been blond as a child, but my hair had turned what one friend called "dishwater blond" and then it had turned an indecisive brown. I decided to change my image and had my hair and eyebrows dyed blond in a Lisbon beauty parlor. For about a week after that, whenever I looked in a mirror I would just about have a heart attack, because someone strange would be looking back at me. Blonds were popular in Latin countries: as we were walking through Lisbon, one young man stared at us so hard he managed to walk straight into a light post and nearly knocked himself out. In Spain, the art of the "piropo" was in full flower. Men didn't pinch women like they did in Italy, but they were expected to follow them and say poetic things about their beauty. There was a joke about a woman who came home in tears because no one had said anything to her on the street.

I boarded with a Spanish family in Madrid, and studied at the University of Madrid in a program supervised and accredited by New York University. The teachers were superb and the experience unforgettable. I studied Spanish history, art, music, literature, linguistics and history of the Spanish language. The art class met in the Prado Museum: we carried folding chairs and sat down in front of the picture we were studying. The museum is vast, and after the class was over I went back and found whole rooms I'd never been in.

I had no trouble with the language. I had been studying Spanish since I was 11, and had had college professors from Spain, so I knew something about the local idioms and customs. I felt right at home. I promptly acquired a Spanish boyfriend, and I was never the least bit homesick, even though I was only 19 and it was my first time away from home and the first time I'd been to a foreign country.

Our classes were interrupted when the university was closed due to student unrest, but NYU simply moved us to a building downtown. At the time, students were not allowed to meet except in the Franco-approved national student association, and public gatherings of more than 2 or 3 students were forcibly broken up. The students were unhappy because of the ironclad tenure rules; there was no way to get rid of an incompetent teacher, and no way for students to even voice an opinion. Some teachers delegated their duties and never appeared in class. I heard about one professor who arbitrarily divided exams into two piles and failed one pile. I knew an engineering student who had been ready to graduate for 3 years except for one class that he kept taking and failing because the professor didn't like him.

The Franco regime was in full swing in Spain. Living under a Fascist dictator was an eye-opening experience. He had executed, jailed, or exiled most of those who disagreed with him. People simply didn't talk about politics. You didn't vote on anything, not even in school for a class president. The Spanish Civil War was recent enough to be a continued presence in the lives of those who had lost family, homes, or careers in the conflict. Brothers had fought against brothers, and men had been killed just because they wore a tie. I can remember asking people questions that they wouldn't answer until they closed the windows and lowered their voices just in case a neighbor might be listening. They remembered ominous knocks on the door in the middle of the night, and men who were taken away and never seen again.

There were things you couldn't do. You couldn't buy a magazine like *Playboy*. The press was censored: the editor of a humor magazine was jailed for printing a cartoon that said, "Keep our country clean" and showed all the priests leaving the country. The newspaper reported that a man was arrested for kissing his girlfriend goodnight in public. Women wore skirts. Once I crossed Madrid in slacks to catch a bus to the country for a hike, and everyone stared at me as if I were wearing a clown suit. Another American student was kicked off a beach for wearing a very conservative two-piece bathing suit that covered more skin than many one-piece suits. Students wore coats and ties, stood when the teacher entered the room, and said "Sir."

There were other things you *could* do. Like walk the streets at any hour of the night without fear of getting mugged or having your purse snatched. You could take the subway anywhere in Madrid for 1 ½ pesetas (about 3 cents), and it cost less to take a taxi across Madrid than it did to take a city bus across Seattle at that time. My total expenses ran only to $100 a month (including room, board, books, transportation and recreation). There were no beggars, no gangs, and very little crime of any kind.

I was pretty well prepared for the foreign lifestyle by the stories of my Spanish professors, but one thing that I hadn't realized was that most of the houses in Madrid were not separate dwellings with lawns, but apartment-style multistory condominiums. I lived with a Spanish widow and her family. In order to host two students, the mother and daughter shared a room, and the college age son put a cot up in the living/dining room after dinner. The other American student and I each had a private room with a balcony looking down into a courtyard between the rows of apartment buildings. We were on the 4th floor (which equates to our 5th floor), and there was an open cage elevator to go up, but you couldn't go down in it. The lady of the house remarked that the other American girl had a funny accent speaking Spanish. I explained that she had a funny accent speaking English, too. She was from Brooklyn.

The maid, Herminia, was a husky peasant girl from Galicia who got a half day a week off. She earned a pittance, slept in a closet, and was saving to get married. She would come back from her free afternoon and proudly show off something like a dish towel that she had managed to buy for her future home. She was always cheerful, and thought herself very fortunate to have such a good job. She was the first awake every morning; she would go down to the bakery, buy fresh bread for our breakfast, and wake us with a hot breakfast on trays in our rooms:

café au lait and toast with butter and marmalade. The mid-day meal was at 2 PM and supper was at 9 or 10. Supper might be gazpacho (cold tomato soup) and an omelet. The mid-day meal was the main meal, and might be pasta, fish, or meat and potatoes, or it might include something interesting like squid in its own ink over rice. There were always two separate courses. We started with two stacked plates and ate our way down: the top one was removed before the second course was served. There was always a bar of fresh bread—you tore off a chunk and ate it without butter. You were expected to keep both hands above the table, never in your lap, and you kept the knife in your right hand as you forked the food with your left. Dessert was fruit, often an orange from Valencia purchased direct from the back of a farmer's truck in the street. You ate most fruits with a knife and fork. I got so hungry for sweets that I would often stop by a bakery on my way home from school and buy something sinful and chocolaty.

Every building had its own "portero," a doorman who kept the common areas clean and kept an eye on everyone who came and went. At night the buildings were locked, and every neighborhood had a night watchman, a "sereno" named in Medieval times for his duty of periodically calling out the hours: "11 o'clock and all serene." The sereno carried a huge bunch of keys that opened the front doors of all the apartment buildings in his area. When you got home late, you stood in the street and clapped your hands; he came running, opened the door and accepted a small tip. Sometimes on cold winter evenings he retreated to a local bar and it took a while to get his attention, but on the whole the system ensured that there were eyes on the streets at all hours, a discouragement to crime. Once I was in an unfamiliar town late at night and found myself in a rather seedy neighborhood in a dark street; I started to worry about running into some unsavory character, but then I turned a corner and saw a group of small children playing tag in the street and decided it was probably safe. Sheep still had the right of way through Madrid on their trips between winter and summer pastures, a right that had been granted in the 12th century for a route that dated back to Neolithic times; one of our students looked out her window early one morning and saw a flock bleating down a major street.

There was a water shortage that year, and for much of the winter the water supply of the entire city of Madrid was turned off early in the morning and didn't resume until late at night. The maid would fill the bathtub with water at night and that would be our supply for the day. To flush the toilet, you had to dip a bucket of water from the tub and pour it down the toilet. One day I was delighted to see a cute little mouse run under the bathtub. I mentioned it to the lady of the house and she was indignant, "We've never had mice in this building.

You must be mistaken. You must have imagined it!" About an hour later I heard her scream and come running out of the bathroom in a panic, yelling, "There's a mouse in there!"

People might not have much money, but they had that old Spanish hidalgo pride. They always dressed well, even if they only owned one dress or coat. The family I lived with would have a seamstress come work in their home twice a year to make them one outfit each for the season from the fabric they chose. The widow would unravel old sweaters and re-knit them. She helped me knit sweaters for my younger sisters; the wool for one cost me a grand total of $2.50. The other was only slightly more and was a beautiful red with golden flecks; my sister was still using it 20 years later. We would knit in the evenings, sitting around the round dining/living room table with a long heavy cloth over it and our knees tucked underneath where we could feel the heat from the little heater that lived underneath the table like a friendly pet dragon.

I think what impressed me the most about the Spanish people is that they got together with friends just for the sake of getting together. They didn't meet to go bowling or to play cards; they didn't need any excuse; they just met to talk. And they didn't go to each other's homes; they met at a bar or cafeteria. There were "tertulias" where a group of like-minded people would meet regularly in a certain corner of a certain cafeteria and would talk for hours over one cup of coffee or glass of wine.

I loved the Spanish espresso coffee. When I got home I looked in vain for a store that sold it or that sold the equipment to make it with. The only way you could get espresso in the US at that time was to import your own machine. Years later, Starbucks happened, and today you can't walk a block in Seattle without tripping over a barista.

Before I returned home I spent the summer traveling all over Spain on dirty third class coal-burning trains and staying in the cheapest hotels and "pensiones." If the official pensions were full, you could always stand around in the train station looking lost until someone offered you a room in a private home. I met my first cockroach in one of those. One pension in Córdoba charged the equivalent of $1.20 for a room and two meals a day and had an indoor outhouse—a closet with a hole in the floor. Also chamber pots. And pitchers and basins instead of sinks and faucets. Who says time travel isn't possible?!

My good Spanish kept me out of trouble. Not so a friend of mine. He once rode a motorcycle through a little Spanish town, parked it by a bridge, and then couldn't find his way back to the bridge. He kept asking people "Where is the bridge?" and they just looked at him real funny and turned away in disgust. We solved the mystery several years later when he told me the story. It seems he had "puente" confused with "puta" and had been asking people, "Where is the prostitute?"

BACK IN SEATTLE

Spain took care of all the course requirements for my major, so my senior year was free for finishing up my pre-med requirements. I did take one graduate level Spanish class in my senior year just for fun: Twentieth Century Spanish Poetry. Since he knew I was going to med school, the professor suggested I write my term paper on "Science and Poetry." At first I thought he was joking, but I ended up doing it—comparing the two ways of apprehending truths about the world, and how creativity applies to both.

My Spanish advisor apparently didn't believe in me any more than the pre-med advisor, because when I passed him one day on campus and told him I'd just received my acceptance letter from the medical school, his jaw dropped and he said, "Wow! When you say you're going to do something, you really do it!"

Nobody encouraged me. Nobody. Ever. All the way through med school, my mother kept telling me it wasn't too late to quit if I changed my mind. And when I divorced my first husband, he shocked me by saying he had never believed I was really going to become a doctor; he said lots of women talked about doing it but never did.

No one actively *dis*couraged me, but I got the feeling that they thought I was a bit strange and that they were willing to humor me and let me play out my little fantasy.

Maybe it was all for the best. Who knows? If I'd had a pushy mother or a physician father who wanted me to follow in his footsteps, I might have rebelled and become a used car salesman—or even worse, a chiropractor!

3

Medical School

I'm just a person trapped inside a woman's body.

—Elayne Boosler

Admissions to the University of Washington School of Medicine were based on grades, scores on the MCAT (Medical College Admission Test), and interviews. They claimed they didn't have a quota, but for some strange reason they just *happened* to find exactly four qualified female applicants each year. Affirmative action hadn't been invented yet; it was 1966. A black woman[1] I knew was rejected even though she had better grades than many of the men who were accepted that year. It was a loss to the profession, because she was very bright, had a wonderful personality, a great sense of humor, had coped with hardships in her life (growing up in Mississippi before Civil Rights), and would have made a great doctor.

The admissions committee asked me questions they wouldn't dare ask an applicant today. "What if you decide to get married?" "What if you have a baby?" They didn't think the State's money should be invested in educating a lowly female who was likely to get married and quit. As it turned out, none of the women quit, but some of the men did.

Despite my anatomical imperfections (the hairless chin, bumpy chest and lack of dangly bits), my other qualifications got me in. I graduated magna cum laude, was elected to Phi Beta Kappa, and won the award as best student in the Spanish department, with a perfect "A" average in my major. They really didn't have much choice: if they'd turned me down they would have had some 'splainin' to do like Lucy.

---

1. I refuse to say "African American" because I agree with Michael Shermer. He says that technically all Americans should check the "African American" block on questionnaires, since the human species originated in Africa.

21

They said they weren't prejudiced against women. But the male students confided to me that the dean had a comedy routine that he performed for them. He would imitate a woman student at the beginning of medical school, acting very feminine and walking with a mincing gait; then he would imitate her at the end of med school—slouching, stalking down the hallway with feet apart and acting like a man.

A woman I know ran into more overt prejudice: on her first day of medical school she was accosted in an elevator by a man who told her she didn't belong there, she was taking a man's place, and she would never finish.

I got a summer job working in the genetics lab, and I got to see my first autopsy before medical school even started. A girl who was my classmate was there too. The deceased had a ruddy complexion from carbon monoxide poisoning. We were both fascinated by the autopsy; but she was more fascinated than I was, because the dead body belonged to someone she knew, the father of a friend of hers. He had killed himself after he was diagnosed with terminal cancer. Not the most pleasant introduction to pathology for my classmate.

FIRST YEAR MED STUDENT

The first day of orientation, they announced that medical students were required to wear coats and ties. I didn't own a coat and tie. I never have owned a tie—except for a Christmas tie with a picture of a Dr. Seuss reindeer—which really wouldn't have been appropriate. For a moment I worried that I was going to be in trouble for noncompliance. Then I realized that they didn't mean me, and that it hadn't even crossed their feeble minds that some of their students might be women. That made me angry, and then I wanted to buy a coat and tie and wear them the next day to make a statement—but I was too chicken. They taught us some basic first aid, because now that we were med students people would expect us to know more than we did.

And then, into the trenches. The first year courses totaled a required 23 credits, compared to the usual 15 or 16 for a full college load. (Undergraduates *couldn't* take more than 20 credits, and to take 20 you had to get special permission from the dean.) The textbooks were massive, the amount of material far greater than any human bean could possibly assimilate, the hours were brutal, and the labs were demanding. The first two years were devoted to lectures and labs, and it wasn't until the 3rd and 4th years that we finally got to see actual patients, rotating through all the major specialties and doing clinical clerkships in several affiliated hospitals.

Everyone wonders about Gross Anatomy. It didn't seem "gross," just demanding. In my class, no one fainted or threw up. We were all too busy learning and getting the job done to think about the macabre aspects of what we were doing.

Our lab was a huge room, with many tables, and on each table a body covered with a white sheet reeking of formalin. We would unwrap only the part we were working on. They called the man in charge something that sounded to me like "deaner" but turned out to be "diener," a word meaning servant in German that is used in English to describe the person in the morgue who is responsible for handling, moving, and cleaning the corpse.

I was assigned to a cadaver with 3 male students, and we spent a full year taking the cadaver apart piece by piece, identifying every tendon, organ, nerve, muscle, and blood vessel. One of my lab partners kept making sexual innuendos and jokes, but I had a stock answer ready for him. "You know what they say about sex: those who can, do; those who can't, talk about it." We developed an easy camaraderie. Terry would point to a stringy unidentified nerve or tendon or something with the forceps and ask, "What would you call this?" and I would answer, "Oh, I think I'd call that one Mortimer." We worked with bare hands, and the formalin the cadavers were preserved in shriveled our fingers and left a penetrating smell that followed us out of the lab and haunted our evenings.

Rumor had it that students in a previous year "borrowed" an arm from a cadaver and drove across the Lake Washington toll bridge. When they reached the toll booth, they extended the arm with coins in its hand and drove off, leaving the arm there. We were admonished to treat our cadavers with more respect. We did.

There's a story about anatomy lab that is supposed to be true, and if it isn't it should be. A woman medical student had a female cadaver, and on the day they were to dissect the genitals, she removed the sheet to find that someone had cut the penis off a male cadaver and inserted it into the vagina of her cadaver. Supposedly she had the presence of mind to turn to her male classmates and ask, "All right, which one of you guys left here in a hurry last night?"

So Gross Anatomy didn't bother me. There were only two things that really bothered me in all of medical school. One was an experiment where you created a wound in your own arm and kept a "skin window" slide on it to study how the healing process progressed. Fortunately, this exercise was optional, and I opted out. I was willing to take their word for how healing worked without maiming myself to prove it.

To show what a total wimp I was, the other thing that really bothered me was when we had to take a sample of our own blood by stabbing our thumb with a lancet. I was determined not to have to stab myself twice, so I did it once with vigor. It took me a long time to build up the courage to stab, but I did it.[2]

We each got a box of bones to take home and study—a disassembled human skeleton. I called mine Yorick. I had always wanted to play with bones. Once on a hiking trip I had found a rotting elk carcass on a riverbank, and I had brought home some of the bones. I tried to boil them to get the flesh off, but the experiment was a failure. Mom said I couldn't do it in the house. I used a Coleman stove in the backyard. I boiled and boiled, but the bones didn't come clean and the odor was appalling.

We studied chicken embryos in Embryology lab. I found one egg that was older than it was supposed to be and was starting to hatch. I took it home and watched the chick emerge. My younger siblings and all the neighborhood kids came to see it. We named it "Shicken." It imprinted on me and followed me around. Mom put her foot down and made us donate it to the zoo when it was a few days old. It was the only pet I had ever had except for some guppies that ate their babies.

In the lab one day, we needed a knife for something. None of the men in my group carried a pocketknife, but I happened to have one in my purse and saved the day! So much for stereotypes! Speaking of stereotypes, our class president did the expected and "borrowed" lab alcohol for the punch at a student party. He also flunked anatomy and had to repeat it!

One of my favorite professors was a psychiatrist, Dr. Thomas H. Holmes. He said medical patients were crazy until proven otherwise, and he emphasized the psychosomatic aspects of illness. He insisted we never use the word "mind" because it was a philosophical rather than a scientific concept. I wrote a term paper on "Creativity, the Poetic Sense, and the Fallacy of Science," in which I bashed science and used the word "mind" repeatedly, but tried to defend my reasons for doing so. The Devil made me do it. I thought Dr. Holmes would probably flunk me. He marked every use of the word "mind" with a red pencil, adding comments in the margin like "Not so!" and "Now, you're clearly in the wrong

---

2.   I'm braver now. After I retired, I developed a cyst in my breast, and I knew it was benign and I didn't want to go to the hassle of making an appointment. Instead, I got a needle and syringe from Wal-Mart and made my husband stick the needle in the cyst and aspirate it while I held the lump steady and provided instructions. He knew if he didn't help I would do it by myself. He's never quite forgiven me. I still wasn't quite as brave as a nurse I knew who lanced her own thrombosed hemorrhoid!

universe of discourse." and "An assumption!" and "Doubt this!" After doing his best to demolish my paper, he gave me an A+ and said, "Unique! Well done! Creative! I enjoyed the dialogue! I've never had a 'lady' medical student with gumption enough to leave the safe middle road of conformity and venture along the lonely, and often dangerous path of originality."

The psychiatry professor's son was a classmate of mine, and people were always asking him if he was going to be a psychiatrist like his father. He insisted he was going to specialize in "diseases of the rich." He started out in general medicine but ended up in—you guessed it—psychiatry. I guess that's about as close to "diseases of the rich" as you can get, except maybe for plastic surgery.

A guest lecturer was announced with an effusive introduction that included praise for his horticultural exploits and his green thumb. When he started to write on the blackboard, we saw that his thumb was wrapped with bright green tape! One anatomy lecturer was ambidextrous: he would take a piece of chalk in each hand and draw both sides of a drawing at once.

An anatomy professor from Scotland told a true story from his homeland. A farmer had picked his small son up by the head, and when he set him down, the boy collapsed and died. The doctors were trying to understand what had happened, and the father demonstrated on his other son—he picked him up with a hand on either side of his head, and when he set him down, he collapsed and died too. Autopsy showed the boys had both inherited a rare condition where the upper two cervical vertebrae dislocated easily when the neck was stretched, and when the tension was released, it allowed a bony prominence to sever the spinal cord. He had essentially "pithed" both of his children just as we had pithed our frogs in biology lab.

One lecturer explained the importance of close observation. He said his own professor had demonstrated the lesson by showing the students how he examined a urine sample. He picked up the urine container, looked at it, smelled it, held it up to the light, dipped a finger in, and licked his finger. He asked a student to repeat the procedure. The student carefully looked at the urine, smelled it, held it up to the light, dipped a finger in and hesitantly tasted it, grimacing. The professor exclaimed, "Aha! You weren't observing carefully. I dipped my index finger in the urine but I licked my *middle* finger."

We heard about a patient who couldn't produce a urine sample and filled the specimen container with the apple juice from his breakfast tray. When the nurse picked it up and looked at it, she said, "Hmm, it's awful cloudy looking." So the patient grabbed it back and drank it, saying, "OK, I'll run it through again."

Some of my classmates revolted and demanded that our professors provide lecture notes covering the essentials of what they were going to say. Then they got a friend to pick up the notes and they skipped the lectures. I never felt right doing that—I was always afraid I would miss something, and besides, if I heard the lecture *and* read the lecture notes, it was reinforcement and I just might remember something.

One day I dozed off in a lecture and when I regained consciousness I couldn't understand what the lecturer was talking about. He kept saying something that sounded like "vitaminny." I finally realized it was his way of pronouncing vitamin E. He was from Canada.

We had one professor who had won some big scientific prize and was world-renowned. The medical school felt lucky to get him, but the students didn't. He was a terrible lecturer because he couldn't get down to our level to explain anything. He would describe complicated experiments and we wouldn't understand what they were meant to prove. When someone asked a question, he wouldn't answer, but would say, "If you'd been listening, you wouldn't have to ask."

ON THE WARDS

After two years of classrooms and labs, we were let loose on real patients. I was too busy staying afloat to notice whether I was being treated fairly, but when I look back, I can see I was at some disadvantage. I can remember male bodies being pressed suggestively against mine in surgery and wondering whether it was really accidental and whether I dared say anything. I didn't; I just tried to ignore it. I missed out on the locker room conversations with the male doctors. I had to put up with teachers showing slides of naked women and making lewd comments. We had our blood tested and I was singled out for having an "abnormal" hematocrit; it was lower than the men's but was actually well within the normal range for a woman. In many ways, little things kept me aware that I was different.

My fellow students were nice enough to me. They talked to me like I was just another student. A few of them asked me out on dates during the first year, before I got married. I don't even remember much teasing, except for one student whose wife was about to have a baby, who kept saying the girls in our class were looking better and better to him. We would congregate in the student lounge during the lunch break. Two of my classmates were talented pianists and would sight-read classical duets at the baby grand in the lounge.

Perhaps the most insidious prejudice was the assertiveness that was expected of the male students. The men were aggressive about pushing in, making themselves noticed, demanding that the resident let them do the spinal tap. I was shy and self-effacing like a well-brought-up female and felt I should wait until the resident offered to teach me a procedure. Because of this, I was often perceived as "not interested" when in reality I was intensely interested and feeling left out. And I was a bit repelled at what I saw as insensitive bedside manners. One evaluator even said I should go into something like radiology or pathology because I would never be good at anything involving direct patient care (which turned out to be precisely my forte).

I remember one male classmate on the pediatric rotation who was very vocal about his desire to specialize in pediatrics. He was constantly asking the staff pediatricians about how to set up an office, where to get a good residency, etc. The next month, on the OB-Gyn rotation, he was suddenly talking about becoming an obstetrician. I asked him why he had changed his mind, and he said, "I *got* my A in pediatrics." I don't know if this kind of behavior was a male thing or a political thing, but I couldn't act that way.

INTERNAL MEDICINE

On an Internal Medicine rotation, I was assigned to a team with a resident and two interns. The resident did his best to ignore me. I went in one Saturday when I didn't have to; the resident knew I was reading my textbook in the call room and waiting for him to tell me if a patient was admitted. I sat there all afternoon and later found out he'd admitted three patients and never called me. And didn't explain or apologize. The interns were nice to me, but they didn't give the grades, and I got the only "D" grade I ever got thanks to that resident. I was crushed. Protesting to the department head did no good whatsoever.

I didn't like what I saw of Internal Medicine. The doctors seemed more concerned with outdoing each other in quoting the latest medical journals than with how their patients felt. In one particularly sad case, the patient had some kind of liver problem and they couldn't pin down a diagnosis. The patient was getting better, and probably would have been fine if they'd left him alone. But they pursued the diagnosis with a liver biopsy. His blood clotting ability was impaired by his disease, and he bled to death. The most disgusting part is that even after autopsy they never did figure out exactly what the liver problem was.

I began to experience a strange phenomenon that I would continue to experience throughout my career. Put one woman in a group of several men. Let her make a suggestion. Watch how her words are entirely ignored. Watch one of the men make the same suggestion a bit later on. Watch the group enthusiastically accept the suggestion from the *man*. I saw this happen over and over, to me and to other women. It was surreal.

One of my classmates was asked to listen to a patient's heart murmur. My classmate applied his stethoscope to the proper place on the chest, and tried moving it to adjacent spots, but couldn't hear a thing. He knew he was "expected" to hear it and was tempted to pretend he could, but honesty prevailed. He said, "No, Sir, I can't hear it." Thank goodness he did, because the professor pointed out that the earpieces of his stethoscope were still hanging around his neck, and suggested he might have a better chance of hearing the murmur if he put the earpieces in his ears.

Another woman student and I were assigned to examine a male patient in third year physical diagnosis. It fell to her to do the genital exam. He said, "Ouch!" She asked, "How long has your testicle been tender like that?" He said, "Only since you squeezed it." She blushed and ended up going into pediatrics.

PEDIATRICS

We had some of our training at Children's Orthopedic Hospital in Seattle. The Chief of Staff at the time was Dr. Jack Doctor. On his first day of work, he went around introducing himself, "Hello, I'm Dr. Doctor." And one nurse responded, "Well I'm Nursy Nurse!" and flounced off.

A patient came into the emergency room there with what appeared to be measles. A medical student looked in the child's mouth and saw what he thought might be Koplik spots, a sign of measles. He asked the intern. The intern said, "I've never even seen a case of measles." He asked the resident. The resident said, "I saw a case of measles once, but I've never seen Koplik spots." It was a great advertisement for the success of childhood immunizations.

They received a phone call from a concerned mother. "I think my child has a fever, but I don't know how to read a thermometer." They tried to teach her over the phone, but she just didn't get it. They tried to find out if there was anyone else available that might be able to read it—no, my boyfriend's not home yet. They determined that the child didn't have any other symptoms and didn't sound very sick. They were about to tell her not to worry. Eventually in the course of the conversation the mother let slip that they usually took the child to King County Hospital for his shunt. He was a hydrocephalic with a shunt that drained into his abdomen to relieve intracranial pressure, and a fever in a patient with a shunt is a medical emergency.

Emergencies can develop quickly in children. One child was taken to his pediatrician's office with a fever. The pediatrician didn't find much of anything, assumed it was a cold virus, and sent the child home. On the way home in the taxi the child started to act sicker, and the mother diverted the taxi to Children's Orthopedic Hospital. The child was admitted, slipped into a coma, broke out in a petechial rash, and was dead 4 hours later of fulminant meningococcal meningitis.

Today many childhood cancers and leukemias are curable. Back then, chemotherapy was in its infancy. One pediatrician used to speak frankly to parents. If they treated the leukemia, the child would live longer but would suffer with multiple hospitalizations, bone marrow biopsies, and drug side effects like baldness and nausea—and would almost certainly die eventually anyway. He gave them another option: not treating, except to keep the child comfortable until he died. Many parents chose that option as the kindest thing to do.

We attended genetics rounds where we saw patients with unusual congenital syndromes. We called them FLK's—Funny-Looking Kids—and tried to match their appearance with a known diagnosis. One day the staff physician asked a new intern about an FLK and he reported back later, "I'm sorry, sir, I've looked in all my books and I can't find the FLK Syndrome anywhere."

After one child had been presented to us, his grandmother asked to speak to the doctors in private, sending the mother and child out of the room first. She said she knew exactly what was wrong with the child. She confessed to us that she had done a terrible thing in her youth. She had been unfaithful to her husband once, and she was convinced that her grandchild's abnormality was her fault because of what the Bible says about the sins of the fathers. We did our best to explain the facts to her, but I don't think we made even a dent in her guilt.

I got to meet a fascinating patient with progeria. These are children who seem to grow old before your very eyes. They never reach adult size; they develop heart disease, cataracts and other diseases of the elderly, and they die young.

My friend Jean Carney was a big success in Pediatrics, because she was the oldest of 13 children. Whenever she needed to know what a child of a given age was like, she could just think of a sibling. Her family was a walking textbook of normal child development. Her father was a doctor, and her mother accompanied him to a medical meeting once. The wives were discussing family size, and one woman opined that no one should have more than two children, because they wouldn't be able to give enough personal attention to any more than that. She turned to Jean's mother and asked, "And how many children do you have, Mrs. Carney?" She answered, "Well, I have a girl who's 22 … and a boy who's 3…." And she hesitated long enough for someone to break in with, "That's quite an age spread." and go on to talk about something else. So she never had to admit to the other 11 children! She was an amazing woman who retained her figure and youthful energy; Jean and I used to stop at her house for lunch en route from the medical school to the downtown hospitals. When you're already feeding a platoon, two more mouths don't matter.

RADIOLOGY—IN THE SHADOWS

I really enjoyed the radiology rotation. There was something cozy about the darkened room where we read the x-rays, the pace was relaxed, and the x-rays couldn't talk back. It was challenging trying to imagine how the shadows related to the anatomy. Once the instructor showed a chest x-ray of a woman and told us she was obviously Chinese. We were amazed. How can you tell that from a chest film? He pointed to the asymmetrical breast shadows and proclaimed, "Wun Hung Low."

On an anatomy exam we were once given an x-ray of a hand and asked to determine the patient's sex. Some students puzzled over the bone structure and complained that the question was unfair. In reality, the answer was easy; you could see the woman's engagement and wedding rings!

One day a fellow student asked about complications of IVP studies. An intravenous pyelogram involved an injection of a radio-opaque solution, and occasionally this can cause a life-threatening anaphylactic reaction. The instructor had just finished telling us how very rare such reactions were when a patient in the next room proceeded to have one. I'm not superstitious, but "speak of the Devil…."

Our pediatric radiology instructor was a paraplegic who had gone through medical school and residency in a wheelchair. One day he showed up for work with a cast on his arm; he had fallen out of his wheelchair playing wheelchair basketball.

Another favorite instructor was a woman who had two small children. One day she was late for class and explained that she had had to go home twice that day. The babysitter called and said her little girl had fallen and cut her head, and she had to go home and take her to the ER to get sewed up. She had barely returned to work when the babysitter called again to say her little boy had fallen and cut his head.... Did accident proneness run in the family? Was it a case of monkey see, monkey do? Or was it just déjà vu all over again?

That radiologist was the only woman professor that I have a distinct memory of. Medical school was a man's world. Full of testosterone and dangly bits. No role models with periods and tits. Hey, that rhymes!

I had some spare time to read in the Radiology Dept. library, and I found an intriguing book on calcifications of the lung. It showed pictures of all the different things that could cause calcifications, including weird parasites. Among other trivia, I learned that the most common cause of miliary (multiple small scattered) calcifications in the lung in Australia was chickenpox pneumonia. For some reason, that fact delighted me and stuck in my head. A couple of months later I happened to be on another rotation where a pulmonary specialist showed an x-ray of miliary lung calcifications to a group of residents and asked them what they thought it showed. They suggested things like TB, Cryptococcus, sarcoidosis. He kept saying no, that's not it. Any other ideas? I said, "Did the patient have a rash compatible with chicken pox?" That was it! He said the residents should be ashamed of themselves, because here this medical student had only been on the rotation for two days and she already knew more than they did!

THE COUNTY HOSPITAL

We did some of our training at the county hospital, Harborview Medical Center (HMC, formerly King County Hospital). Some of the patients we met there belonged to an underworld of society I'd never encountered in my sheltered middle class life. In the Emergency Room, the staff kept a list of interesting actual "chief complaints" transcribed from the medical records of their patrons. Here are some of them:

> Says she has 3 vaginas, 4 ovaries and a bicarbonate uterus.
> Tickling penis.
> Screaming.
> "Aren't I in Hollywood and this a movie set?"
> "I was walking down a tunnel that was cold [at 2 AM] so they picked me up and brought me here for a checkup."
> Said to have put hard [sic] thru a window on purpose.

"I'm pregnant by my cousin and my mother said she going to press charges of Sagittarian rape against him."

From a call to the Crisis Clinic: "Will the green pills [chloral hydrate] affect my coil and make me pregnant?"

Was sleeping in woods and bug crawled in ear.

"A bread loaf in my head."

"Started coughing and shaking chills as soon as I came in the door."

Was found directing traffic.

"Stomped on by a bunch of hippies."

Was chasing mother with a butcher knife.

Brought by cabbie because unable to pay cab fare; was admitted for a cold so Welfare would pay cab fare.

Attacked with fingernails by an unknown person.

Transported via ambulance from the VA hospital because he was complaining of chest pain.

Fell in rose bush while eloping.

Found by police with pants down due to rapid pulse.

Found washing in Plaza Hotel Fountain.

"Can't remember."

Possible head pain.

Had eaten pumpkin seeds.

"Sick."

Chest pain for three months (age 20)

Said to be a human being by some—Reported to also have feelings.

Said to have been shot in shoe; discharged to Nordstrom's.

Cue stick broken over head—discharged to Seattle Sports Supply.

Ate a raw apple.

"A guy grabbed me from behind and bit my ear off.... What d'you mean did I save it?"

"Been searching for his soul."

Said to have been cured by God via the light bulb while waiting in trauma room T3.

Otitis media secondary to bread mold.

Discharged self from nursing home a month ago.

No crutches—stolen.

Bitten yesterday by dog in both arms—has swelling in right groin—could it be due to dog bite?

Tried to pay cab fare with appointment slip.

Called police because someone was trying to break into his hotel room.

Found nude in street—reason given: "I had to urinate."

Stuck sponge in vagina and unable to retrieve it for 2 weeks.

Found in a hole—multiple skull fractures, bilateral Battle's sign.

Bothered by invisible person.

Said to have right leg, alcohol on breath.

Said to have been kicked by a pig 24 hrs ago and still bleeding.

Cast on for 9 months.
Been sitting in a tavern all day.
"Oh my God!"
Gave address as Harborview Medical Center.

We learned what a Gomer was. It comes from the acronym "Get Out of My Emergency Room" and refers to a category of hopeless patients including alcoholics, psychotics, the homeless, and other ne'er-do-wells who are frustrating to try to help because they either can't or won't cooperate. The hospital staff kept a list of various things these feckless patients had actually done, and assigned each of them a Gomer Point Rating.

1. The admitting note from the ER ends with "sorry."—10 points.
2. Patient's clothes are refused by the laundry and subsequently have to be destroyed—13 points.
3. Admitting orders include, "Bath STAT"—2 points.
4. Patient is referred to as John Doe for longer than 36 hours—4 points.
5. Patient has been evicted from 4 nursing homes of ascending classes in as many months—8 points.
6. Patient is refused admission to any and all King County nursing homes—11 points.
7. Patient sent back from nursing home on the day of transfer there—15 points.
8. Patient's ulcerations deeper than 1 cm. If only on buttocks—5 points; if elsewhere—10 points.
9. Patient has hip fracture older than 3 weeks at time of admission for fracture—6 points.
10. Spikes temp. the night of transfer to nursing home—8 points.
11. Discovered to have guaiac [test for blood] positive stools the night preceding transfer to a nursing home—8 points. If sent anyway—2 points.
12. Sent back from x-ray without barium enema having been accomplished—10 points.
13. If catheter straight drainage tubing is under more than 10 pounds tension without complaint from patient—5 points.
14. BUN greater than age; head-holding; bilateral palmomental, snout, suck, forced grasp or plantar extension reflexes; jaw clonus—3 points each when accompanied by at least 2 other Gomerisms.
15. Admitted to nursing home before the age of 46—14 points.
16. Found to have lice under cast when cast is windowed—4 points.
17. Lice on patient survives 5 treatments with Kwell—8 points.
18. Patient is able to remove Foley catheter from bladder while the bag is inflated to 30 cc.—15 points. While in full restraints—21 points.
19. Patient destroys spica cast—12 points.

20. Removes IV—1 point.

21. Removes a cutdown—2 points. Between midnight and 4 AM—4 points. If hypotensive—8 points.

22. Toenails can't be cut with a pair of clippers or a drill—3 points.

23. Patient is Caucasian who is thought to be a Negro on admission—4 points.

24. Urinates on roommate, physician or visitor—8 points. On med student—2 points.

25. Semi-formed guaiac-positive stool is found more than 10 feet from bed—8 points.

26. Fluid balance consultant gives up—2 points.

27. Requires emergency tracheostomy for aspiration on ward—4 points.

28. Patient sent to nursing home for rehabilitation to permit further workup at Harborview Medical Center—15 points.

29. Brain herniates after lumbar puncture when opening pressure was <60 mm.—10 points.

30. Femoral puncture required to get blood samples for daily pro-time—12 points.

31. Intern's workup is less than one page long—2 points.

32. Abdomen is higher than head despite 30 degree catch of bed; or if patient diureses more than 75 pounds—2 points.

33. Found in bed with another patient—3 points.

34. Ward resident irately calls ER resident upon patient's arrival to floor—5 points.

35. Patient with unstable cervical fracture gets out of bed to remove weights from halter traction—10 points.

36. Coprophagia[3]—6 points.

37. Sequel to 36[4]—10 points.

38. Appears to have continuous Babinski reflex due to curling of toenails—5 points.

39. Panniculus [apron-like fold of abdominal fat in a morbidly obese person] equal to half the size of the patient—2 points. Equal to size of patient—4 points.

40. Drinks own vomit—15 points.

41. Defecates in student doctor's bag—5 points.

42. Jumps from 9th floor and lives—5 points.

43. Adjusts pacemaker while trying to turn down radio—5 points.

44. Drinks guaiac test kit—3 points.

---

3. This means eating feces, shit, poo, BM, excrement, number 2, or whatever euphemism you prefer.

4. Use your imagination.

I was helping with a trauma case one day when the resident in charge ordered me to put in a urinary catheter in a male patient. It's a simple procedure in a female, but in a male it requires a certain amount of manipulation of private body parts and an adjustment to different angles. I had learned to do this on a comatose patient, and thought nothing of it. After I was finished, the resident said, "I didn't think you'd really do it!"

A patient who had overdosed on a narcotic was left on a gurney in the hallway and we were instructed to keep reminding him to breathe every time we passed. He was conscious enough to breathe when told to do so, but if you didn't keep reminding him, he would stop. I guess you could call this a form of "talk therapy."

A former psychiatric patient reported to the hospital because she had started hearing voices again. She had enough insight to realize the voices weren't real. I wondered why she did when others apparently didn't.

I was appalled to find out that poor patients had to take the bus to the hospital while poorer patients could call a cab and Medicare would pay for it.

MISCELLANEOUS MEDICAL ABERRATIONS

On the psychiatry rotation, I was assigned a new patient to work up. I had the astoundingly bad luck to draw a deaf-mute man who had become violent and had broken up some furniture in his brother's apartment. He couldn't hear or talk and I couldn't do sign language, so the only way we could communicate was in writing. To top it off, he had lost his reading glasses, so I had to print my questions in large block letters. I finally gave up and just wrote WRITE DOWN THE STORY OF YOUR LIFE AND WHAT HAPPENED TO MAKE THEM BRING YOU TO THE HOSPITAL and I left him alone for a couple of days. He produced a manuscript that made it clear there was absolutely nothing wrong with him. He'd had a sort of temper tantrum over something that angered him. Hey, he couldn't *talk* about it, and he had to express himself some way! So my one and only psych patient wasn't even a psych patient and was admitted due to a misunderstanding. I did learn something about communication, I guess.

We saw one of the oldest babies on record. A woman had been pregnant in her 20s and never had the baby. It had died and calcified. She carried a large calcified lump of fetus in her abdomen for 50 years before it was finally surgically removed.

An OB patient dropped her baby in the toilet when she was expelling her pre-delivery enema. It was fished out and cleaned off. No harm done. Got a shitty start in life, but hey!

Another OB patient kept us entertained during her labor. A young, unmarried woman, she regaled us with tales from her job repossessing cars for finance companies. When people wouldn't relinquish them, she got to break into them, hot-wire them, and steal them back. She explained how much harder a trunk was to break into than a car door. She told us how she could get into different makes and models of cars in record speed.

The gynecology prof told us about the most memorable couple he had seen for infertility. He examined the woman and found she was still a virgin after several years of marriage. He made careful, delicate inquiries, and discovered they had had difficulties with penetration at first but had kept trying until they managed to dilate her urethra and were having intercourse in her bladder. That is a piss-poor way to try to get pregnant.

An intern had a 3 year old daughter. He would call her during his 36 hour shifts whenever he got a chance. She would tell him to come home and he would explain that there were sick patients who needed him and he had to stay and take care of them or they might die. One day she demanded, "You come home, Daddy! Let dem people die!"

An instructor told us one day that he'd read in the news that one brand of birth control pills had been found contaminated with small amounts of LSD. We believed him and were shocked. Until he continued, "So you can take a trip without the kids."

A patient in the clinic, a young man who had been living in his car, found me attractive and asked if my wedding ring was for real or if I just wore it to discourage suitors.

A classmate explained the proper etiquette for doing a pelvic exam. The doctor says, "At your cervix, Madame." And she answers, "Dilated to meet you, Doctor."

We got to go on Public Health field trips and visit the homeless shelters, the TB clinics, and the prostitutes in jail. The investigators kept a first-name file for prostitutes for monitoring VD. If a man tested positive for gonorrhea and only knew he'd been with a girl named Mary he met in the Rainbow Tavern, they could find her. The jail had a rotating door: a prostitute would be picked up, spend a couple of days there, and go right back on the streets until next time.

We got to visit a state home for hopeless children, where we saw a bedridden child whose head was as big as the rest of her body: a hydrocephalic vegetable.

We visited the state mental hospital where Dr. Walter Freeman had once performed prefrontal lobotomies with an ice pick through the eye socket with no sterile precautions.

There was a fake heroin epidemic in Seattle when I was in med school. Something was being sold on the street that everyone believed was heroin, but it wasn't. People experienced the rush, the letdown, and the craving just like they were supposed to. They thought they were addicted, but they turned out to be just suggestible.

MARRIAGE

During my first year in med school (I was 21) my younger brother and sisters announced that I was now officially an old maid and they started asking me when I was going to leave home. After spending my junior year in Spain on my own, it was hard to come under my parents' discipline and house rules again. So I got a scholarship and a student loan and moved into an apartment. My Dad didn't try to stop me, but he told me he thought it was financially foolish, and he said once I moved out I could never move back. I never wanted to.

My first apartment was one room with a pull-down Murphy bed. A friend gave me a copy of a book, *The Impoverished Student's Guide to Cookery, Drinkery and Housekeepery* and I set up housekeeping. Mom gave me a few old dishes and pans. I'd use them all up before I washed anything—it was more efficient that way. One day there was a cockroach on the kitchen counter. I was too squeamish even to squish a spider, and I wasn't anxious to learn what kind of obnoxious liquid gunk exuded from cockroach corpses, so I opted for the temporary expedient of covering it up with a pot lid. Then I was afraid to pick up the lid. There it stayed for a week until my father came by for a visit and I got *him* to lift the lid. Oops, there was nothing underneath! The cockroach was eventually located hiding up in the rim of the pot lid, and Dad sent him to cockroach heaven.

Within a matter of months my boyfriend from Spain came to the US and we were married. Although he was a college graduate, he spoke not a word of English (just Spanish, Latin, Greek, French and Catalan), so he had to enroll in language classes and take a menial job. He gradually learned to speak respectable English, although there were occasional glitches. He brought home a can of dog food from the supermarket for dinner once. He tried to tell me about the insect that had flown into the room—a beeblebum. He earned enough to keep us afloat, along with my student loans and summer research jobs.

His name was Pancracio Celdrán Gomariz. By Spanish convention, the mother's last name follows the father's, so the "last" name falls in the middle; so I became Mrs. Celdrán. That mother's surname convention got my Spanish professor in trouble. His full name was Marcelino Peñuelas Company. "Company" is a Catalan name and is pronounced "com PAN-yuh"—but of course, Americans assumed it was the name of his business. The university administration told him he'd have to stop advertising his business in university correspondence, so he finally gave up and changed his name to Marcelino C. Peñuelas.

We were married in a civil ceremony. The judge required that a bilingual friend be present to make sure the groom understood what he was getting into. We borrowed my Dad's car for a one-day honeymoon trip to the mountains—I had to be back that night to feed the cells in my cell culture experiment in my research job. It was a year or so before we could afford our first car, a $600 VW bug. It looked just like Herbie in the movie, even the same color. I had never driven a stick shift and my husband had never driven a car, period. I had my Dad give me two quick shifting lessons, then practiced stopping and starting on a hill until I got the hang of it. I felt superior because a high school friend had a VW and she was still so afraid of hills that she had mapped out routes all over Seattle where she could avoid them.

Our first apartment had a kitchen so small the refrigerator had to stay outside in the dining area, and the bedroom was made out of a former closet, with a wall-to-wall mattress on the floor. The top of the mattress was level with the low sill of the window, and on warm nights when the window was open, we'd have to be careful not to roll right out the window and down two stories to the sidewalk.

The apartment was in the University District on "The Ave"—which was a center of hippie life second only to San Francisco's Haight-Ashbury district. We didn't have a TV—but there was plenty of entertainment just looking out the window at the colorful clothes, the eccentric people, and the drugs exchanging hands in plain view. Pancracio wore a suit and tie and was frequently mistaken for a "narc" because no one else dressed so formally. One boy never wore shoes, and would slosh through the gutters in bare feet in the rain. Motorcycles would gather in front of the café across the street and would rev their engines late at night. One crazy guy would scream and threaten to take off his clothes whenever he thought someone had insulted him. A crowd would gather, and he would rip off his shirt. Never went all the way, though. Darn!

We knew a number of Spanish-speaking people that we could socialize with while my husband's English was still shaky. My favorite Spanish professor came to our apartment for dinner one night with his wife and brought a visiting celebrity: the Spanish novelist Ramón Sender. He had fled Spain during the Spanish Civil War after his wife was brutally murdered by Franco's followers, and he refused to return to Spain while Franco was alive. We were having a pleasant dinner until he discovered that my husband had once belonged to a Franco-government-approved youth group. Then he shouted, "If I'd known that, I never would have set foot in your house!!" My professor friend had to pacify him.

One day I looked out the window and saw a man holding his little daughter so she could pee on the sidewalk. I thought, "Gee, I've never seen that happen in this country, but I used to see it a lot in Spain." Sure enough, I met the man the next day: he was a Spanish naval officer here on some kind of student exchange.

We eventually got tired of our apartment's space limitations, the summer heat (we were on the top floor with a flat roof and no insulation), and the fact that we had to park on the street several blocks away. We found another apartment in an old house that was subdivided. We still had to park on the street, but could usually find a place in front of the house or nearby. The owner lived on the second floor: she was an elderly Christian Scientist, but she was able to forgive me for my delusion that illness was real and she applauded my desire to help people as a doctor. We got what had been the living room/dining room/kitchen of the original house. The dining room became the bedroom, conveniently located between the kitchen and living room, with a cardboard closet in the corner. We had our own bathroom, but to get to it, we had to go downstairs and through a common area with a coin-operated washer and dryer. But it was definitely an improvement. The kitchen was big enough to accommodate the refrigerator and more than one person at a time, and the mattress was on a bed frame instead of the floor.

We bought our first furniture, a refurbished mahogany dining room set, at the Goodwill store for $70. Since the "dining room" was now a bedroom, we had to put the table in a corner of the living room. I used that set for over 30 years, through 7 moves and 2 broken and repaired table legs. We only ate out once a week—at my mother's house! When I wanted a couple of throw pillows, I bought cloth remnants and sewed them myself to save money. I remember budgeting one dollar a day for food and managing to stay within my budget. I started collecting china that they gave away at the grocery store, one piece a week. I don't remember feeling deprived or unfortunate. We could get out of the city on weekends because gas was cheap, especially for a VW. School was all-consuming, and life was good (when I could steal a moment from studying to remember I was alive).

Medical Student Hard at Her Studies, Christmas 1969

In the summers I managed to get research trainee jobs, and the summer before my senior year I really outdid myself. I managed to get research grant money to pay for a summer vacation in Spain! My psychiatry professor, Dr. Holmes, was the co-developer of the Holmes-Rahe Social Readjustment Rating Scale, which measured the relative stress of various life events. For example, the death of a spouse rated 100 points, while spending Christmas alone rated 12 points. It had been validated for Americans by asking large numbers of people "If the stress of death of a spouse is equal to 100 points, how many points would the stress of a change of job be? Of a serious illness? Of the birth of a child? etc." We wondered whether people in other cultures would have the same perceptions of stress. So I translated the questionnaire into Spanish and took it to Spain.

Since I was now getting a military paycheck (see below) I could finally afford a down payment on a new car, so we arranged to pick up a new Volvo in London, drive it to Spain, and ship it home to Seattle at the end of the summer. We rented a furnished apartment in Alicante, with a view of the Mediterranean on one side and of the Castle of Santa Barbara on the other. There were no laundry facilities and no such thing as a Laundromat, so I learned the backbreaking joys of washing bed sheets in the bathtub. One day I looked down from the balcony and saw two and only two vehicles in the parking lot. My new Volvo was parked beside a rustic cart hitched to a donkey!

We visited my husband's friends and relatives and drove all over Spain. Everywhere we went, we had people fill out the questionnaires. It was fun and easy. The hard work came when I got home: I had to turn it into a Senior Medical Student Thesis. First I had to collate the data, learn how to do Fortran programming, and run a statistical analysis. In those days, the computer was a room-sized monster in a Computer Lab across campus. You punched the data on punch cards, left your deck of cards for the technician to feed to the monster, and came back the next day to find that it "would not compute" because you had put a comma in the wrong column. The statistician gave me a block of punch cards that constituted a subroutine—all I had to do was put it in the right place in the deck, and it would automatically spit out Spearman's Rank Coordination Coefficient numbers, whatever they are. We found lots of small differences, but overall our data showed that Spaniards essentially perceived the stress of different life events very much the same way Americans did.

In my senior year I joined the military through the Senior Medical Student Program. This sounded like a really good deal. I would be on active duty during my senior year, drawing the pay and allowances of a second lieutenant, but I wouldn't have to wear a uniform or report to anyone. The end of poverty! I couldn't resist. My father's first reaction was, "I didn't raise my daughter to be a soldier!" I didn't exactly want to be a soldier; I had no motivation other than to earn money. I would be obligated to serve for three more years, but I figured if I didn't like it, all I would have to do is get pregnant and I would be automatically discharged. A double standard was in effect: men who went into this program were already obligated to two years' military service by the draft, and they incurred one additional year of payback for the Senior Medical Student Program; since I was not draftable, I incurred a 3-year payback obligation.

I had to go down to the nearest Air Force base for a physical, but I had no other contact with the military until I graduated. Except for a check in the mail once a month. I applied for an Air Force internship, which was highly recommended by our advisors. Since the military didn't have private staff physicians, the interns had more control over their patients than they did in many civilian programs; and since the staff in military hospitals came from all over the country, interns were exposed to a variety of philosophies.

I got my orders to report to David Grant Medical Center at Travis Air Force Base, California for my internship. The orders had all kinds of funny abbreviations in them that I didn't understand, like PCS and NLT.[5] My father remembered some of them from his Army experience in WWII, and I had to go to the ROTC office on campus to get a translation of the rest of them. I was a second lieutenant until the day I graduated, a first lieutenant from then until my internship started (a matter of days) and a captain from the first day of internship. When I was going through inprocessing at Travis, a young lieutenant asked me how long it took me to get promoted to captain, and I was ashamed to tell him.

VACATION

When my classes ended, I managed two camping vacations: one before the graduation ceremony and one after. On the first, my husband and I had some differences of opinion about what to do and when, so on the second vacation, I decided to bring company along for moral support.

After graduation we took off again with my 18 year old brother and 13 year old sister. They kept an ongoing diary of the trip. It was titled "The Trip—Offishul Recurd" (They could spell better—that was an attempt at humor).

It started out with considerable detail:

Mileage 16486 = 0.	Seattle (Blech) lv. 8:000000 0'clock. Stop at Village Shell, pump air pressure up to 30 lbs. Lv. Seattle 8:30 and 25 seconds.
7.4 miles.	Mercer Island (more Blech) End construction
12.7 miles	Eastgate. (Even more blech) Started raining.
18.1 miles	Issaquah (Icky Squaw) Highway crossed East Fork Issaquah Creek Crossed East Fork Issaquah Creek again More East Fork Issaquah Creek More East Fork Issaquah Creek More East Fork Issaquah Creek More East Fork Issaquah Creek More East Fork Issaquah Creek More East Fork Issaquah Creek

---

5.   Permanent Change of Station, and No Later Than

| 31.4 miles | North Bend (Bent)
Harriet yawned.
Tree—4,857,392 ½ needles
Rocks |

At 88.8 miles, they opened a package of cookies and started keeping track of the cookie mileage.

101.5 miles	Thorp. 22 cookies et
109.5 miles	Ellensburg: we shoulda stopped an got a Ellensburger
114.2 miles	Kittitas. 28 cookies Passed Ditch Witch Truck Passed same bus again some more
130.9 miles	Would you believe East Fort Issaquah Creek? Ginkgo Pet [Petrified] Forest next rt.
135.5 miles	Vantage
135.3 miles	arr. Ginkgo Pet Forest. 37 cookies lv. Ginkgo Pet Forest. 40 cookies
144.0 miles	Wanapum Dam (Damn it) Saw Dam—I'll be dammed. Saw fish viewing room without fish Water

By 338.7 miles, we had arrived in Idaho and gone through 100 cookies, for a cookie mileage of 2.5 miles per cookie. There was a cryptic first entry for Idaho

IDAHOOOOOOOOOOOOOOOOOOOOOOOOOOOOOOOps
Prepare to write you weren't supposed to write that that's the question. What's the answer? The answer? Stop dictation. Dictators are bad. Weather clearing up whoopee.

At 377.3 miles, we arrived at the Farragut State Park Campground.

Stopped and spended nite. Saw deer. Eated hot dogs, potatos and onions. Sleeped. It rained. Eated oatmeal (blech). Still raining. Leave Farragut. Come back for hatchet. Leave again.

We drove all the way through Glacier National Park without seeing it. The diary includes a drawing of the park showing only clouds and fog, with a glimpse of a small section of hillside that was pronounced to look like "Africa tilted." It rained a lot. We stopped at the Museum of the Plains Indians. "The plains in the plains are mainly full of rain. The rain in Spain falls mainly in Montana." The trip diary entries become sparser and even less informative.

760.8	Bynum
	it's clearing up?
774.2	Choteau
	halp! It's getting dark.

After that, the diary deteriorated even more. It indicates that we visited Lewis and Clark Caverns, Virginia City, and JELLYSTONE National Park. On the back of one page is a drawing of a certificate:

BIRCH JOHN SOCIETY[6]
This is to certify that
___Peter Potty___
is an official member of the Birch John Society
and is hereby entitled to free overnite accommodations
in any John in the whole world and Canada.

[Crude drawing of outhouse]

IN T.P. WE TRUST

So much for diary keeping. Judging from this experience, you can probably be very thankful that I didn't keep a diary, even though it means many of my life events are lost to history and others may be misremembered.

After the diary fizzled, the trip deteriorated some more. We had a flat tire. Then we started through the mountains near Ouray, Colorado and the car quit. We rolled backwards downhill for about two miles to a garage in Ouray. We were stuck there for two days waiting for them to send a part by Greyhound bus. We managed to check into an old hotel with only half a wall between the rooms and entertained ourselves by playing Frisbee in the street and "horsing around" on a trail ride.

---

6.   The John Birch Society was an anti-Communist organization. There was a popular song about "if your Mommy is a Commie then you have to turn her in," and "meeting in the john, in the john, in the John Birch Society."

Ouray, Colorado. Not the best place for a Volvo to break down

By the time the car was fixed, the charm of this vacation had pretty well evaporated, so we drove through the night and arrived early the next morning at Travis Air Force Base in California, about halfway between Sacramento and San Francisco. We rented an apartment in Vacaville and slept on the floor in our sleeping bags that night. We checked out San Francisco, then put my brother and sister on the bus to Seattle. My husband got a job in an onion factory, and I started my internship.

4

Internship

Behind every successful woman is herself.

> —*bumper sticker*

At last! I was a real doctor and a real "Air Farce Ossifer"! Sort of. At least I had the diploma and the uniform. You can't actually legally practice medicine until you have completed a year's internship and passed a licensing exam. My internship was what was called a Rotating 0 internship. It had required rotations through the major specialties (internal medicine, surgery, pediatrics and OB-Gyn) plus electives like orthopedics, dermatology, neurology and ENT.

ORIENTATION

Since we interns were coming from different schools with different graduation dates, and since all internships were required to begin on July 1st, they didn't have time to send us to the usual basic training course. We got a quick in-house orientation instead. A master sergeant taught us a few military essentials like how to salute, when to salute, who to salute, when to keep our hats on, and how to wear the uniform. I was confused about the ranks; I had some vague idea that you progressed from private to sergeant and then to lieutenant. I had to learn that the enlisted men and noncoms were a whole separate species from officers. It still doesn't make sense to me that you are a second lieutenant first and a first lieutenant second. Even after this orientation, it was the better part of a year before I got it all straight and learned to distinguish a staff sergeant from a tech sergeant. At least I was better informed than the wife of a staff sergeant I worked with. All she knew was that there were lots of different kinds of sergeants. She saw a man in

46

uniform in front of her in line at the commissary, and she didn't know what the stars on the shoulder meant. She asked him what kind of sergeant he was. The general was not amused.

New Doctor/Captain/Intern Reporting for Duty[1]

Our instructor talked about the men's uniform in great detail, but said nothing about the women's uniform. Since I was the only woman, I didn't want to monopolize class time for my sole benefit, so I waited until the end and then went up and asked him about the women's uniform. His answer was, "I don't know; we've never had a woman before; you could go ask one of the nurses." Thanks a lot! As a result, I didn't realize that the only earrings allowed were a small pearl or a small gold ball. Several months into my internship, a nurse was kind enough to tell me I was wearing illegal earrings.

---

1. Notice that I am wearing two ribbons. 14 years later, after three promotions, I will still be wearing only two ribbons. More about this later.

Doctors were notorious for being un-military. Our neurologist wore his hair too long, but got away with it because every time someone would call him on it he would reach up and feel his hair and look surprised and say, "I didn't realize. Thank you for telling me, Sir; I'll get a haircut right away, Sir." And then he wouldn't.

The internship was grueling. We were on call every third night, and rarely got much sleep on call, so the second night we would go home and crash, and that left one evening out of three for everything else in our lives including food shopping, house cleaning, laundry, studying, and recreation. It all passed in a kind of blur. I didn't keep a diary, but I did put a few cryptic notes on an engagement calendar, and a lot of the weekend days indicate "slept all day." I managed to stay awake enough weekends to visit San Francisco, Sacramento, Point Lobos, Yosemite, Lake Tahoe and other nearby sites of interest.

The chief resident on surgery used to ask the interns, "Have you had time to eat or take a crap today? If you have, then you're not working hard enough!" He claimed that he got home so seldom that he had to show his ID card before his wife would let him through the door. One resident was constantly complaining that he didn't have time to spend with his wife and kids, and talking about the importance of family; naturally, he was the one who took up with a nurse and divorced his wife. We would start rounds at 7 AM, spend most of the day in the operating rooms, and break out between cases to rush to the wards and do the workups for the next day's patients. They said an ideal surgeon would come equipped with an indwelling bladder catheter and Supp-hose. Standing all day left my feet and legs aching long into the night.

Call Rooms

There was some concern about having a woman in the internship program. I was only the second woman intern in Air Force history. I was really conspicuous: Travis didn't have (and as far as I know had never had) a single other woman doctor assigned in any capacity, even as a civilian consultant. The first woman intern, two years earlier at another Air Force hospital, had caused a scandal by having an affair with a married resident; he was thrown out of the program and she wasn't. They were watching me to see what I would do. They needn't have worried: I was securely married and besides I was too tired from the 36 hour shifts to think about fooling around.

On my first rotation, internal medicine, there was a call room with two beds for the intern and resident right on the ward. It was quite public: the nurses would walk in and wake whichever doctor they needed. There was a private bathroom to change clothes in, so there was no embarrassment about a female intern and a male resident sharing the call room. No one even said anything except for one older surgeon who made some comments about how lucky the resident was to get to "sleep" with me. I just ignored him.

One of the staff doctors left a stack of old *Playboy* magazines in the call room; his wife had made him clean them out of the garage because she was afraid the kids would find them. When we had a few spare moments, we would look through them. Maybe the guys enjoyed looking at the pictures; I don't know. But I do know we all enjoyed reading the better jokes to each other out loud. One time we were surprised by a giggle—the nurses at the nursing station had been listening to us over the intercom.

My next rotation was OB-Gyn. Of all the specialties; wouldn't you think that would be the most accepting of women? They had a call room for four doctors, so it was even less private than the two-doctor internal medicine call room. And we were so busy we didn't get to spend much time there anyway. I never dreamed there would be any problem. Apparently one of the wives complained, and I was banished. The only place they could find for me to sleep was a makeshift cot in a treatment room. It wouldn't have been so bad, but the lights were connected to the circuit for the newborn nursery next door, so I couldn't turn the lights off without consigning the whole newborn nursery to darkness.

YES, I REALLY AM A DOCTOR

In 1970, people didn't expect to see a woman doctor, especially in a military hospital, and they tended to assume I was something else. The women's uniform at the time was a light blue cotton pinstripe material similar to what the Red Cross volunteers wore, so I was frequently mistaken for a volunteer. I was also mistaken for a nurse, a lab technician, and practically everything *but* a doctor. This was hard on me, because the ink had hardly dried on my diploma, and I was still trying to convince *myself* that I was really a doctor.

I wore a white coat over my uniform, with a name tag that said doctor on it. I made a point of always introducing myself as "doctor." It didn't do any good. People refused to see the tag or hear the introduction, because it didn't match their preconceptions. I would introduce myself as doctor, spend an hour doing a complete history and physical on a new admission, explain to the patient what we planned to do for him in the hospital; and then, as I was leaving the room, he would ask, "Are you a nurse?"

I was tempted to answer "No, I'm only the cleaning lady, but I always wondered what it would be like to be a doctor, so I borrowed this white coat and nametag." Or "No, I'm the doctor's wife; I'm just filling in so my husband can play golf." Or simply, "No. Are you a patient?"

A patient was sitting in the lobby one day with his 3 year old daughter when he saw me pass through the hall. He pointed me out to his daughter, saying "That's my doctor, honey." She turned to him with a disgusted look and decreed, "Oh, Daddy! That's not a doctor; that's a lady!"

When I was assigned to the newborn nursery, part of my job was to talk to all the new mothers about child care, the well baby clinic, where to call if they had any questions, etc. One morning I had made the rounds and had specifically introduced myself as doctor to each new mother. Later, the OB resident checked with his patients before discharge and asked if the doctor from the nursery had been around yet to talk to them. Every single woman said, "No, just some nurse." He went storming into the nursery to chew the nurse out for doing the intern's job, only to find out that that "nurse" was me.

When I was on the OB rotation, they got busy and had to call me in at the last minute to deliver a patient I hadn't previously seen. She was a black lady with a strong accent. She kept asking the nurses, "When de doctah comin'?" They pointed me out in the scrub room at the sink. She kept saying, "Oh, now, you joshin' me. Dat ain't de doctah! When de doctah comin'?" I proceeded to give her a spinal anesthetic, perform an episiotomy, deliver the baby, and sew her up. Through the whole thing, she kept protesting, "You not de doctah. When de doctah comin'?" Three days later, when she was discharged with her baby, she stopped me in the hall to say, "Ah just wanted you to know: Ah really believe you de doctah now!"

I got so frustrated I was tempted to get one of those sandwich boards with huge letters saying "I AM A DOCTOR" to see if anyone would notice *that*. I'm sure they wouldn't have.

EMERGENCY ROOM DUTY

There was an MOD (Medical Officer of the Day) assigned to work the ER each night. All the staff doctors shared this duty in rotation, and an intern was assigned to work with them. Some of them were subspecialists who hadn't seen general medical patients in years. One colonel told me, "You see all the patients. I'll be in the call room if you need me, BUT YOU'D BETTER NOT NEED ME." I managed not to. We had to work all day before the night shift started, and we had to work the following day, so we hated to get up for a trivial problem that should have waited for a regular appointment. One night I got up at 2 AM to see a lady with a headache. I asked how long she had had it. About 3 hours. Had she taken an aspirin or anything for it? No. Why not? Because she was waiting to see if it would go away.

Another woman wanted us to see her dog. We told her we didn't do dogs, and suggested she call her veterinarian. She said, "I wouldn't THINK of waking my veterinarian at this time of night!"

A woman came in and said she'd had a rash, but it went away. What was it?

Another patient was referred to a veterinarian. She brought her child in; the doctor asked her what was wrong, and she said, "You're the doctor, you tell me." He handed her a prescription slip with the name of a veterinarian and told her, "*I don't treat patients without a history.*"

Some mothers were very demanding: "I want penicillin for my child's cold." The doctor asked her, "What kind? Pen VK? Bicillin? Oral, intramuscular, aqueous? How many units?" She said, "You're the doctor; you're supposed to know that." And he countered, "Yes, and aren't I supposed to know *when* to prescribe it, too?" She got the point.

One night a patient came into the ER with a penile discharge. He was too embarrassed to tell the female nurse what his problem was; he said he would only talk to the doctor. She called me and watched the patient's face fall as he saw who was walking down the long hallway towards him. He did manage to get over his shock and let me examine and treat him; but I don't think he was too happy.

There was a nearby naval station at Mare Island that tried to turf[2] patients to us whenever possible. "Please examine this patient. I can't do a pelvic exam because I don't have a female chaperone." They didn't stop to think the patient's husband could have very well acted as chaperone. "Our lab isn't open at night." when the test could well have waited until the next day. We dreaded their calls, and came to refer to it as Nightmare Island.

---

2.   Slang for finding a way to get rid of a patient and make someone else responsible. One way to turf is to put the patient's bed in the "orthopedic" position—as high as it will go. The hope is that the patient will fall out of bed and break something so you can transfer him to the orthopedic ward.

There was a condition we called "terminal seizures." Heavy-drinking soldiers returning from their tours in Viet Nam would have a long binge of a farewell party, and during the many hours of the trans-Pacific flight they would dry out. By the time they arrived at the air terminal at Travis to catch their connecting flight, they would be in full alcohol withdrawal and would have an alcohol-withdrawal seizure in the terminal. They would already be waking up by the time we picked them up with the ambulance. We would evaluate them to rule out anything more serious and usually discharge them in a couple of days none the worse for wear. One of the interns hadn't heard about this phenomenon. He was sleeping in the call room in the main hospital, and when he heard "terminal seizures" on the phone he thought the patient was in the midst of dying, so he panicked and didn't take time to dress. He went running down to the ER building in an embarrassing state of dishabille.

One ER patient was an Army private named General Jones. Yes, "General" was his first name. He told about an experience he had while visiting another base. He didn't know how to get from one place on base to another, so he called the number listed for transportation, and said, "This is General Jones, how can I get to building 106?" They sent a staff car.

One memorable wound I treated was a lawnmower injury to the leg. Can't remember how it happened, but the wound was a large one and was filled with tiny pieces of grass. I spent about an hour picking them out one by one with a forceps. One night I lost my temper with a patient's husband. He was a high-ranking officer and he was trying give me orders and tell me how to treat his wife. I realized he was just anxious about his wife, but I finally snapped at him, "What medical school did you go to?" and he quieted down.

An overweight young woman came into the ER with regular abdominal contractions but she and her mother both loudly insisted she could not possibly be pregnant. Even after a full term baby duly made its appearance by the traditional route they kept protesting she hadn't done anything to get pregnant. Where did they think the baby came from? Parthenogenesis? Immaculate conception? And then there was the young man who delivered his wife's baby in the front seat of a Volkswagen bug on the way to the hospital—it was a breech birth and he admitted he did have a little trouble getting the head out.

We didn't have much trauma in our emergency room, so we were sent to work a few evenings in a civilian ER in Sacramento. I hated it. The civilian doctors weren't particularly helpful: they made comments like, "How do you like my bed?" and "Come up and sleep with me [in the call room]." We didn't know anyone there, and were thrown into situations we really didn't know how to handle.

It was "front lines" experience with little teaching. We saw a different type of patient there: the dregs of a city. Alcoholics, street people. One man came in with seizures, and he still had the unopened pill bottle in his pocket from the previous night when he'd come in with seizures. How can you help someone who won't lift a finger to help himself? Another patient came in with his ear torn almost completely off. He was so drunk that I was able to sew the ear back on with no anesthesia. He thought his injury was funny and he kept making jokes throughout the procedure.

ON THE WARDS

The C-5 transport plane had just been added to the Air Force inventory. It was a BIG plane. The flight path put it right over the hospital when it took off; the ground shook and the noise was deafening. You couldn't hear yourself think. If you were listening to a patient's chest with a stethoscope, you just had to stop and wait until it passed.

Another occupational hazard was the new carpets. They interacted with the soles of military shoes to produce an impressive blue electric flash when you touched a doorknob. It hurt. I learned to take a key from my pocket and touch it to the doorknob to avoid the pain. I also let other people go through doors first whenever possible. Doors were an issue. Some men were stuck on "ladies first," while others were programmed that rank went first, and still others thought that staff doctors should precede interns and residents regardless of rank. Much jostling and confusion and blue sparks every time a door got in our way.

Today x-rays are digital and readily available on computer systems. Back then, they were more of a challenge. We held x-ray rounds each afternoon where we would look at all the films that had been taken on the patients on our service. About half the x-rays would be in the box for our service where they were supposed to be. The interns had the fun of tracking down the rest—looking in the files, in the to-be-filed stacks, the wards, the radiologists' offices, on the floor, under the secretary's lunch, etc. We got pretty good at it; we would have contests with the radiology techs and we could usually find a film before they did.

My most unforgettable patient was an old Navy man with Korsakoff's syndrome. This is a condition where chronic alcoholism damages the brain so that the patient has a faulty memory and "confabulates" or makes up stories to compensate. These people can be difficult patients. His chart read, "This 68 year old white male was dumped at our emergency room from the doors of a speeding ambulance …" He had a lung abscess. Normally we would have treated him with IV antibiotics, but he couldn't remember what the IV was for and kept pulling it out. So he got intramuscular penicillin shots twice a day. These are quite painful; but since he could never remember the last one, every shot was the first as far as he was concerned, so he had no complaints.

If you asked him what he was doing in the hospital, he would say, "I was on this ship when it was commissioned, and in a while I'm going to go down and fire up the boilers and set sail for Pearl [Harbor]." or "Me and John went up to Oregon to see about buying some pigs, but we couldn't find any we liked, so we came back here." He liked to parade around the ward naked, and when he found out the nurses objected, he would wrap the sheepskin pad from his bed around his waist. One day he pulled a wastebasket out into the middle of the ward and proceeded to defecate in it in full view of a dozen other patients. After a month of treatment, the abscess wasn't healing, so they eventually did a biopsy and found out he had active TB and had been exposing everyone on the ward. Oops!

A new drug for Parkinson's disease had just been approved by the FDA: levodopa. On my neurology rotation it fell to me to write the first prescription for levodopa ever filled at our hospital. The patient was a little old man who had difficulty writing, a tremor, and a slow, uncoordinated gait. He had a great response to the medication and would run sprints down the hall to show off. One reported side effect of the drug was an increase in libido, and sure enough!—one day we found him in a private room flirting with a woman patient, holding her hand! She had an advanced brain tumor, and I'm not sure she knew what was going on, but he had a big smile on his face and seemed to be enjoying himself.

A patient on the orthopedic ward was recovering from a gunshot wound. He was a security policeman who had somehow managed to shoot himself in the foot while cleaning his weapon. As I looked through his medical record, I discovered a psych consult from three years earlier that said, "This man should never be allowed to carry a weapon." I guess the message didn't get through to the security police. Rumor had it that recruits who scored lowest on the entrance exams were assigned to be cops or food service workers.

One of the psych patients got out a window and walked all around the hospital on a ledge, peering in windows and scaring the patients. Another patient went AWOL from the hospital and turned up in a civilian jail on pot charges.

A woman was worked up for a seizure disorder and found to be faking. Predictably, when we tried to discharge her she staged a seizure and lay thrashing in the middle of the hall. We just stepped over her and went about our business until she finally got tired and decided to get up and leave.

One day a directive came around: our pharmacy is short on penicillin; please try not to prescribe it.... Um, OK (!?).... How about sending the patients a directive not to have infections that required it? At night, we could "raid" the pharmacy in the ER; we had a key and could pretty much take whatever we wanted for our patients (or even ourselves). Quaalude was new and it and Darvon were still on the open shelves; they weren't yet considered drugs of abuse. It can take a while to realize a new pain medication is habit-forming; when heroin first came out it was advertised as a non-addictive alternative to morphine!

Once a week they would let the drug representatives set up a display in a room we could visit. We called it "metabolic rounds" because they always had free doughnuts. We pretty much ignored their advertising spiels, but we got lots of free pens, paperweights, free samples, and gadgets from them. I remember a little box of 12 pill bottles that Smith, Kline and French handed out that included samples of diet pills, tranquilizers, pain pills, etc. many of which contained amphetamines and barbiturates. Not controlled substances at the time.

Staff doctors often had additional duties. One was the Rabies Control Officer. I asked him what that involved, and he told me about the required meetings, reports, etc. He said all he had actually accomplished in his 3-year tenure was to identify rabies in 3 skunks and a cow! I had a mental image of a cow running amok and foaming at the mouth. I guess you could say we had "mad cow disease" even back then.

One of the OB residents was an incorrigible practical joker. When he learned that a new Chief of OB/Gyn was coming, Dr. Wesp, the resident told everyone he knew the man from a previous assignment and his name had been mis-spelled: it was really Dr. Werp. When Dr. Wesp arrived, all his paperwork, his name stamp, and the plaque on his door all read "Werp." He didn't think it was funny.

The same resident called Labor and Delivery one night pretending to be the husband of a patient. He said, "My wife's not having contractions or anything, but there's this funny blue cord hanging down between her legs: is that anything to worry about?" The L&D nurse realized he was describing a prolapsed umbilical cord, which is a medical emergency. The blood supply can be cut off when the cord is caught between the baby's head and the mother's pelvic bones, and the baby can die. The treatment is to put a hand in the vagina and push the baby's head up to relieve the pressure and to do an immediate C-section. The nurse told the man to bring his wife in immediately. Then she called the intern on duty who called the resident on duty who called the staff obstetrician on duty who called anesthesia and a surgery crew. They all came in and sat around anxiously awaiting a patient who didn't exist.

Another doctor played a practical joke on the Armed Forces Institute of Pathology. They are renowned for being able to identify almost anything. He had a pet octopus that died, and he cut a chunk out, labeled it "left lower quadrant mass" and sent it in as if it were a surgical specimen removed from a patient's abdomen. Weeks passed. Finally the report came: it identified the specimen right down to the exact species of octopus and ended "Don't ever try a stunt like that again!"

Z SERVICE

The staff surgeon who made wisecracks about the residents "sleeping" with me, Dr. Z, was not particularly well liked; he was older and a bit out of date, his expertise was suspect, and he was always in a bad mood. He would positively abuse the residents, even the chief resident, saying things like, "God damn it, only an idiot would take such small stitches! No, damn it, don't make them *that* big! What the *hell* do you think you're doing?"

We had a medical student extern whose newborn son developed pyloric stenosis. This is a narrowing of the outlet of the stomach from overgrowth of the surrounding muscle, causing projectile vomiting. A simple operation is done to snip the muscle. Since it was a medical student's son, Dr. Z thought he should do the operation instead of the residents. This should have been a routine procedure, but there were unexpected complications. The residents did all the other surgery that month; they never had a complication with *their* pyloric stenosis surgeries.

There was an "A" service and a "B" service in the surgery department. Once a month there was an M and M meeting. Not to eat candy, but to discuss every surgical case that had occasioned morbidity or mortality. That month, the statistics were something like:

"A" service: 51 cases, 2 morbidities.
"B" service: 62 cases, 1 mortality, 1 morbidity.
"Z" service: one case, 1 morbidity.

It seems that every time someone tries to do things "better" for a doctor or a doctor's family, things go wrong. The wife of a doctor had twin boys, and the staff pediatrician volunteered to do the circumcisions, which he hadn't done in a long time. One of them resulted in bleeding complications requiring electrocautery. None of us residents or interns had any complications with the circumcisions we did.

One of my fellow interns became the father of premature twins. Their condition was touch and go for a while—one of them stopped breathing in the middle of the night when I was on duty and I had to resuscitate him. Meanwhile, the wife had a hysterectomy along with the C-section and developed complications. They had carefully identified the ureter on each side so they wouldn't cut it, but it turned out she had two ureters on the left side and they had cut the one that was functional. So they had to open her back up a couple of days later in an emergency operation. And the poor intern had another child at home and was still working his 36 hour shifts! It's a wonder he didn't develop post-traumatic stress syndrome. Only back then there wasn't any such disease, so he didn't know he was allowed to decompensate.

I had to get a physical exam in the Flight Surgeon's Office for some military requirement. I managed to get away from the ward long enough to get the preliminaries done—BP, hearing, visual acuity, blood tests, etc. but then they said the flight surgeon was busy and I'd have to come back another day. I protested that it was hard enough to get away from my duties once, and twice was unreasonable to ask. The corpsman asked me if I was healthy. I said I thought I had to be pretty healthy to be surviving a stressful internship. He said OK and faked the paperwork.

HUSBANDS CAN'T BE DEPENDENTS

I discovered that all married men had "dependent" wives, even if they worked and made more money than their husbands; but a woman couldn't have a dependent husband, even if she actually provided 100% of his support. I only got a single officer's housing allowance, so I made less money than if I had had hair on my chest instead of boobs. My husband got a military ID card that was good for the commissary and the base theater, but not for the Base Exchange or for medical care.

It wasn't just the military that had this attitude. I applied to Geico for car insurance as a military officer, but they informed me they couldn't insure me because I was not head of the household. It made no difference who my husband was or whether he was working. If he'd been a mentally incompetent quadriplegic, he still would have been head of the household. Oh, the power of those dangly bits!

Women in the military really couldn't have dependents back then. If you got pregnant you were automatically discharged. No appeals. If you married a man who had a 20 year old child from a previous marriage, that meant you technically had a dependent so you couldn't stay in the military.

Another intern told me it was only fair for women to make less money, because they couldn't serve in a combat zone. No Viet Nam for me. I never understood that policy. Doctors were noncombatants. And I knew nurses who had served in Viet Nam; one had picked up a rifle and defended her patients when the hospital came under attack.

I was personally glad I didn't have to go over there to be shot at, but I couldn't approve of the policy that exempted me. When people asked me if I thought women should be sent into combat, I would say, "No! But then I don't think men should either." Unfortunately, sometimes people *are* sent to war, and I see no reason to exempt women, especially in an all-volunteer army. The only consideration should be whether the individual woman is qualified for the particular job.

I told my friend that maybe I should make more money than he did, because every time he saw a woman patient, he had to take a nurse away from her other duties to act as chaperone. I didn't need a chaperone even for pelvic exams and Pap smears. I could manage the whole thing by myself; and I frequently did, rather than wait until a nurse was free.

I never used chaperones when I examined males, either. You may call this a double standard, but the legal reality was that female patients had sued male doctors for inappropriate conduct but no male patient had ever sued a female doctor. Some of my male patients were a bit embarrassed to be examined by a woman, but they got over it. One was just amused—I was about to do a prostate exam on an old retired geezer when he started laughing. He told me he was remembering his first rectal exam when he was a naive young recruit fresh off the farm. The doctor had told him to bend over and spread his cheeks, and he bent over and pulled the sides of his face out with his hands. He didn't have any idea what was coming!

Have you ever heard the term "short arm" inspections? It was an old military tradition where the men lined up and presented their penises to be examined for VD. If they still had that duty, I was never called to perform it. Probably a good thing, as some of the arms might have tried to stand up and salute me.

Rectal exams are ideal for a practical joke: a male doctor stands behind the patient, has him bend forward over the exam table, and inserts his finger into the patient's rectum while a colleague slips into the room unnoticed and places *both* his hands on the patient's shoulders.

NURSING NOTES

I discovered I had one advantage over some of the other doctors: I was willing to listen to nurses. I actually read their nursing notes, and sometimes I learned important facts that the patient hadn't told the doctor. The nurses spent more time with the patients and were less threatening, so patients tended to open up more. I also was not ashamed to ask the nurses for help in writing orders. For instance, if I had a 6 month old patient and didn't know what a 6 month old was supposed to eat, I'd ask the nurses, "What kind of diet orders do the doctors usually write for a 6 month old?" They knew, they were happy to be asked, and they were glad to be appreciated and respected. Some of the male doctors felt like they had to maintain an air of superiority and be perceived as knowing more than the nurses. I didn't feel superior to anybody. I was just trying to survive and help the patients. I also realized that a smart nurse who has been on the same ward for years may know more than an intern who has just started a rotation on that ward.

The one time I was unhappy with a nurse was when the Chief Nurse brought some VIP wives around for a tour of the pediatric ward. One of our favorite patients, a sweet child with leukemia, had died during the night, and we were devastated. It seemed like the nicest kids were the ones who got the terminal illnesses. The ward nurses were busy tying up the loose ends after his death, and no one was standing ready to greet the tour as instructed. The Chief Nurse chastised the ward supervisor for not obeying orders, and was very nasty about it. The ward nurse humbly apologized. Then the Chief Nurse flippantly asked her to show the visiting wives "some interesting patients." I wanted very badly to tell them to step into the next room and look at the "interesting" dead body of the leukemia patient—but I bit my tongue.

One little boy was being evaluated for a genetic disorder and had to have a lot of blood tests. He would patiently let them stick the needle in his vein, wouldn't flinch or complain of pain, but when he saw the red blood appear in the syringe he would start screaming. I always wondered what was going through his mind. Maybe something like the child who cried because the nurse took his temperature and wouldn't give it back.

The pediatric ward tended to be noisy. There was usually a baby crying somewhere. After a while we tuned it out. Visitors would say, "How can you stand that noise?" and we would say, "What noise?"

We had a hemophiliac patient on the ward, and they called me one night because he had a nosebleed. I had visions of a continuing hemorrhage that just wouldn't stop, and a fatal outcome. Instead, I discovered that nosebleeds in hemophiliacs are just like nosebleeds in other patients: you pinch the nose for 5 minutes and they stop.

We learned to examine urine for signs of disease. One sign was "casts" of clumped cells that retained the shape of the vessel they had filled. One of our instructors showed us a good example under the microscope and said, "Look at that cast. What a cast!—I can see Marilyn Monroe, and John Wayne!"

We learned to look for the "O sign" where the patient's mouth hangs open; that's a bad sign. Worse is the "Q sign" where his mouth hangs open and his tongue hangs out one side. In women, we learned to look for the "positive lipstick sign" as an indication of recovery.

We learned to start IVs in veins that were barely visible, on the tops of baby feet, on baby scalps, wherever was available. I swear one pediatric resident could insert a needle that was bigger than the vein he put it in. Sometimes adult IVs were even harder, for two reasons: they complained, and they had big rubbery veins that looked easy but that made the needle bounce off to the side. I had a rule of 3; after 3 attempts I would ask someone else to try. Sometimes the nurse could do it when I couldn't. I was really embarrassed one day when I had to start an IV on a staff physician who had been admitted with some kind of cancer; I stuck him 3 times painfully without success and had to call for help. He was polite and understanding about it, but I thought he probably wanted to kill me.

RhoGam shots for Rh incompatibility (to prevent "blue babies") were still relatively new. When I ordered one for an OB patient, the nurse informed me nurses were not allowed to give those shots. I informed her that doctors might be "allowed" to give shots, but that medical schools didn't teach them "how" to give shots. I had never given one before. So she stood out in the hallway with me and described what I was supposed to do, and I went in the patient's room and did it. It was easy. The patient thought I was a pro.

SURGERY

I learned how important expectation is in the perception of pain. We had two hernia patients on the surgery service the same day; they had exactly the same operation. One was a 2 year old boy, the other a 28 year old man. Right after surgery, the child was standing up in his crib asking to be taken out. Someone who didn't realize he had had surgery took pity on him and put him down on the floor, and he proceeded to run up and down the hall and play. He never complained of any discomfort. He didn't know it was supposed to hurt. The 28 year old man, on the other hand, was still moaning and groaning several days later when we took out his stitches; he could hardly turn over in bed.

I have long, slender fingers; the surgical gloves did not seem to be made with me in mind. I had a choice of using size 6 ½ and having my palm scrunched up, or of wearing a larger glove and having it droop off my fingertips. Sometimes they didn't have any gloves as small as 6 ½, which settled the dilemma neatly. Another problem in the spring was my hay fever. You can't wipe your nose when you are scrubbed in. One day I had mucous draining down so profusely all I could do is try to lick it up under the mask before it could drip down my chin. You couldn't stop in the middle of an operation to visit the restroom, so some fluid management planning was necessary to avoid emergencies.

I didn't get to participate in locker room discussions, because I had to change clothes in the nurses' locker room. But I did get treated to plenty of jokes during surgery. They weren't always politically correct. We were near San Francisco, so one surgeon told us a two-part joke about two homosexuals driving across the Bay Bridge. One said, "Look at the ferry." And the other said, "I didn't know we had our own Navy." The second part of the joke was that they got so busy watching the ferry they ran into a truck in front of them. One homosexual got out to try to pacify the truck driver. He started to apologize, when the huge driver got out of his truck, glared down at him with arms akimbo and said, "Fuck you, buddy!" He ran back to his car and told his partner, "It's all right, dear! He wants to settle out of court!"

I got to assist the plastic surgeon. One operation was a subcutaneous mastectomy. He made a small incision under the breast and managed to remove the entire breast through it. As the assistant, I was holding the edge of the incision up with a retractor and couldn't see a thing. Not even the surgeon himself could see what he was doing—he worked mostly by feel. He would tell me to watch and let him know if he cut through the skin. I *think* he was joking.

I assisted with nose jobs. You stick a chisel in the nose and hit it with a hammer to remove pieces of bone and cartilage. The patient is awake; he feels no pain, but can feel the vibrations of the hammer blows. Then he walks around looking like a raccoon for a couple of weeks afterwards. I decided I liked my nose just the way it was, thank you.

I learned to do bunions. First you squeeze all the blood out of the leg so there is a bloodless field to operate in. You peel the skin back over the bunion, take a hammer and chisel to the excess bone until it is pleasingly flat, then suture the skin back together. I bet a 10 year old could learn to do it.

I got to do a shoulder operation all by myself, with the orthopedic surgeon talking me through every step of it. I'd never even seen the operation done. I used chisels and saws and things I'd never used. After the initial incision, when I was getting ready to cauterize or tie off the bleeders, the surgeon told me not to bother—just put a towel on it, insert the retractor, and the pressure will stop the bleeding. I followed instructions; it worked. The surgery was a success. I did wonder what the patient would have thought if he knew who had done his operation.

I learned to scrub my hands with the little brush until they felt raw. I learned to hold my hands up and let water drip off my elbows. I learned to let the scrub nurse dress me and snap the gloves on my hands. I learned not to contaminate the surgical field. I learned not to scratch my nose. I learned to tie knots with one hand. I learned to hold a retractor steady. I learned to cut the suture as close as possible to the knot without cutting it so close it would unravel. I learned to take out an appendix. I learned to dictate operative reports. I learned to avoid the tip of the Bovie cauterization instrument after I saw a surgeon burn himself with it. I learned to make sure the patient was anesthetized before making the incision; one day the chief resident was in a slap-happy mood due to sleep deprivation, and he asked the anesthesiologist "Are you ready?" and proceeded to slit the patient's abdomen from xiphoid to pubis without waiting for an answer (fortunately the answer was yes).

Surgery was not my favorite rotation. Surgeons seemed to be gluttons for punishment and only partially human. They never slept, ate, peed or went home. They cared more about cutting than about the patients. One bragged, "Find me a patient, any patient; and I can find something to take out."

There is a rivalry between surgeons and internal medicine specialists. The internists like to think they are the intellectuals and surgeons are mere plumbers. The surgeons insist that they are the only ones who can actually fix things instead of just supplying pills. There is a joke about an internist and a surgeon who visit a

Chinese restaurant where there is a fish tank in the lobby. As they are waiting to be seated, the internist rests his forehead against the glass and seems to be concentrating. After a minute, all the fish start swimming in formation, doing loops, rolls and other tricks. The surgeon is impressed and wants to know how he does that. The internist explains that it is just superior intelligence, mind over matter. The surgeon tries. He rests his forehead against the tank and concentrates. Nothing happens. The fish keep going every which way. After a while, the surgeon starts opening his mouth and going, "Glub, glub."

Another rivalry joke is about the internist, the surgeon, the radiologist and their dogs. They are bragging about whose dog is the smartest. The internist calls his dog, "Here, Osler! Go out and find 3 sticks." The dog leaves, comes back with 3 sticks, lays them down in a row and barks 3 times." The surgeon says that's pretty good, but his dog is even smarter. He calls his dog, "Here, Halsted! Go out and find enough sticks to make 5." The dog leaves, comes back with 2 more sticks, lays them down beside the first 3 and barks 5 times. The radiologist is not impressed. He calls his dog, "Here, Roentgen. Show these guys what *you* can do." Roentgen screws the other two dogs, takes all their sticks and goes home early.

I did my first bone marrow biopsy with the hematologist supervising me. I had finished when the patient asked me when I was going to start. The hematologist was impressed by my painless technique, and thought my medical school had trained me well. I didn't tell him that I had never done one before; at my medical school not even the interns got to do bone marrows, much less the students.

The staff internist was quizzing us one day about the various causes of heart failure. He described the symptoms of beriberi, hoping one of us would recognize that this form of malnutrition can be a cause of heart disease. He asked, "What would you think if the patient had these symptoms?" I answered, "I'd think he was bery, bery sick."

A woman kept coming into the ER with severe headaches, and she claimed that only shots of Demerol provided relief. We didn't want to create a drug addict, and we suspected that she was exaggerating or that her headaches were psychosomatic. The psychiatrist arranged to have her get a shot of sterile salt water instead of her usual Demerol. Lo and behold!—the placebo worked just as well as the narcotic! The psychiatrist sat down with her and explained, saying "I can't understand it. If you have real pain, why did you respond to a fake medicine? Do you think maybe there could be a psychological component to your headaches?" After a long talk, he was congratulating himself that he had been able to give her some insight into her problem. But as he left the room, she said,

"Next time I get a headache, can I have another one of those placebo shots—it really worked great!"

We admitted an active duty enlisted man age 20. He'd gone to Sick Call with cold symptoms, and no one had worried much about him until he came back a week later still complaining. At that point, they did a blood count and discovered he had fulminant leukemia. He was admitted and was dead in less than 24 hours. He had a wife and child.

A patient in Intensive Care had drunk himself into liver failure with massive amounts of beer. He went through withdrawal, had hallucinations, pulled out his urinary catheter without deflating the bulb, and died late one night of complications of alcoholic pancreatitis with a massive abdominal infection. I had to tell his wife he was dead.

Delivering babies was fun, because the results were happy. I learned to do a spinal block, and to do a paracervical block where you reach up into the vagina with a humongously long needle and inject anesthetic on either side of the cervix. I learned to use forceps, do episiotomies, and sew them up. I got in trouble one day for not doing an episiotomy. The patient had had several babies, and she begged me not to cut. There was plenty of stretch, and the delivery went just fine. At the time, the accepted wisdom decreed that every woman should have an episiotomy to (1) prevent an uncontrolled tear, and (2) minimize stress on the baby, so I got reamed out for not following the rules. We know today that that was nonsense. I did the right thing. We also routinely treated swelling in pregnant patients with water pills, but by the time I started my residency a few years later, we had learned that that was likely to do more harm than good. Times change, science progresses, medical practice improves, doctors learn.

LITTLE OLD LADY WITH JOKES

Looks can be deceiving and first impressions wrong. We had a sweet, innocent-looking elderly grandmotherly lady on the internal medicine ward who surprised us all by passing out copies of her list of X-rated one-liners:

> Two old maids opened a cat house. They sold 8 cats the first day.
> The gigolo in the leper colony was doing real well until his business started falling off.
> Cuddle up a little closer; it's shorter than you think.
> All light headed gals are not blondes, by cracky!
> Did you hear about the cannibal who passed his grandma in the woods?"

"I can't get over a girl like you, so reach up and answer the phone."
You can have your cousins—of all my relations I like sex the best.
The fastest 4 handed game in the world is when it slips out.
It's sure hard to be good—in fact, it's got to be hard to be good.
She was only a farmer's daughter, but she couldn't keep her calves together.
Height of passion—2 old maids playing squat tag in an asparagus patch.
She was an angel until she swapped her harp for an upright organ.
Where there's a wilt there's no way.

This is just a sample; if you're a glutton for punishment, the entire list can be found in Appendix 1.

WOMEN AREN'T RETAINABLE

I loved looking at x-rays, seeing inside the body and interpreting what the shadows meant. I decided I wanted to be a diagnostic radiologist. I thought it would be a good specialty for raising a family, since it had more predictable hours than most. I applied to the radiology residency at David Grant. I was not chosen. After the decisions were made, one of the staff radiologists confided in me; he was black of skin and also purple of face due to a large birthmark, and perhaps his own experience of prejudice made him more sympathetic. He said he thought I should know that my qualifications were better than those of the men who were chosen, but that the selection board had been instructed to deduct points for women because women were not considered "retainable" in the service. I had the last laugh, because of all the men who were selected that year, not one stayed a minute beyond his payback requirements, and I stayed for a full 20 years and retired as a full colonel. The experience did lead me to wonder—if this was an example of the Air Force's accuracy of prediction, would the target be the safest place to hide during a bombing mission?

Since I wasn't selected for a residency, my only remaining options were to get pregnant so they would discharge me or to serve three years as a general medical officer. The latter option seemed more attractive at the moment. As we finished the internship, we got to request our choice of assignments. I asked for Torrejón Air Base in Spain as my first choice. Instead, I got another, smaller base in Spain that I had never heard of: Moron Air Base, near Seville in southern Spain. I was insulted. Just because I wasn't "retainable" enough to get a residency didn't mean I was so stupid I belonged on a base for dummies! Then I realized it wasn't "MO-ron" but the Spanish word "Mo-ROAN," with an accent on the second "o". I was reconciled except for a small nagging fear that my friends might spend the rest of our lives teasing me that I used to work at a base for mental defectives. When one of my friends heard I had been assigned to Spain, he said, "That's impossible. The Air Force never does anything as rational as sending someone who speaks Spanish to Spain!"

I didn't realize it at the time, but the Air Force had done me a favor. I was forced into primary patient care and discovered I had a real knack for it; I was happier interacting with patients than I would have been sitting in a dark room looking at pictures. It wasn't the first or last time that I found that I was fortunate not to get what I thought I wanted.

At the end of the year, we had a group photograph taken in the blue dress uniform (instead of the everyday khakis), and they had to send fully half of the men back because there was something wrong with their uniforms—like the wrong color socks, improper placement of insignia, or missing insignia. They were afraid we would embarrass them at the graduation ceremony, so they made us practice walking across the stage, saluting with our right hand, accepting the diploma with our left hand, thereby leaving the right hand free to shake hands with the general. The practice went well, but in the actual ceremony, the first person on stage was a pediatric resident accepting a special award, and he managed to salute with his *left* hand. The funniest thing was he didn't even realize he'd done anything wrong!

5

A General Medical Officer in Spain

○ ○

Whenever you are ignorant of a soldier's complaint, you should first take a little blood from him, and then give him an emetic and a cathartic—to which you may add a blister. This will serve, at least, to diminish the number of your patients.

—Francis Grose:
Advice to the officers of the British Army, 1782

Finally, school was out. I was a real, fully trained, licensed doctor and I was on my way to Spain!

The Air Force pays for a moving company. The movers packed our belongings and put everything in a big sealed shipping container for overseas transport. They would pack EVERYTHING including the contents of your trash cans, so you had to be sure you didn't overlook anything that could rot and smell. There were a few items they couldn't take; one was a motorcycle. One enlisted man I knew really wanted to take his motorcycle, so he took it apart and left a wheel in the bedroom, an engine in the dining room, a fender in the closet, etc. They would ask, "What's this?" and he would say, "Oh that's just an old part I'm keeping."

The moving men told us about another military family whose move was a real CATastrophe. The kids were unhappy that their cat couldn't go overseas with them, so they managed to sneak it in the shipping container with a bowl of food and water, not realizing how long the trip would take. The result was a dead cat, a great stink, and furniture frantically clawed to smithereens—which the insurance wouldn't pay for because it was the family's own fault.

I decided to drive across the US, ship my car from an Atlantic port, and catch a military flight from the East Coast to Spain. There were a couple of problems with this plan. In the first place, my husband was not considered a dependent, so he couldn't get on a military plane and they wouldn't pay his way. If he wanted to go to Spain with me, that was his problem. It was entirely up to him to get himself there.

The other problem was that I couldn't get on a military plane without dog tags, and they had never issued me any. I said fine, I'll just have to get some. Where can I get a set of dog tags? They said, "You can't. The machine that makes them is broken." A typical military Catch-22. As it turned out, no one ever asked to see my dog tags, and I didn't get a set until several years later. Did you ever wonder why dog tags come in pairs? It's so they can leave one on your dead body and keep track of the body count with the other. A happy thought, no?

So, dogtagless, I set out on a month's camping vacation with my husband. We climbed Lassen Peak, drove to Seattle to visit my family, drove cross-country stopping at every national park we could fit into our route, visited relatives in North Carolina and New York, and finished with a visit to Sturbridge Village in Massachusetts. I took my husband to the airport in New York for his commercial flight, delivered our camping gear to West Point for shipment to Europe as "hold baggage," delivered my car to the port in New Jersey, took a bus to McGuire AFB, stayed up all night waiting for a plane, flew to Charleston S.C. on a canvas bench in the back of a C141, and spent a couple of nights in the Charleston VOQ (Visiting Officers Quarters) awaiting my overseas flight.

The VOQ rooms were shared by two officers. My roommate told me she had once checked into one of these rooms after her assigned roommate was already in bed asleep. She was considerably quiet and kept the lights low and got into bed without awakening the roommate. The next morning, when she awoke, the light of day revealed her roommate to be a man! The same thing almost happened to me later in Spain—they assign so many male officers to rooms that they sometimes forget that an officer just might happen to be a woman.

Finally I caught my overnight flight to Madrid—a C141 with all the seats facing backwards.[1]

I arrived to a warm welcome: my cousin Bill, who I hadn't seen since I was 5, was stationed in Madrid. He and his family met my plane, entertained me, fed me chuletas and sangría, and delivered me to Iberia Airlines for my flight to

---

1. The Air Force puts the seats in backwards because they believe it is safer in a crash, not because they're trying to keep the troops from knowing where they're going.

Seville that evening. My husband and my military sponsor[2] met me at the airport there. My husband had rented a temporary apartment, and the next day we rented a SEAT 600 to use until the ship came in with our car a month later. SEAT was the Spanish version of the Italian Fiat, and the 600 model made a VW bug look big. No air conditioning, of course. Better than walking, but not by a whole lot. After my month-long odyssey, I was ready to go to work.

Leaving Grandparents' house in Poughquag en route to Spain

---

2.   When you move to a new base, the Air Force automatically assigns someone to be your sponsor. He is supposed to write you a welcome letter, tell you anything you might need to know, answer questions, and assist you with things like finding housing and getting settled in.

THE BASE AT MORÓN

The original American air base was right next to Seville. Franco made them move, supposedly because the planes made too much noise and people in Seville were complaining. That didn't stop him from immediately converting the old base to a civilian airport using the same runway. He used the same tactic in Madrid, where the old American base conveniently became the new Barajas International Airport, and the Americans had to rebuild a few miles away at Torrejón. Franco was a ruthless negotiator. He once met with Hitler, who wanted his support in WWII, and Hitler came out second best. Adolf reportedly said he'd rather have all his teeth pulled than have to talk to that man again.

Morón was about an hour's drive to the east of Seville, in a rolling Andalusian countryside of humble farms, whitewashed villages, ruined hilltop castles, ranches with fighting bulls, and acres of olive trees and sunflowers. It was not named after a mentally deficient person, but after the nearest town, Morón de la Frontera. The name translates as "mound or hill on the frontier," referring to the frontier between Moorish and Christian Spain.

The base was actually a Spanish base; Americans were tenants and were responsible for air traffic control. The Spanish Air Force had a fleet of jet fighters they had purchased from the US. Rumor had it that they had lost too many planes by pilots ejecting, so they had removed the parachutes from the planes. I doubt if that was true, but it said something about Spanish attitudes. We had no planes of our own stationed there, but an air-evac flight landed there twice a week, once to and once from Torrejón, our base at Madrid, where there was a big Air Force hospital. When my sponsor, the dispensary administrator, had arrived at Morón three years earlier, they had told him not to unpack his bags because the base was closing. It kept shrinking but it never did close. By the time I finished my three year tour, I was the last doctor there and I was not replaced; it remained an aid station manned by corpsmen.

We eventually got down to only 120 military personnel and a handful of dependents. There was a movie theater, BX, commissary, post office, a seasonal pool, a bowling alley, and a combined officers' club/enlisted men's club/chow hall. A visiting team leader commented, "The first night we were here, we had dinner at the club, went to a movie and went bowling. The second night we discovered we had already done everything there was to do the first night."

We had an elementary school, but the high school kids had to go to boarding school at another base. We couldn't deliver babies, so when pregnant women neared their due date, we had to send them to "The Stork's Nest" in the hospital at Torrejón to await delivery. Occasionally we had a miscalculation. There was more than one wild ambulance ride to the nearest hospital in Seville when a woman went into labor prematurely.

The biggest excitement we had was when the base commander's horse got loose from his carport stall and the security police cars drove all over the grass trying to round him up. The commander also got into some kind of trouble involving flying horse feed in from Morocco on a military plane.

The vice commander wasn't into horses or anything else that involved effort. He was a very laid-back, friendly type. Once, in the commander's absence, he was summoned to answer a complaint from a visiting general. The general was staying in our VOQ (Visiting Officers Quarters) and was unhappy about what he perceived as lax discipline and unmilitary behavior and dress on our base. He opened the door of his room to see our vice commander standing there in Bermuda shorts, a colorful Hawaiian shirt, and flip-flops, pleasantly asking, "What can I do for you?"

Base security was provided by the Spanish Air Force, and it was worrisome. A visiting friend from America showed his Washington State driver's license at the gate and they thought it was military ID and waved him through. Anyone who wanted to get on base illegally could have driven in across the unfenced fields just out of sight of the gate. When there was heightened security, they assigned their troops to patrol around our base housing with submachine guns. It was good odds the guy with the gun was an 18 year old semiliterate recruit who had polished off a liter of wine at dinner.

I was not eligible for base housing, because only officers with dependents were eligible. At this point, my husband had returned to school to work towards a PhD. He attended the University of Seville, in a historic building that formerly housed the Royal Tobacco Factory—the very building that Carmen comes out of in the first scene of the opera. He had no income and was in fact absolutely dependent on my support. The Air Force didn't care. Husbands couldn't be dependents. Period.

A VILLA IN SPAIN

For the first year, I rented a villa in the little town of Alcalá de Guadaira, about halfway between Seville and the base. The name means "the fortress on the river Aira" in Arabic. There was a castle on a hill, an old Arab mill, and one traffic policeman at the major intersection instead of a stoplight. To give directions, you would say, "Turn left at the traffic cop." I was giving our pharmacy tech a ride home one day when we passed a shabbily dressed old man riding a donkey through town. He waved at us, and the pharmacy tech told me it was his landlord.

My villa was a real bargain. It even had a name: the Villa Isabel Macarena. Several bedrooms, a dishwasher, a garage, a swimming pool, and a large surrounding garden with flowers and lemon trees. The gardener's services were included in the rent, which was around $125 a month. I got a cleaning lady to come in for 25 cents an hour. It even had a telephone! (More about this later). The road was unpaved, and they kept tearing up the access road so I would have to drive home via a garbage dump and puddles.

The author smelling the roses in the garden at Villa Isabel Macarena

Thanks to the Guardia Civil, Alcalá de Guadaira was a safe place to live. The Guardia Civil are the Spanish national police, a corps dating back to Ferdinand and Isabella's time. They dress in green uniforms and black patent-leather pseudo-tricorne hats, they work in pairs, and they are assigned away from their home province so they won't play favorites. They don't put up with any nonsense.

Shortly before I arrived, there had been an incident where the Guardia Civil stopped a car driven by an American dependent. He tried to argue with them, and then tried to walk away. They shot and killed him for resisting arrest. No questions were asked.

They knew where we lived. When an American home was burgled and guns stolen, they promptly found the guns and returned them. When an American child failed to get off the school bus as usual, they knocked on the parents' door to make sure there was no problem (there wasn't, she'd just arranged to stay at a friend's house).

There was only one thing wrong with my new home: it was designed as a summer house and had no central heating. In the winter we burned olive wood in the fireplace and kept a portable butane heater running in whatever room we were in. I would leap out of bed in the morning, light the butane heater, and retreat under the covers until the room had warmed up enough to venture out again. I opened the closet one day to find a heavy growth of green furry mold on my favorite beige shoes.

I dreaded a second winter there, but fate had a wrinkle in store for me.

SPANISH TELEPHONES

Spain had a nationalized telephone service under Franco. It was enough to make you really appreciate AT&T. They were reluctant to string new lines until they had enough customers to pay for the construction, so it was common to have to wait as long as seven years to get a phone installed in a new house. And they charged a huge fee to transfer telephone ownership to a new person, so everyone's phone number stayed listed in the directory under the name of the first person who had the phone. In consequence, the directories were useless.

My college Spanish professor told us about an encounter a friend of his had with the Spanish telephone system. He was traveling through Madrid and thought he would take the opportunity to phone an old acquaintance in Valencia. He tried all day to get through on the phone without success. He decided it would be easier just to get on a train and go there. He did. They invited him to stay overnight. He ended up staying for several weeks and marrying the daughter of the family! He thanks defective Spanish telephony for a happy marriage.

I tried to call a specialist in Germany once and found myself talking to someone in the Pentagon who was also trying to call Germany. We had a nice conversation.

My mother called right before Christmas. She had never phoned overseas before, so my first thought was that she was calling to tell me about some family crisis. The connection was terrible, and I could barely tell who was calling and couldn't hear what she was saying. I rushed to the dispensary to call her back from another phone, and this time I got a clear connection. She said she had just put the Christmas tree up and was calling so I could see how nice it looked (over the phone!?).[3]

Not everyone could find a house with a telephone, and even those who did ran into problems. In one small town where some of our staff lived, there was a live operator who only worked a day shift, so the phone system didn't work at night. One of our doctors had no phone, so they had to provide him with a large two-way radio when he was on call. He could hear the base calling, but got such poor reception that he had to climb up on the roof to carry on a conversation. Since few of our off-base personnel had phones, we had to have another system to notify them if they were needed in an emergency. We set up a Paul Revere recall system. The base would call someone with a phone, and that person would drive into Seville, or wherever his route was, and knock on the doors of people without phones. That involved having keys to all the apartment buildings so he could get in at night to knock at the apartment door.

So I was lucky to have a reliable phone in my villa. I got a call one night for a patient with a nosebleed that wouldn't stop. I got in my car and discovered I had a flat tire. Because of the way my car's jack was designed, it was impossible to get it to work where the car was, in dirt ruts. I eventually found an American neighbor with a conventional jack and got the tire changed, but it was still a half hour's drive to the base, and I was afraid the patient might bleed to death before I got there. I called to check before I left, and fortunately the nosebleed had decided to stop on its own.

SEEING PATIENTS

My first day of seeing patients was Friday the 13th of August, 1971. But that's OK, because we were in Spain. They don't believe Friday the 13th is bad luck; they think Tuesday the 13th is the one to watch out for! On Sunday I went to a bullfight at the famous La Maestranza bullring in Seville; Sunday the 15th was the unlucky day for those bulls.

Morón had a dispensary with several inpatient beds, a lab, pharmacy, x-ray, a fully staffed dental clinic with a dental lab, several medical corpsmen and nurses,

---

3.   Mom had an eccentric sense of humor. After she visited, my staff told me, "Now we understand."

and an administrative staff. A pediatrician left shortly after I arrived, leaving only 3 doctors assigned. My boss was partially trained in internal medicine and the third doctor planned to become a surgeon; neither had any experience with children or OB/Gyn, so I became the de facto pediatrician and obstetrician/gynecologist. I didn't mind. I was also pressed into service as a translator.

Most of the women and children seemed pleased to have a female doctor. The men didn't seem particularly pleased, but they accepted me. Possibly because they had no choice. The Spanish dependent wives loved me. They would come in and start to explain their problem hesitantly in broken English, "I ... small pain ... here ..." and when I would ask, "¿Prefiere hablar español?" they would erupt into a torrent of rapid-fire Spanish with evident relief.

One memorable inpatient was a non compos mentis elderly dependent mother-in-law awaiting air-evac transfer to a nursing home in England. Every time a male walked into her room (whether doctor, corpsman, or lab tech) she would start screaming, "Don't touch me! Get out of here! Go find yourself a woman of the streets!"

We saw a fair amount of infectious hepatitis, so when a woman came in with bright yellow skin, I first thought she was jaundiced. Then I realized two things didn't fit. She wasn't sick, and the whites of her eyes were still white (the eyes usually turn yellow before the skin). It turned out she was trying to lose weight and had been eating a lot of carrots! She had carotenemia, which is harmless but which really looked funny on her, since she had bright orange-red hair and pale skin that let the yellow shine through. She looked as if she had been colored with the wrong crayons in a child's coloring book!

I prescribed wart medicine for a woman but the pharmacy couldn't make up the solution that day because they were out of one of the ingredients. When she came back two weeks later to pick up the prescription, she no longer needed it—her warts had vanished! Another patient outdid her: he made an appointment for a wart, and when he tried to show me where his wart was, he couldn't find it—it had vanished!

A father brought his small son in. While waiting to see the doctor, he threw up in the men's room. The father came running out yelling, "My son's vomiting blood!" Investigation showed that the "blood" was only the strawberry shortcake he'd been eating. It was fortunate we were able to examine the evidence; in med school I saw a patient who got a complete GI workup for hematemesis (vomiting blood) before they found out he had really only vomited clear liquid over a red floor!

A woman came screaming through the front door in hysterics one afternoon, with a small child in her arms, "My baby's dying!" The child had fallen out of a shopping cart in the commissary. It didn't even have a bruise. The mother happened to be Puerto Rican, so someone on our staff made up a politically incorrect diagnosis that we used henceforth as a handy label for people who tend to over-react: PRS, Puerto Rican Syndrome.

I think the PRS diagnosis even snuck into a couple of medical records, which was a mistake. Like "gomer" in medical school, doctors have lots of unofficial terms that are best omitted from permanent records. I heard about a doctor who was kicked out of his residency program for writing, "This 51 year old SHPOS was admitted …" His supervisors had never heard that acronym before, so they asked him to explain and he had to tell them it stood for Sub Human Pile of Shit.

Doctors have a macabre sense of humor; it's a way of coping with a difficult job. One of my colleagues said of a not-too-smart patient, "He only has two neurons connected by one synapse, and if that one ever becomes syphilitic, he's done for." Another colleague invented the 7P syndrome: Piss-Poor Protoplasm Poorly Put together with a Poverty of Potential.

A mother brought her son in because his behavior was out of control and she thought he might be hyperactive or have something else wrong with him. Sure enough, he bounced all over my office, kept getting into things, and ignored his mother's attempts at discipline. I established the real diagnosis (and cure) by gripping him by his upper arms, sitting him down on a chair, looking him straight in the eyes, and saying firmly, "You don't act like that in my office. Sit right here and be quiet." He was good as gold for the rest of the visit.

I learned a lesson in placebos from the pharmacy tech. He discovered that two different brands of allergy pills came from the same factory and were identical except that one was coated red and the other green. We'd prescribe one, and it would seem to work well for a while, but then the patient would decide it wasn't helping any more. We would switch them to the other brand, which always seemed to work better, whichever way we switched.

The x-ray tech had little to do. One day he had a migraine headache, so he lay down on the x-ray table, put a wet cloth on his forehead and tried to take a nap. The Spanish cleaning lady came in, flipped on the lights, saw what she thought was a dead body, ran out of the building screaming, and refused to ever work there again.

The flat roof developed a leak. The water entered at one point on the roof and filtered through layers to drip at an entirely different point on the ceiling inside. When it was raining, they couldn't work on it, and when it wasn't raining, they couldn't find the leaks. For months, we had buckets and basins sitting all over the floor. To get from the front door to the front desk, you had to run a slalom course. One of the nurses got an electric shock from trying to answer the wind-up emergency phone while standing in a puddle. Another nurse was hit on the head when the waterlogged ceiling let go of a light fixture. I have a picture of her sitting at the front desk wearing a protective helmet the next day. What might have been a small problem had turned into a large one. When they finally got around to fixing it, they had to put in a whole new roof at great expense.

Our brand-new ambulance quit on us during an emergency run. We had rushed into a small town to pick up a patient with severe chest pain. We thought he was having a heart attack. We got him on a stretcher and out the door only to find that the radiator was boiling over and the ambulance wouldn't start. We were forced to improvise, and we ended up taking the patient back to the base in his own VW, with his wife driving, a corpsman in the back seat with the patient, and me in the front seat leaning over the back trying to feel the patient's pulse. Probably not the smartest thing to do, but it all worked out. We stabilized him, got an emergency air-evac plane in to transfer him to the hospital at Torrejón, and heard that he broke out in a rash the next day. It wasn't a heart attack; it was herpes zoster (also known as shingles). Shingles usually causes a painful rash limited to one side of the body. Sometimes the pain precedes the rash by a day or two, but it is practically unheard of for it to cause pain on both sides of the chest like his did. Oh well!

It was months before we could get the ambulance fixed. They couldn't get the right part until one of our NCOs finally called an NCO friend at a stateside base and made some kind of an unofficial trade; the part came in on the next plane. I didn't ask for details. While we were waiting for the part, we had to make do with a stretcher on the floor of a van.

They warned us that it was bad news if an American died off-base, because of all the international legal entanglements. So they suggested that if we ever went on an ambulance run and found a dead patient, we should pretend he wasn't dead yet, perform CPR en route, and not declare the patient dead until we were back on the base on "American" soil. Fortunately, the situation never arose.

For ambulance response on base, we used the old military "crackerbox" field ambulances that could carry four stretchers. One of our corpsmen got a call for an emergency on the flight line one day, and climbed in the crackerbox only to find it wouldn't start. He switched to the other crackerbox and made it only as far as the end of the driveway before it quit too. He did the only thing he could—he drove his own car to the flight line to get the patient. Instead of praise for his initiative he got a reprimand for illegally driving a private vehicle on the runway.

One day we learned that we were going to have an open ranks inspection. I had no idea what that meant. It turned out we had to put on our dress uniforms and white gloves, line up in the parking lot according to height (this meant a lot of jostling around and standing back to back to compare), position ourselves an arm's length apart, and MARCH over to where we would be reviewed by the base commander. I had never marched in my life. The enlisted men had to teach me which foot to start with and how to right face and left face and about face without getting my ankles tangled. I even had to learn how to "ten-hut" and "at ease." And this was after I had been on active duty for three years! Just one more disadvantage of the way I stumbled into the military through the back door.

BASE HOUSING

I was dreading the thought of shivering through another winter without central heating, but a bit of good luck came to my rescue. The personnel numbers on base had become so depleted that they now had more officer houses than officers. They had to put single officers and non-officers in the vacant houses. I got one.

A Spanish moving company was contracted by the Air Force to move us on base. Their methods looked primitive: they packed my good china in straw in flexible baskets. I held my breath. Our friends recommended we have a few old *Playboy* magazines to give the movers as tips; they were not available in Spain and were highly prized. I guess they did the trick: there wasn't a single chip or scratch on anything; it was my most damage-free move ever.

My new house had a gardener too—he grew tomatoes, onions, and garlic for us in a garden behind the house, he brought us braided garlic chains to hang in the kitchen, he mowed the lawn, and he knocked on the door every Saturday to ask which of our two cars we wanted washed.

The housing was duplex, and a dentist lived in the other unit. Shortly after I moved in, his 5 year old girl knocked on my door and asked if I could come out and play! It was a large house with two bathrooms, three bedrooms, and a maid's room behind the kitchen. A nice house—except for the termites! I discovered the pesky little creatures boring out of a door frame, and I caught one in a pill bottle. I'd never met a termite before, so I looked them up in a book for a positive identification, then I reported them to the base civil engineering department. They informed me emphatically that I couldn't possibly have termites: they were only flying ants. They were quite condescending. Yeah, don't listen to me; I'm only a woman! No dangly bits! What do I know? I took my pill bottle with the captured insect to them in their office and asked, "Is this a flying ant?" and they said, "By golly, you have termites!"

There were some other problems. The furnace quit 12 times in two weeks. When it did work, it would hesitate, leak gas for a while, and then erupt with huge flame right past the paper tape the workmen had patched it with. Somehow, it never started a fire. Once we returned from a trip to find a moldy bathroom and a screeching furnace fan. The bathtub faucet was stuck and dripped constantly; they never did manage to fix it, and then they had the nerve to try to blame me for the resulting rust stain when I moved out.

I noticed that every other officer had a sign in front of his house with his name and rank on it. I never got one. I felt left out. Finally I mentioned it to the captain in charge of civil engineering, and at lunch that day I found him putting up my sign himself.

For a while I rode my bicycle to work. My silly hat kept falling off, so I rode without it. Someone told me I couldn't do that because without a hat I was "out of uniform." I asked the Chief of Security Police what would happen if I got caught—would I get a ticket? He said, no, don't worry—he never wore *his* hat when he rode *his* bicycle. He was a gentle man who had joined the Air Force to play the clarinet in the Air Force band. I asked him how he ended up as a policeman, and he told me he often wondered the same thing.

No More Dispensary

As the base down-sized, we lost our status as a dispensary and were down-graded to a medical aid station. In stages, we lost our inpatient beds, our dental clinic, our x-ray tech, and the other two military doctors. Since I was the only military doctor left, I automatically became the DBMS (Director of Base Medical Services). They hired a Spanish civilian to back me up, Dr. Mesonero, an obstetrician/gynecologist who had trained in the US.

We were assigned a van with a standard column-mounted shift. We were supposed to put a minimum mileage on it each month to justify keeping it. So the corpsmen would take it to the flight line when no planes were due in, and they would drive it up and down the flight line to rack up mileage. They decided I should have a military driver's license to drive it, so they took me over to the motor pool supposedly to take a test. My master sergeant and theirs had a great time chatting, and before I knew it I had a military driver's license in my hand without having taken any kind of a test. I had driven a floor-mounted stick shift, but I didn't even know how the gears went on a column-mounted shift. I guess I could have figured it out if I'd needed to, but I never did have occasion to drive the van.

I also had to get an emergency generator operator's license. There was a big generator behind our building that could be fired up if we had a power outage. They gave us a class essentially telling us first you flip this switch and then you turn this knob. Big deal. I kept that card proudly in my wallet for many years. Never had to start the generator, of course.

Every time it rained heavily, the water would get into a siren on a pole, and a false alarm would go off, but we learned to ignore it. We had another kind of electrical alarm when Spanish civilian workmen came to our clinic to fix something. The plugs on their equipment were designed for the local 50 cycle, 220 volt electricity, and they wouldn't fit into our American-style outlets, so they just stripped their plug and insulation off and stuck two very long ends of bare wire into a wall socket in our hallway. When I saw it a little sign popped up in my brain: Fire Hazard? I called the base fire chief. He came over, kicked the wires out to the accompaniment of flying sparks, declared, "I guarantee you *they'll* never work on this base again!" and stomped out.

We had a direct emergency line to the control tower. Our pharmacy tech was buddies with one of the air traffic controllers, and they would use the emergency line for critical messages like "Your wife said to remind you to pick up bread on your way home." Once they called us to respond to an inflight emergency and our nurse asked what kind of plane it was. They didn't know, so they told her it was a B-One-RD. She hadn't ever heard of that model before. We had to explain to her that B1RD spells bird and is military lingo for an unidentified aircraft (a UFO?). One day when we were really busy, the emergency line rang to demand our ambulance for a simulated emergency. I almost told them we would send them a simulated ambulance.

When our x-ray tech left, he taught us all how to take and develop x-rays and left us a "cookbook" of settings for each type of film. I took an x-ray of my purse for practice. We didn't have an automatic processor. We had to go in the darkroom and dip the films in tanks, and then did authentic "wet readings"—the films would actually drip on the floor and we had to put a towel down to catch the drips.

When I had been at Morón for two years, I got a letter in the mail informing me that I would be promoted on a certain date. By the time the letter reached me, it was already three weeks past that date! Apparently at that time medical officers were automatically promoted to major after three years in grade as a captain. I didn't know that. It was a pleasant surprise. On the other hand, it was an unpleasant surprise to find out I'd been wearing the wrong insignia for three weeks! Their sloppy approach certainly didn't make me feel like I was very important in their scheme of things.

By 1974, a "busy" day consisted of 12-13 patients; on a light day I might only see 2. It was just me and Dr. Mesonero, the Spanish civilian physician, and there was no point in us both being there. When he was on duty, I went home. I was essentially working only 2 ½ days a week, plus being on call half the time.

Things got so boring we had to make up ways to entertain ourselves. We knew what time the bus arrived from Seville, and we had a lookout to see if any potential patients got off and headed our way. We played cards and board games in the conference room. Once when we were playing the board game "Life" a corpsman put a sign up on the front door saying, "Closed for Life." We were getting so little use out of the building that some wag made up a real estate ad offering it for sale as a country villa. The guys would play volleyball out behind the building and park an ambulance by the court with the radio on. If we needed one of them, we would call them on the radio: "Front desk to volleyball court, front desk to volleyball court, do you read me?" The guys got so bored they even learned how to do each other's jobs just for the hell of it. It was not unusual to find the pharmacy tech in the lab doing a blood count. One corpsman took up knitting and made himself a sweater while manning the front desk.

The dental clinic was no longer staffed, but they had left their equipment. Once, for a joke Christmas gift for my brother, we used dental modeling compound to make a cast of our biggest sergeant's clenched fist with his middle finger extended. We painted it gold and called it the Goldfinger award.

The pipeline for medications was erratic, but our pharmacy tech was a good trader. He'd find something left over from when we had inpatients, something we were never likely to use again, and he'd drive down to the Navy base and swap it for whatever we needed. Periodically he would call me in to do a required inspection of out-dated medicines. Most of them were still OK because they had been stored properly and the dates are overly cautious. I had no idea how to tell if they were still good, but he explained the rules: if the pills didn't show any visible sign of deterioration they should be safe (except for certain things like nitroglycerine that we know don't last). So we would go through the shelves opening bottles and deciding whether they "looked" OK.

The Navy base, Rota, was in Cádiz, about 80 miles to the south. Since we no longer had inpatient beds, we had only two choices: an air-evac plane to Madrid or an ambulance ride to Rota. One night I was called out at 10:30 PM for a woman with a possible intestinal obstruction; we took her to Rota, and I got home at 5:30 AM. Another night I was called out at 2:30 AM for a woman whose husband had beaten her with a camel saddle. One patient broke his ankle playing basketball and was brought in with his foot at a 90-degree angle to his leg. We had to splint it in that position and ship him to an orthopedic surgeon. One night I was called out at midnight to suture lacerations after a car hit a telephone pole and knocked out all the lights on base. The patient also had a hip fracture, and we took him to Rota.

Rota and Morón were locked in a mutual delusion that the grass was greener on the other side. Each base was convinced the other had better stuff in their BX and commissary, so caravans of cars would pass each other on Saturdays as each went to the other to shop. Most of the food in our commissary came on military trucks, but some items were bought locally. For two long months we couldn't get eggs at all, because the Spanish chickens had salmonella or something.

Things like stereo equipment and cameras were available on base at a much lower price than on the Spanish economy. It was an irresistible temptation for black marketers. I heard that the dollar value of stereo equipment sold on American bases in Spain was twice that of all the stereo equipment sold in the entire rest of the country. The OSI[4] caught one entrepreneur after he bought 3 lawnmowers. He lived in an apartment.

On such a small base, people know and help each other. Once I got a tire pumped up by the fire truck when the pump at the service station quit. One night when I was buying a ticket for the movie, the box office guy (who was also the mail guy) told me I had a package at the post office. He went over during the movie, opened up the post office, and when I left the theater, he handed me my package.

I had to take the x-rays into Seville every 3 weeks to be read by a Spanish radiologist. If I made a mistake, I might not find out about it until 3 weeks later. The only time I missed something potentially serious was on an x-ray of a boy's arm. I hadn't realized that his fracture extended into the joint, which made a difference in how it should have been treated. I felt terrible. I called the orthopedic surgeon at Torrejón, and he helped out, not only with the patient, but with my conscience. He reassured me that no one was immune from mistakes, that an occa-

---

4.   Office of Special Investigations, sort of like an Air Force FBI.

sional mistake was a fact of life that doctors had to learn to live with, and that I should forgive myself and carry on.

Considering I was fresh out of an internship, with little experience, I managed pretty well. If I didn't know what to do, at least I could do an adequate history and physical and communicate the results to a specialist over the phone. One of my patients told another patient she really respected me because I was honest enough to say, "I don't know, but I'll try to find out." And then I *would* find out.

We had great phone access to consultants and I learned a lot from them. Once I had a young boy who broke his upper arm. All he did was throw a baseball, and his arm just snapped. It was visibly bent. I x-rayed it and looked up the fracture in my fracture book, and it said he would require an operation to open up his arm and put in a steel rod. I called the orthopedic surgeon to arrange a transfer, but he said not to bother. He told me how to realign the bone and put it in a splint. I tried, but it could not be aligned. The orthopedist said to just put it in a sling and it would heal OK and eventually realign itself through bone remodeling, since the boy was still growing. He was right; the kid did fine and avoided the trauma of air-evac, hospitalization, and surgery.

WATERGATE

One day our Spanish physician, Dr. Mesonero, had a few free moments between patients and reached for a medical journal to read. It was on a small table behind his desk. He felt for it and it didn't feel like a medical journal. It felt more like a lizard. He looked around, and there was a big lizard sitting on the table, 18" long from nose to tip of tail. The good doctor departed the office precipitously and notified the staff.

A chase ensued, and the lizard was eventually trapped under an upturned butt can (a big red metal container for cigarette butts). This was the most exciting thing that had happened all year, and the whole staff convened. They got the butt can turned upright and covered it with a lid so the lizard couldn't escape, and then they didn't know what to do. Someone suggested a hamster cage and brought one in from home. Now, how to get the lizard into the cage?

How about sedating the lizard? Someone remembered a container of ether left over from the old days. They poured a little in the can. The lizard kept running around the bottom of the can. They poured a little more in. No effect. They ended up pouring the entire container of ether into the butt can, and finally the lizard was still. They were afraid they had killed him. They were also afraid to reach in and touch him to find out. The lab tech got an asbestos glove from the lab and reached in with his gloved hand. He lifted the immobile lizard slowly, and just as he got it even with the top of the can, it erupted into violent thrashing activity and he let go.

The lizard was running every which way all over the lawn, one corpsman was chasing it with a broom, others were jumping on the hood of the ambulance to get away from it—it was like the Keystone Kops! They did eventually get it in the hamster cage somehow, but by then we had all collapsed in hysterical laughter.

We enjoyed our new mascot; we identified the species (a jeweled lizard, *Lacertus lepida*), took an x-ray of it (which I still have), and someone suggested we name it Watergate—because it was found where it wasn't supposed to be. We kept it for a couple of days, but we didn't know what to feed it, and the commissary didn't carry Lizard Chow, so we gave it its freedom.

A DIGRESSION ON FOOD

Spanish food is not as well known as French and Italian, but it's equally good. I don't know why it hasn't caught on. It has nothing whatsoever to do with Mexican food, and isn't spicy. It's heavy on tomatoes, onions, olive oil, and garlic. When you ask for a tortilla in Spain you get an omelet. And a "taco" is a generic term for swear words. They have no idea what an enchilada is. And what we call Spanish rice, they call Cuban rice—and they serve it as a mound of plain rice topped with tomato sauce and maybe a fried egg.

They make a delicious tortilla española, a huge thick omelet made with potatoes and onions. They put slices of this in a loaf of bread for a portable lunch. They also make sandwiches of jamón serrano, a mountain ham similar to prosciutto, and of queso manchego, a strong goat cheese.

The wine is wonderful, and everybody drinks it. Children start out with a small splash of wine in a glass of water, and the proportion of wine increases as they get older. I learned to always ask for the house wine, because they used the best small local wineries that did not export but that were often better than the name brands. The best white wine I ever had in Spain was in a restaurant where the wine was cheaper than the bottled water. Speaking of bottled water, one popular brand proudly announced on its label that it was radioactive!

In the evenings, people go for tapas—bar snacks—which can be quite elaborate and can be a meal in themselves. You wash them down with small glasses of wine, and you throw your napkins, shrimp peels and cigarettes on the floor.

I went to a restaurant that served sparrows and another that served fried blood. Actually, this was quite tasty. They let the blood coagulate, cut it into cubes, and fry it in olive oil with garlic. It has the flavor of liver but almost melts in your mouth. I tried one snail, just to say I had done it, but I couldn't get used to the idea of eating something with eyes. I ate squid, octopus, and blood sausage, but never tasted the big barnacles that were widely available. Once I had stew made with meat from the tail of a fighting bull that had been killed in the arena the day before. Sort of like macho oxtail soup.

When my parents visited, we went to a restaurant with "pig's trotters a la mode" on the menu. They meant pig's feet "in the style of" some Spanish province. My mother ordered it in a fit of nostalgia—she had eaten pig's feet as a girl in North Carolina. She was relieved to find that it didn't come with ice cream.

Sangría was popular—a red wine punch made with lemon and other fruits and sometimes a splash of brandy. It was dangerous stuff. You'd be guzzling it down thinking it was lemonade, and when you'd go to get up, your legs would have turned to spaghetti.

Gazpacho was another of my favorites: a cold tomato soup with oil, vinegar, sometimes green peppers, cucumber, onion, and garlic. And bread crumbs. It was a refreshing and nutritious dish for a summer dinner. Every chef made it from a different recipe, but I never tasted one I didn't like. When I took my daughter to Spain a few years ago, they even had gazpacho on the menu at the McDonald's in Madrid.

The Spanish dish par excellence was paella (pah-EL-yah). It's made in a large flat round pan with two handles; it contains bright yellow saffron-colored rice and an assortment of seafood, chicken and other ingredients. They liked to fix it for every special occasion. I had it so many times I got a bit tired of it. Once we visited relatives of my husband in a small village where the homes had no ovens. They fixed us a big paella, took it down to the communal oven, and carried it back through the streets when it was done.

In Segovia we ate at a restaurant famous for its roast suckling pig. Simple, crunchy on the outside and juicy melt-in-your mouth on the inside. A real treat and good enough to make you forget all about cholesterol.

We used to take visitors to a bar that served criadillas. They would ask what we were ordering and we would say, "I'm not sure exactly how you translate it, but it's really good." After they tasted it and said how much they liked it (everyone did) we would tell them they had just eaten a slice of fried bull's testicle.

We visited friends in the Canary Islands and got to spend a night with their relatives in a tiny fishing village on the southern coast of Gran Canaria. The house was right on the beach. We watched the fishing boats come in and had an unbeatably fresh fish fry on the flat roof of the house in the moonlight, with the waves lapping softly 20 feet away. For breakfast we had freshly baked bread flavored with anise. Then they decided to slaughter a goat for us. A doctor in their family was elected to do the honors—he'd never slaughtered an animal before, but thought he was qualified. He dragged it into a vineyard, slit its jugular vein, gutted it, skinned it, dismembered it and grilled it outdoors for a picnic. We got to watch the whole process.

IG INSPECTION

Every couple of years there would be an IG (Inspector General) inspection. A team would come and look into every aspect of our operation and give us an extensive "report card." These inspections generated much anxiety. They were supposed to be unannounced, but there was a grapevine that could usually give us some warning that they were at the next base down the line and would be heading our way soon.

Our techs cleaned out the ambulance very thoroughly to get ready for the dreaded inspectors, but they forgot to put the equipment back in. When the inspector looked in, he found nothing but a fire extinguisher. He said, "Nice fire engine, but where's your ambulance?"

We were technically supposed to have all kinds of committees with meetings and minutes, but we had downsized so much we didn't have anything to meet about. They let that go.

They quizzed our personnel to see how they would respond in an emergency. They took our best corpsman into the ER and asked him what he would do if the doctor asked for particular pieces of equipment. Every time they would name one, he would reach and say, "It's right here." And it wouldn't be. It seems the other techs had reorganized the ER supplies when he was off duty, and he hadn't been briefed yet. We explained, and they understood.

They asked another technician a series of questions about patient care and he answered several correctly and then got one wrong. At that point, I stepped in and informed the inspector that he wasn't a medical corpsman; he was the lab tech, who wasn't supposed to know *any* of the answers. They were impressed.

Capt. Celdrán at her desk

Before leaving, they quizzed the enlisted men, "How do you like having a woman for a boss?" I guess they expected to hear complaints, but my guys responded better than I could have wished. They didn't even understand the question. "We usually work under nurses who are usually women; now we work for a doctor. What difference does it make whether it's a man or a woman? Why are you asking? Is there a problem?"

We passed the inspection with flying colors.

HUMAN RELATIONS

The Air Force was integrated, but there had been some racial incidents in military dorms, so shortly after I arrived in Spain the Air Force instituted a program to teach tolerance to the troops. They called it "Human Relations" training (which predictably led to a joke or two). They sent a team to Morón to train us. Everyone had to go. They wanted to have a mix in each group, and there were only three women assigned to the entire base—me, a nurse, and one enlisted woman. So we each had to attend more than once.

I enjoyed the classes. They pointed out that we are all prejudiced in various ways, and it may be very hard to overcome, but we can at least learn to be aware of our prejudices and not let them interfere with fair treatment of others. They pointed out that blacks may be prejudiced against whites and whites may be prejudiced against blacks, but that both black and white men agree on one thing: they are both prejudiced against women. I was glad to hear that; I thought it was just me because maybe I had halitosis or something. It explained a lot of things.

It was discouraging to hear the generally poor opinion of women, but there were redeeming moments. They discussed whether there were any jobs a woman couldn't do. One man said he didn't think a woman could be a taxi driver; another man jumped up protesting, "My mother was a taxi driver and she was a good mother!" One man said women belonged in the kitchen; another told him, "I hope when you come in with a broken leg, Dr. Celdrán tells you she can't treat you because she has to go back to the kitchen!" One man said a woman couldn't be a garbage man and lift heavy garbage cans; the enlisted woman said, "Bullshit! I used to work as a butcher and carry hind quarters of beef—do you know how much they weigh?"

One instructor tried to get us all to experience prejudice by picking on something different about each of us. He pointed to a Puerto Rican lieutenant sitting next to me. He said (in a very disparaging tone) that that guy was a "foreigner" and he asked me how I would like it if that guy started talking Spanish. I answered, "Pues a mí no me importaría un pito, porque yo le entendería exactamente igual."[5] The poor instructor was flabbergasted—he had no idea what I had said or what to do next. I felt sorry for him. No I didn't—I thought it was pretty funny.

One of my favorite jokes illustrates just how deeply-ingrained prejudice can be. On a school bus, some black kids and white kids were trading racial slurs, and the bus driver decided to put a stop to it. He parked the bus and ordered all the kids off. He said, "From now on, no white kids or black kids are allowed on my bus—only green kids." He started down the line of kids. "What color are you?" "I'm black." "Then you can't get on my bus. Only green kids are allowed on my bus. What color are you?" "I'm white." "Then you can't get on my bus. Only green kids are allowed on my bus." Finally the kids started to get the idea. "I'm green." "OK, then you can get back on the bus." "I'm green too." "I'm green." "We're all green!" The bus driver said, "OK, everybody back on the bus: dark green in the back, light green in the front."

I can't claim to be entirely free of prejudice (nobody is), but I can claim to be oblivious to race. One afternoon someone asked me if I had seen a black airman

---

5.   Translation: Well, it wouldn't make a bit of difference to me, since I would understand him just as well.

that morning with a certain illness, and I remembered seeing an airman with that illness, but for the life of me I couldn't remember whether he was black, white, or chartreuse!

DRUGS

It was the 70s, and even Air Force personnel were known to occasionally indulge in a mind-altering substance. In my humble opinion, some of them *needed* to have their minds altered, although perhaps not in the way they chose. Some drugs that were legal in Spain got our troops into trouble, because you could buy narcotics over the counter with no prescription. If you asked a Spanish pharmacist to sell you a nonprescription headache remedy, it might well contain a whopping dose of codeine and show up positive on a drug test. Or a sleep remedy might be full of barbiturates.

Drugs like marijuana were illegal in Spain but were widely available, mostly smuggled in from Morocco. More than once we had to quickly ship a suspect back to the States before the Spanish police could jail him. One of our troops returned to us after a short residence in a Moroccan jail, malnourished, with lice, and with nothing good to say about his hosts. When we visited Morocco we were warned never to leave our car unguarded, because smugglers would sneak drugs into cars and later retrieve them in Spain. A friend of mine had his Volvo practically disassembled by Spanish customs on his return from Morocco: they took off the door panels and even disassembled his air conditioner—which they left in pieces because they couldn't figure out how it went back together.

While I was at Morón, the Air Force instituted mandatory drug tests. They supplied us with random number tables and a system to randomly pick patients by social security number. The patient had to be actually observed urinating into the bottle, because otherwise he might substitute a drug-free sample of someone else's pee. Our prim and proper old maid nurse caused quite a sensation when she announced, "I volunteer to be the pecker checker."

It took us a while to appreciate how much of a sense of humor she really had. One day there were two brooms propped against the wall and someone said, "Colonel Bemis, you're double-parked." She went right along with the joke, picked up one broom and said, "You're mine." Picked up the other broom and said, "Why, you're mine, too. How did you get here? I thought I left you home in the garage."

She was a LtCol and was the highest ranking woman on the entire base. I was only a captain (and later a major). But I was her boss because doctors outrank nurses. It was really hard to explain to people why a captain could give orders to a LtCol. Heck, it was hard enough to explain to Spaniards that women could have rank in the first place; there were no women in the Spanish military. They really didn't know what to make of us. I was picking up tickets for a commercial flight once at the Madrid airport and they kept looking around for the Captain who was supposed to get the tickets. I had to tell them three times it was me.

The other drug problem was the perennial one: alcohol. We had mandatory briefings for personnel suspected of overindulging. One sergeant did *not* want to be there. He had been reported by a friend for regularly consuming mass quantities of beer after work. He insisted he didn't have a problem and didn't need to listen. He sat sideways in his chair and told us with his body language that he was not really there. Something apparently managed to filter through despite his precautions. A month later, he had stopped drinking, joined AA, and started his own campaign to keep others from succumbing to temptation. He would hang around the officer's club and enlisted club and report on who was drinking, and he made rather a pest of himself.

An AA group met on base, and I attended many of the meetings as medical advisor. The members would gather around the coffee pot with their cigarettes and observe, "We haven't stopped; we've just switched drugs." Alcoholics are not depraved bums; some of them are very bright, likeable people who have managed to function in demanding jobs even while drinking heavily. I heard some hairy stories. One guy had been in the Navy and every time he got a promotion he would get busted and have to start up the ranks again. He drove a truck back and forth between England and Spain and half the time he was so sloshed he couldn't even remember which country he was in and which side of the road he was supposed to be driving on. One member recounted his experience when he first stopped drinking. He went to a party determined to stick to Coca-Cola, but a very attractive woman kept rubbing up against him and cooing, "Come on, take a drink! Just one little drinky-poo won't hurt. Be a sport! Come on!" He finally told her, "I'm sorry, but I just can't drink alcohol; the doctor said it would interfere with the medicine I'm taking for my syphilis." She vanished.

THE ATTRACTIONS OF SEVILLE

Spain celebrates Easter in a big way, especially in Sevilla. First they have Semana Santa (Holy Week). There are religious clubs, "cofradías" in each parish that plan all year for the big processions. Each church has one or more images—usually big statues or tableaus of Christ or the Virgin—that are mounted on big platforms that they carry through the streets in a long, circuitous route to the main cathedral and back. A succession of different churches marches day and night all week. There is music from marching bands and from flamenco singers who spontaneously break out in "saetas" from balconies along the route. There are grandstands outside the main cathedral, and streets along the routes are crammed with onlookers. Some marchers are penitents who carry a cross or walk barefoot to fulfill a vow. Most of the cofradía members carry huge candles (the candlelit processions at night are really something to see) and they wear an outfit that looks just like the KKK costume—gown and tall peaked hat with cloth hanging down to cover the face and only tiny holes for the eyes. Each cofradía has its own color; it may be black, green, or any color, but some are white like the KKK.

One of our patients was a black woman from the Deep South who knew nothing of Spanish customs. She took the bus into Seville to do some shopping, and when she got off the bus with her children, the first thing she saw was a group of cofradía members walking down the street towards her on their way to a procession. As luck would have it, their cofradía's color happened to be white. She panicked and ran, certain that the KKK had followed her all the way to Spain and were about to get her.

After the serious religious stuff, it's time to party. Semana Santa is followed by "Feria," a spring fair. Families and other groups set up a tent city of open-fronted "casetas" (with tables, chairs, a bar and a dance floor). They dress in flamenco garb, ride horses up and down the avenues, stay up all night, invite each other into the casetas, drink a lot, eat snacks, play the guitar, clap their hands to intricate rhythms, sing, and dance sevillanas. I loved watching the kids—even those who were barely old enough to walk were dressed in miniature versions of the adults' costumes and already knew the dance moves. Some of them could really dance up a storm.

There were treasures of history and art everywhere within easy reach. You can visit the world's largest cathedral[6] in Seville; it features Columbus' tomb and preserves the Moorish patio of orange trees and the Giralda tower of the mosque that

---

6.   St. Peter's in Rome is bigger, but isn't technically a cathedral.

it replaced. You can go to the royal (Alcázar) palace next door and stand in the very room where Columbus pitched his project to Queen Isabella. You can wander through the ruins of an entire Roman city just outside Seville at Itálica, birthplace of Seneca and two Roman emperors, Hadrian and Trajan. The little town of Carmona has a well-preserved Roman necropolis complete with banquet halls and vomitorium; the rest of the Roman city is still there but has been overlaid with modern buildings and can't be excavated. A weekend trip could take you practically anywhere in the southern half of the country: Granada with its Alhambra, Córdoba with its Mezquita, the mountains, the beach. People pay good money to travel to Spain to see those things, and we were already there.

Most of our troops got out and met the locals and enjoyed life in Spain. One joined a Spanish club to pursue his hobby of radio-controlled model airplanes; another scoured the countryside with his metal detector on weekends looking for Roman coins. But we did have a few young recruits who were away from home for the first time and were seriously intimidated by the idea of a foreign country. I encountered one young airman who had been at Morón for a year and had only been off base twice, and one of those times was because the chaplain took him.

I later met a nurse who had been stationed in Spain and had hated it. She said it was the only country she'd ever been to that she didn't like. She said the people were ignorant and dirty and unfriendly. She went on and on, and couldn't find a single good thing to say. A mutual acquaintance revealed the truth: she said the same thing about every single country she went to. Except for the occasional incorrigible sourpuss like her, most people loved being assigned to Spain.

MY STAFF

The master sergeants of the Air Force are the ones who really keep things running. I was totally unprepared to run a military clinic, but our MSgt told me what to do. One day I was called to attend something called a Battle Staff meeting. I had no idea what that was, but I reported as instructed. All the high-powered officers of the base were there. Halfway through the meeting a MSgt came in and notified the commander that I didn't have a security clearance so I shouldn't be there. They needn't have worried; I didn't understand enough to have picked up any secrets. They gave me an application to apply for security clearance. I had to report every address I'd ever lived at and all the foreigners I knew, and swear I didn't have any Communist contacts or secret indiscretions like homosexuality that could be used to blackmail me. I was cleared.

One of our corpsmen had worked in a minor surgery clinic and had removed toenails under supervision by a surgeon. We had a patient who needed this procedure for a badly ingrown toenail. I'd never done one. I'd never even seen one done. I should have sent the patient to a surgeon at Torrejón, but that would have meant a plane trip and a week off duty. So I took a chance and let the corpsman do it. All went well.

The same corpsman had had experience on a psychiatric ward and he was big, black and intimidating. We had a patient one night who had slashed her wrist with a broken glass ashtray as a suicide gesture. She was hysterical and wouldn't let me near her, but she was willing to let him treat her. He sewed up her wound.

His hobby was buying and repairing antique clocks; he was going to open a clock shop when he retired. He went to the flea market in Seville every weekend and found some real treasures. One clock was so rare the only other known example was in a museum. The flea market dealers begrudgingly respected his bargaining ability, calling him "el judío negro"—the black Jew.

A tech sergeant in Environmental Health was a very capable man with a college degree. I asked him why he hadn't applied for a commission as an officer. He answered that he wasn't qualified to be an officer because his parents were married to each other.

He once sent an inquiry up to headquarters and got it back with the answer written on the bottom of the inquiry itself. It was accompanied by two full sheets of paper: *two copies* of a letter saying "We have answered your letter on the letter itself to save paper."

He told me about the time he inspected the Officers' Club at a base in the Philippines. He lifted up a floorboard behind the bar and discovered swarming rats. He closed the Club until the health hazard could be resolved. The base commander called him into his office and demanded, "Who told you you could close my club?!" He replied, "The rats did, Sir."

One of our corpsmen was on duty alone when a mother brought her child in with a spider in his ear. The corpsman was afraid of spiders, but he coped. He made the mother kill the spider. I laughed the next morning when I read how he had written up his report:

> Patient complained of foreign body in right ear.
> Physical exam: A small spider seen in ear canal.
> Disposition:
>   1. Hydrogen peroxide drops to ear.
>   2. Spider still "holed" up.
>   3. Hydrogen peroxide drops instilled again.

4. Spider not moving.
5. Before 3rd application of hydrogen peroxide, spider crawled out.
6. Mother alerted. Spider seized.

CULTURAL DIFFERENCES

Some Americans acquired Spanish wives. This led to some strange situations, because they didn't speak the same language. One young man brought his betrothed in for the mandatory blood test, gave her first name, but didn't know her last name. He had to ask in atrocious Spanish, "Hey you what name?"

I frequently had to brief parents about their child twice; once in English for the father, and again in Spanish for the mother. If I just told one of them, the message would never reach the other. One little toddler didn't like what we were doing to him, and he came out with, "¡Coño!" (Spanish for cunt, frequently used as an obscene expletive). Mom turned bright red, because it was obvious which parent he'd learned *that* word from.

One of our enlisted men married the town whore; his buddies all either had slept with her or knew someone who had, and they agonized over whether they should tell him or whether maybe he already knew and didn't care. I hope she took the opportunity to reform. Incidentally, Air Force regulations said if one of my enlisted men wanted to get married, he had to ask for my approval! I didn't think it was any of my business, and I wasn't about to refuse anyone permission.

One day I saw a young Spanish woman with multiple vague complaints: headache, backache, fatigue, insomnia, etc. I knew she and her two children had come back to live with her parents in a small Spanish village while her husband was on an "unaccompanied" assignment where dependents were not allowed. I asked her one question: what's it like going back to live in your parents' house after being on your own all those years in the States? She burst into tears, unloaded on me, and never mentioned her physical symptoms again. Instead, we talked about better ways to cope with her difficult living situation.

I learned some Spanish expressions they hadn't taught me in school. "Hacer aguas menores" and "aguas mayores" (to make minor waters and major waters) apparently referred to peeing and pooping. "Hacer uso de matrimonio" (making use of matrimony) means what you might guess. "Caca" means feces. I was surprised to hear a vendor in a park in Seville shouting "almendras" (almonds) when what he was offering was actually peanuts. I inquired, and he said he couldn't very well call out "peanuts" because the Spanish word for peanuts is cacahuetes, and he would have to shout "caca—huetes."

WIESBADEN

I had arrived at Morón in August 1971. By November 1972, I was the only military doctor left, and had become Director of Base Medical Services by default. I suspect I may have been the first female DBMS in the Air Force, but I have no way of knowing. As DBMS, I had to attend a conference in Wiesbaden for all the DBMS's and Chief Nurses of all the U.S. Air Force bases in Europe (USAFE). I was the only female DBMS, of course, and there was one male Chief Nurse, from a base in Turkey. In the morning we all met in the same room and after lunch the doctors and nurses split into two separate groups. As I sat down, a helpful doctor informed me that the *nurses* were meeting in the other room. I said, "I know," and just sat there and let him figure it out.

I got invited to dinner with the nurses—I think they felt sorry for me—and got to hear their serenade to the lone male nurse:

> We're here because we love ya'
> We love ya' cause you're good.
> You're good because God made you.
> We wish to Hell we could.

Nurses were a raunchy bunch. Wait till you read about the male stripper in a later chapter.

MORE MONEY!

In 1974 the Air Force started paying bonuses to physicians, around $10-13,000. I already was earning enough to live comfortably, so I went home to Seattle for a visit and invested my bonus in real estate. I knew other doctors who had their bonuses spent on luxuries before they even received the check.

Around this time I got another pleasant financial surprise due to a class action lawsuit. The suit had been filed claiming that the military policy on dependents was discriminatory to women. Well, of course it was! Nevertheless, legal legerdemain convinced the court that it wasn't. But eventually justice prevailed and the verdict was overturned on appeal.

The military's incredibly stupid defense was that most wives are dependents and most husbands are not dependents, and it would be too cumbersome to try to figure out who was actually dependent, so the easiest thing was just to assume all wives are and all husbands aren't. After the court decision, the DOD decided all spouses, male or female, would be considered dependents whether they actually were dependent or not. They eventually reimbursed me for all the dependent housing allowances, my husband's travel expenses to Spain, and everything else I had missed out on because of their discrimination.

When I had been at a steadily shrinking Morón for nearly 3 years, the Air Force decided they didn't need a doctor there at all and the aid station could be managed by independent medical corpsmen. I was transferred to Torrejón Air Base, just north of Madrid, to fill the vacant position of GMO (General Medical Officer) there.

I was leaving because there was practically nothing to do, so of course on my last day of work I saw 17 patients and had to work late.

6

Torrejón—Working in a Hospital Again

o o o o o o o o o o o o o o o o o o o o o o o o o o o o o o o
The art of medicine consists in amusing the patient while
nature cures the disease.

—*Voltaire*

I was back to medical civilization. Torrejón had a busy hospital, with an ER, out-patient clinics, inpatient wards, operating rooms, delivery rooms, internists, general surgeons, orthopedic surgeons, obstetricians, pediatricians, a psychiatrist, a pathologist, flight surgeons, a physical therapist, a urologist, and even a dermatologist. I was the only military GMO assigned, although there were a couple of Spanish civilian doctors to help share the workload. I was Chief of the General Therapy Clinic, in charge of military sick call and all non-specialist outpatient appointments. And I had admitting privileges. I was delighted.

When I first got there, they even had a woman doctor! Not a military woman doctor, just a civilian employee, wife of a military internist, and she left right after I arrived; but it was the first woman doctor I had even *seen* in over three years!

We used to joke about VOQ syndrome—it seemed that whenever anyone was coming or going to a new assignment and moved into temporary quarters on base, everyone in the family would get sick. Probably something to do with the stress of moving and the exposure to new germs. Anyway, it happened to me too: I had a terrible attack of hay fever my first week at Torrejón; couldn't stop sneezing, and my nose ran like a faucet. They even gave me a steroid shot in an attempt to suppress it. I thought "Oh, no; if it's going to be like this the whole time, I'll never survive." But miraculously, after the first week I was back to normal and never had another bad attack.

Allergies are strange critters and I still don't begin to understand them. At Morón I was getting allergy shots twice a week for a while. Sometimes they can cause a serious anaphylactic reaction, and I was worried that I might have a problem when no other doctor was around. One day after my shot I started getting short of breath and dizzy and almost panicked. Then I realized, "You idiot, you're just hyperventilating!" I slowed my breathing down and the symptoms went away.

My first day of work was Monday, July 8, 1974. My first admission was Friday, July 12, and was my own fault: a woman had a bad reaction to the Fiorinal I had given her at sick call. Not exactly a promising start. I didn't work for long the first time around. On July 18 I left for a long vacation trip to Egypt.

I came back from Egypt with Pharaoh's revenge (diarrhea) but went to work anyway. Our Spanish civilian, Dr. Atocha, was out sick and I had to cover his patients as well as see walk-ins and supervise a nurse practitioner in training. The next day Dr. Atocha left at 10 AM with a headache again. It was like we were having a competition to see who could be sickest. I won. By that night I had a fever and was so dehydrated they had to admit me to the hospital for IV fluids. When I was discharged, I *still* had diarrhea; they hadn't found anything wrong, but they empirically gave me some antibiotics and it eventually resolved. I suspect my recovery was in spite of the antibiotics, not because of them.

LIVING IN MADRID

We found an apartment in Madrid near a subway station and convenient to the highway leading north from Madrid to the base. Driving to work meant fighting rush hour on one of the busiest highways in the country. I would start up the on-ramp with a car on each side of me trying to crowd its way into the one lane. I would have to butt my way in between other cars to get onto the highway. I used to say they should give me combat pay for driving to work.

Our 4th floor (5th the way Americans count) apartment was spacious, with several bedrooms and a maid's room. It had a phone which remained listed under the name of the original occupant of the apartment many years before. We had a cleaning woman come in once a week; we heard that another family's cleaning lady was so thorough she managed to scrub all the chrome off the faucets with steel wool. Ours was more intelligent.

When we moved into the apartment, the tiny elevator was not big enough for furniture, so the moving men rigged a big pole between our balcony and the one above, with a pulley sticking out, and they airlifted all our furniture. I took a photo of my upright piano swinging in midair from this ingenious apparatus four stories above the ground.

When we moved in, the kitchen sink was not connected to the drainpipe. There was a small gap that leaked water. I didn't know anything about proper plumbing repairs, but I had some epoxy glue that I used to fill the gap, and it worked great. I often wondered what would happen if they ever needed to disconnect the pipe.

An electrician came to install a transformer for the whole apartment to step down the electricity from 220 volts to 110 volts so we could operate our American appliances. My college physics came in handy, because I knew enough to calculate that he was trying to give us far more capacity than we needed, and I got him to install a smaller, less expensive transformer.

Our building was one of several in the neighborhood that were supplied with heat and hot water by one central plant. The system was not well designed, because there was no way to cut off the heat for individual apartments if they stopped paying their bills. Would you bother paying your bill if you knew you'd keep getting service anyway? So of course, lots of people didn't bother to pay their bills. Eventually the system went bankrupt.

For several months that winter we had no heat or hot water until the buildings had each installed their own new boilers. We used portable heaters and managed not to get frostbite, but it was a nuisance to heat water on the stove for baths and washing hair. There were two other doctors who lived in the same area, and for once we all appreciated the chance to pull ER duty because it gave us a warm place to sleep and a chance for a hot shower. As I remember, they finally got the heat working just about the time they usually shut it off for the summer anyway.

There was a tiny grocery store across the street. I could shop there and leave my purchases at the check-out and a few minutes later a boy would deliver them right to my door. It was a short walk to a subway station that would take me anywhere in Madrid for pennies.

EMERGENCY ROOM ANTICS

The ER was covered by the MOD (Medical Officer of the Day, or as we affectionately called it, Mother of the Day). It involved a 24 hour shift; there was a bed in an on-call room, but no guarantee you'd get to use it. All the doctors had to take turns as MOD, even the pathologist, who hadn't seen a live patient since medical school. When I was leaving the hospital one evening, I passed through the ER just as the pathologist was seeing a child with a simple asthma attack. He had no idea what to do, and I stopped long enough to tell him. Another time the pathologist was called up to the OB ward to deliver a baby because the obstetrician hadn't arrived yet. I happened along and was recruited by a worried nurse. I scrubbed in just in time to bail the pathologist out. When I came into the delivery room he was standing at the foot of the table with his sterile gloves on, hands up in front of his chest, white as a sheet and shaking like a leaf.

One night a woman came in asking for a pregnancy test. That wasn't exactly an emergency, and the test wasn't accurate until several days after the deed was done, so we asked how long she thought she might have been pregnant. She looked at her watch and said, "About 30 minutes."

One man complained that his foreskin hurt when he masturbated; I told him there was an easy solution to that problem. Another man came in (to the *Emergency Room!*) to ask if he could have a circumcision. He had heard that it was a good idea, and wanted to have it done while the Air Force would pay for it. A quick exam showed that he had already had a circumcision. I don't know *what* he expected us to cut off!

A mother brought her child in for a common headache which had already stopped by the time they got there. Instead of getting mad, I tried to find out why she did such a silly thing. I found out it wasn't so silly: he had had a head injury earlier and she was truly alarmed because she had heard that a headache might mean he had suffered a concussion or other brain injury.

A 4 year old girl had an ear infection and just to make conversation I asked her, "What did the doctor give you last time?" She answered, "Ampicillin, 250 mg four times a day for 10 days and Sudafed one teaspoon three times a day." I stood up and offered her my chair: "Here, you know more about this than I do."

One evening an enlisted man came in and asked the MOD to evaluate him because when he went to sick call earlier he hadn't been allowed to see a doctor; he'd just been seen by some nurse. The MOD looked at the medical record and discovered that that "nurse" was me. He reamed the patient out, telling him that "nurse" was a doctor who knew more about his illness than the MOD did.

A patient came in with an overdose of Darvon and alcohol and stopped breathing. We got some Narcan into his vein and revived him. I saved his life, and he never even said thank you.

One of the nurses came to me and asked a special favor. Would I give her a penicillin shot? It seems a man had shared something with her, and she was embarrassed to ask one of her fellow nurses to administer the remedy. I'd never given a penicillin shot before, but she got it and told me what to do, so I did. She was grateful. She lamented, "It's not fair. I've never done anything like that before, and the one time I slip, I get the clap!"

Corpsmen sewed up most of the simple lacerations in military ERs; they took pride in their ability and were meticulous. I kept hoping a patient would ask for a doctor to sew up his wound. I would have said I'd be happy to if I could remember how, but I hadn't sutured a wound since 1970; then I would ask the corpsman how many he'd done since 1970 and I'd let the patient decide.

People used to debate whether women should work in an ER—were they strong enough? What if a drunk patient got belligerent? Actually, I suspect patients were less likely to misbehave in the presence of women. One of our corpsmen was a slender, petite, delicate-looking blonde female. It would have been interesting if a belligerent patient had challenged her: she held a black belt in judo.

There was a big fuzzy black and yellow caterpillar that appeared in great numbers in the spring in the Madrid area. We started getting patients in the ER with rashes. Apparently the caterpillar hairs came off and floated through the air and caused an itchy rash in susceptible people. They would break out even without any direct contact with the caterpillar. One day there was a picnic on base and we had a regular epidemic of itchy, rashy people. One little boy had picked up caterpillars with his fingers and collected them in a bucket; he didn't break out, but his Mom did just from picking up the bucket to empty it. All we had to treat it with was Calamine lotion. We moved our entire supply of Calamine lotion to the front desk and stopped bothering to sign patients in. We'd take a quick look, say caterpillar rash, hand them a bottle of Calamine lotion, and move on to the next patient.

A woman told me her high school age daughter had been planning on a career in nursing. Then one night she came into the ER and saw me working there. She was electrified, and told her mother it had never occurred to her before that a woman could be a doctor, and now that's what she wanted to do.

ATH—6 TENTS, 4 DAYS

Torrejón had an ATH—an Air-Transportable Hospital. It consisted of several big wooden pallets of supplies that could be unloaded from an airplane and quickly transformed into a tent hospital complete with operating room and wards, sterilizers, refrigerators, a lab, pharmacy and even a dental chair. If it deployed, doctors, technicians, and other personnel were supplied from the base to go with it into the field. No women had ever been assigned to the ATH.

Then I transferred in. The required staff of the ATH included one general medical officer. And who was the one and only GMO at Torrejón? Little ol' me. They had no choice but to put me on the ATH. This caused great consternation and alarm.

[In a hushed, ominous voice] "What about restroom facilities?" I don't know, but when you're backpacking or climbing mountains, you can always ask the guys to look the other way, and presumably the ATH would have some kind of latrine set up with a modicum of sanitation and privacy.

"The guys like to take their shirts off sometimes." So what? I promise not to be offended, and I hope you don't think I'm going to take *my* shirt off.

"The guys like to swear and use bad language sometimes in the field." Do you think they know any words I haven't heard? If they do, I'd love to learn them. I speak Spanish and know the swear words in that language too.

"Women aren't strong enough." Bullshit. Maybe it took two average women to lift something one macho man would try to carry by himself, but maybe there would be fewer back injuries that way. There wasn't a single task involved that the average woman couldn't accomplish.

Playing MASH—that's me on the left, beside a very tall internist

We were never actually deployed, but we had exercises where we would set up the ATH on base, spend a few days there and have a disaster exercise with pretend patients. I loved the chance to be outdoors doing something new and exciting. We had to practice lifting and carrying litters: ready, set, LIFT. The two guys on one side were taller than the two guys on the other side; they lifted with greater vigor, and the patient tumbled off. Oh, yes—we were supposed to fasten the litter straps first!

We played war and pretended to treat patients in the tents. They came to the ward tent to get the next patient for surgery and found his bed empty—he had to pee, and had walked over to the base Laundromat to use the restroom there.

Since they *had* to take me, they gave in and took a female nurse and a female corpsman too so I wouldn't feel lonely (or so I would be properly chaperoned?). After the first ATH exercise with women, the ATH unit commander held a debriefing and asked the men how it had worked out having women on the team. They were sort of like, "Duh, what difference does that make? Why are you even asking?" No one had any complaints. In fact, the enlisted men commented that they *preferred* me because the male doctors hated it and were always sneaking off back to the hospital and hardly did any work, while I had enjoyed the whole experience and had pitched in and helped with every phase of the operation, including erecting the huge WWII era tents and carrying supplies to and from the pallets.

When we had these exercises, I had to wear fatigues. There was just one fatigue uniform, designed for men, and I wore men's combat boots and a men's baseball-type cap. The first time I wore it for an exercise, I noticed that the portero (doorman or concierge) of my apartment building did a double-take and then sort of stared at me but didn't say anything. The day after the exercise ended, when I reverted to the blue uniform, he approached me hesitantly and said shyly, "You know, I like *that* uniform much better." I told him I did too.

DISASTER EXERCISES

We had periodic recalls, where personnel would notify each other by a phone chain at some ungodly hour of the night and we would have to dress in our fatigues and report to the base. Then we'd sit around and twiddle our thumbs until time to start our regular workday. One internist was tired of these games and decided not to play. When they phoned him he simply turned over and went back to sleep. Which meant that no one else down his chain got the notification. He was punished, of course.

In disaster exercises, we had to triage patients in the field and again on arrival at the hospital. There were four categories: "Immediate"—those who required immediate lifesaving attention, "Delayed"—those who required substantial treatment or surgery but could tolerate some delay, the "Walking Wounded"—who could be patched up and sent back to battle or used to help with other patients, and the "Expectant"—those who would die no matter what we did or whose treatment would divert resources that could have saved more lives. A patient might move from immediate to expectant or vice versa depending on the workload and personnel available. And in wartime, resources would have to be assigned to get some of the walking wounded back in action even if it meant some of the more seriously wounded would die. This is a harsh reality that seems inhumane but is a necessary part of war and is intended to save more lives in the long run by winning the battle.

The triage officer could use his judgment to pretend that a pretend patient had died. One surgeon who was assigned to triage patients on arrival at the hospital simply declared everyone dead at the door. No one in the hospital got any patients to play with. Next time we had a new triage officer!

In the field, we could load 4 patients into each field ambulance. One doctor had 6 patients waiting, so he loaded 4 into the ambulance and rolled the other two off into a ditch, declaring them dead. When the ambulance returned later for another load, he had 2 vacant spaces, so he went back to the bodies in the ditch, felt their pulse and decided they weren't dead after all.

It was always interesting to have a pretend psych patient. They had great fun doing whatever their idea was of what a crazy person might do. One pretend psych patient stood out in a major intersection directing traffic and directed all the emergency vehicles off in the wrong direction. I always wanted them to have the base commander be the one to pretend to freak out. It would have been interesting to see if his subordinates would realize he wasn't acting right and would dare to override his command. I wondered if they would even notice.

We had two big "crackerbox" field ambulances. One was a Dodge whose letters had been rearranged so it read DOGDE. I was assigned to ride in one of the ambulances in these exercises. That presented a problem. If we were called out during the day I wouldn't be wearing the fatigue uniform. The step up into the field ambulance was quite a stretch, and my everyday uniform had a tight skirt. It was practically impossible to get up there without exposing my private anatomy to public view. And of course, it wasn't exactly practical to run around in a field examining patients on the ground while wearing a short skirt and trying not to display my undergarments. I really needed some kind of uniform with trousers. The nurses had the option of a white pantsuit uniform, but as a doctor I was not allowed to wear whites. And I couldn't wear fatigues for everyday duty. I was pretty much stuck. I was in the unique situation of an officer whose duty called for pants but who was required to wear a skirt. I soon discovered that there was a blue tunic and pants combination that the flight nurses were authorized to wear on air-evac flights. I asked for and received special permission to wear it. I carried a letter in my wallet from the Surgeon General of USAFE authorizing it. I loved it when the IG team came. They would solemnly inform me that I was out of uniform and was going to be written up in their report, and I would say no I wasn't and show them my letter. I wrote a letter to the Uniform Board suggesting that they make the flight nurse uniform legal for female doctors, but before they had a chance to act on it, a pantsuit version of the class A blue uniform was authorized for all women, so my problem was solved.

Just one more instance of being part of an organization that wasn't really prepared to include women. And one more time I was made to feel "different." I longed for the day when no one would even notice whether a doctor was male or female.

Uniform regulations had other curious provisions. Women could carry an umbrella but men couldn't—men were assumed to be waterproof. At that time, the regulations said that the skirt could be worn 2 inches above the knee if one had attractive legs; otherwise it should extend to the top of the knee. It didn't say who got to decide whether your legs were attractive. The regulations also specified "appropriate" undergarments. Probably because some women had started going braless. One older master sergeant challenged an enlisted woman because she appeared not to be wearing a bra. She was wearing one, but it was a soft material with a natural look. She said, "I am too wearing a bra!" and she lifted her shirt to *show* him. He was majorly embarrassed and I doubt if he ever dared question a woman's attire again.

PLANE CRASH

One night when I was on duty in the ER there was a plane crash. Normally, the tower would alert the ER and the MOD would go out to the crash site; then the flight surgeon on call would be contacted to take over and help with the accident investigation. On this occasion, we didn't even know that a plane had crashed.

We heard messages over the radio to the effect that "We seem to have lost contact with an aircraft." And "There seems to have been some kind of explosion beyond the end of the runway." We sort of expected to be called out for the explosion, but they never asked for our help, so we figured maybe they'd seen something off base that didn't concern us.

Suddenly the flight surgeon blew into the ER and commandeered an ambulance. He had been at a party, and somehow he had learned there was a plane crash before we had. We could hear the radio transmissions from the emergency vehicles and we spent the rest of the evening listening to events unfold with one screw-up after another. The crash site was visible from the tower, but it was off base, and nobody knew how to get to it. It took them over two hours to find it. The convoy of fire trucks, ambulance, etc. set off down Spanish country roads through little villages in the dark and the rain. One of our fire trucks hit a telephone pole in a village and knocked it down, putting itself out of commission in the process. The plane had crashed in a valley where the radio reception was bad, so the only way to communicate between the base and the crash site was by relaying via the radio of an ambulance parked at the top of an overlooking hill. There was mud and confusion everywhere. Over the radio, we heard someone shout, "We're up to our *assholes* in mud out here!" This was broadcast loud enough for all the patients in the emergency room area to hear. An ambulance got stuck in the mud, and by the time they finally got it loose, they couldn't get it started because the driver had returned to the base with the ignition key in his pocket. They thought they had identified all 7 of the bodies from the plane, but these were so fragmented they got the count wrong. What they thought were 3 bodies were actually only 2, and when daylight arrived they found another body that had been thrown clear of the crash site.

We learned later what had happened. A military plane, a KC 135, had started its descent into Torrejón and had mis-heard its instructions from air traffic control. They told it to descend to 4000 feet and the pilot responded, "Roger, descending to 2000 feet." The altitude of Madrid happens to be 2100 feet, and the pilot should have read his charts and known this. Anyway, the tower didn't realize the pilot had repeated the altitude wrong, the air traffic controller didn't say anything, and the pilot proceeded to fly into the ground and smear parts of the aircraft and crew over a mile or so of Spanish countryside.

That was one of those accidents they say was caused by flying at an altitude lower than that of the ground. It was caused by miscommunication and pilot error. My father insisted that *all* airplane accidents were due to pilot error: the error was getting in the airplane in the first place.

DR. MUDDLE

I was Chief of the General Therapy Clinic for a while, but then I was displaced by a new arrival: an elderly DO (Doctor of Osteopathy) who had been recruited directly from civilian practice and given the rank of full colonel. I'll call him Dr. Muddle. He knew nothing about the military, very little about medicine, and didn't even know how to pronounce the name of his car—he called it a MER-suh-deez.

Things deteriorated rapidly under his mismanagement. Dr. Muddle refused to see patients for the first few days while he "got the clinic organized." He organized a new GP inpatient service and put himself on the schedule to cover it the first weekend. I had one inpatient; Dr. Muddle failed to make rounds, and no one saw my patient all weekend.

One day our Spanish civilian doctor was out sick, and we had no one assigned to cover walk-ins. It was total disaster in the clinic; no one asked for help, there was no call schedule, no joint rounds.

I did way more than my share of the work. The civilian doctors were frequently out sick; they often arrived late and left early. One day Dr. T "overslept" until noon, and I had to see all his morning appointments along with my own. One day one of them was out sick and the other went home at 3:30, while I stayed until 7:00 pm. One week I kept count: I saw 59 patients more than Dr. Muddle did. He couldn't keep up with his appointment schedule, and I often had to see 3 or 4 of his patients, who had been waiting for as long as two hours. One day 31 patients showed up for sick call and I saw 20 of them; my total patient count for the day was 45—the corpsman at our front desk brought me a rose as a prize for seeing so many patients.

Dr. Muddle was the only DO on our staff. DOs are trained to do spinal manipulations, and the rest of us wanted to know what that was all about. We asked him to give a talk about it at a staff meeting. He rambled on with a lot of vague nonsense, said absolutely nothing, couldn't even begin to explain what he was doing when he cracked a back, and after only 10 minutes he said, "I don't know what else to say."

Dr. Muddle would see a patient or two at sick call in the time it took me to see 6 or 8. If a 19 year old man came in with chest pain, he would personally escort him to get an x-ray and EKG and stand by just in case he might be having a heart attack—he'd spend an hour or more with someone who obviously had benign chest wall pain and only needed some aspirin. Whenever I tried to complain that

I was getting the bulk of the workload and sick call was running late, he would change the subject and talk about the weather.

Sick call was always a logistical problem, and we tried to discourage patients from using it when a scheduled appointment would be more practical. One day a man came in late for sick call with a problem that wasn't really urgent, and the nurse at the desk managed to get him in. She jokingly told him "You owe me a bottle of wine for this." The next day he showed up with a bottle of wine for her, with a ribbon around it.

Some patients were hesitant about seeing a woman doctor on sick call. They were told they could either see me now or make an appointment later with the doctor of their choice. They usually gave in and saw me. After the first time, when they had gotten over the initial shock, they would come back and *ask* for me.

MISCELLANEOUS ANNOYANCES

Once a month we had to assemble in the cafeteria and sit through Commander's Call and listen to announcements and military stuff that we found quite boring. One time I was sitting next to an obstetrician named Dr. Fine. He leaned over and whispered in my ear: "I've invented a new douching solution. I'm going to name it Finasol after myself. It's going to consist of alum, LSD and the 7 herbs and spices from Col. Sanders' Kentucky Fried Chicken…. to make you uptight, outa sight and finger-licking good!" I practically choked trying not to laugh out loud and disrupt the meeting.

For one Commander's Call we got to go on a field trip to the flight line and the air traffic control tower. I had never seen those things before. I had no idea that I would be seeing much more of them later. At the time I didn't have the slightest inkling that I would some day be a pilot and a flight surgeon.

One of our pediatricians had been stationed in Turkey, where he was a flight surgeon. People would ask him, "Why would the Air Force want a pediatrician for a flight surgeon?" and he would answer, "Have you ever known any pilots?" One day in Turkey, a patient was unhappy with his treatment and demanded to see the commander. The pediatrician said, "Of course, you can see the commander." He stepped outside, stepped right back inside, and said, "Hello, I'm the commander." He claimed that good pediatrics consisted of benign neglect of children and emotional support of parents. He also claimed that giving vitamins to healthy children only produced expensive urine.

The hospital commander had a rule that his doctors couldn't stay home sick. They either had to go to work or be admitted to the hospital. The pediatrician was always catching the latest bugs from his patients, and he did *not* like the idea of being admitted to the hospital. One day he staggered through his duties with a fever of 104 degrees.

We had to get cholera shots twice a year in Spain. They aren't very effective, but they do help reduce the severity of the illness a little, and there was some cholera in certain areas of the country. At Torrejón, they had an outbreak of hepatitis that was traced to a broken sewer pipe in base housing that affected people in the neighboring houses. When I went in to get my next cholera shot, they told me the requirement had been dropped, and I didn't need a cholera shot—unless I was going to base housing!

We had a bomb scare. Someone found a suspicious unclaimed bag under a chair in the terminal. The bomb squad took it out to a field and blew it up. Only to find out after the fact that they had blown up someone's extra socks and his transistor radio.

Since the Palomares incident in 1966, when two American aircraft collided over southern Spain and dropped four thermonuclear bombs,[1] Spain did not allow overflights of Spanish territory by planes carrying nuclear materials. Nevertheless, we still had to regularly carry out Broken Arrow exercises so we would know how to respond to a nuclear accident that couldn't possibly happen in the first place.

We had to train with gas masks that didn't have effective filters. The good filters were in storage somewhere, and they would supposedly be issued if we ever really needed them. We wondered how long that would take, whether there were enough filters, and whether they really worked.

My faithful Volvo, bought new in 1969, was becoming a problem. It quit during a trip. After repairs, it never was right again. It would be going 60 mph down the highway and then suddenly wouldn't go over 25. And then it would again. It became increasingly obvious that the Spanish mechanics didn't understand it, so I reluctantly replaced it with a new Fiat. I sold the Volvo to an American who worked on his own cars; he tinkered with it over a weekend, replaced the sparkplugs, cleaned things he said looked like they'd never been cleaned, and had it purring like new.

---

1.   They didn't explode, and no one was injured, but cleanup was expensive and there was a lot of bad press.

I had problems with the Fiat right away. It idled way too fast; I took it back to the dealer and asked him to adjust the automatic choke. He saw a presumably ignorant female, so he tried to tell me that was the way all automatic chokes worked. I blew up. I informed him that I'd driven lots of cars with automatic chokes and I knew very well what they were supposed to do. I demanded that they fix it, for free. They did. I grew to hate that lemon of a Fiat and even to fantasize about leaving it unlocked in the hopes that someone would steal it.

One day I got an official computer printout ordering me to report for a routine dental exam on a certain date. In order to clear my own appointment schedule, I had to get permission in writing from the hospital commander and personally take it to the appointment desk so the clerks could block an hour off from my appointment list. This seemed so Mickey Mouse. Wouldn't you think even a lowly appointment clerk would be capable of recognizing an order for a required appointment? One of our doctors said that was the difference between the Air Force and the Boy Scouts—the Boy Scouts had adult leadership. A nurse did him one better: she said the Air Force is like a condom; it gives you a sense of security while you're getting screwed.

SPANISH MEDICINE

I majored in Spanish, I married a Spaniard, some of my best friends were Spanish, and I loved Spain. I knew individual Spanish doctors who were top-notch. Nevertheless, I couldn't help developing an unfavorable opinion of Spanish medicine in general. Keep in mind that this was the early 70s and the situation has improved vastly since then.

An American child in a boarding school complained of a sore throat and they called in a Spanish doctor. He examined her at the bedside, listened to her chest with a stethoscope, felt her abdomen, did no laboratory tests, and concluded that she had scarlet fever that had affected her pancreas and possibly her heart. He prescribed a month of bed rest on a diet of nothing but fruit and bread. Her parents brought her to me for a second opinion.

None of this made any sense to me. Scarlet fever is a strep infection, and no throat culture had been done to identify strep. Rheumatic fever is a result of strep infection and can damage the heart valves, causing a murmur, but I had no idea how a bedside exam could determine anything about the pancreas, and I couldn't fathom the diet recommendations. I examined the child, tested for strep, heard no heart murmur, and found absolutely nothing wrong with her.

I thought perhaps I'd heard a garbled story, so I phoned the Spanish physician to hear his version first hand. I asked what he had found on exam, if he had heard a heart murmur, and why he had recommended what he did. He mumbled something to the effect that once a cousin of his had died of scarlet fever and you couldn't be too careful. He was obviously an idiot who had no idea what he was talking about. I bet he hadn't read a word since he graduated from medical school back in the Middle Ages. I almost asked him if he still used leeches.

I heard horror stories about Spanish medical education; I had no way of verifying them, but they did seem to fall into a common pattern. In the US, students have 3 or 4 years of college and usually a bachelor's degree before they apply to medical school. Admission is highly competitive. After four years of medical school, a year of internship is required and the student must pass a written test before getting a license to practice medicine. If he decides to specialize, he spends two to six more years in a residency program, then passes a board certification exam. In Spain, anyone with a high school diploma was automatically accepted to a 7 year medical school program. No internship was required and no qualifying exam; anyone with an MD could open a practice. If he wanted to specialize, he would work for a specialist for an undetermined period of time; whenever he felt he had learned enough he could hang out his own shingle as a specialist.

We had spent a year dissecting a cadaver shared by 4 students; one Spanish doctor told me the only dissection he did in medical school was when he and 3 other students got part of a forearm to dissect. We bought our own microscopes and carried them to class for regular use; one Spanish doctor told me he had only looked through a microscope once during his entire medical school career, when a special demonstration was set up. We spent the last two years of medical school on the hospital wards caring directly for patients; I was told it was possible to graduate from medical school in Spain without ever actually having touched a patient.

A woman was told she had diabetes, fallen kidneys, and a couple of other serious problems requiring surgery; I found absolutely nothing wrong with her. A child who was probably autistic was given a medicine to make his brain grow—a medicine that does not cross the blood-brain barrier so it couldn't even get to the brain, and even if it could get there it wouldn't know what to do. Numerous patients told me they suffered from low blood pressure, vague "liver" complaints, and other diagnoses that didn't fit into my scientific paradigm.

A man was in a car accident and sustained a large laceration to his arm. We would have cleaned it out with thorough irrigation and would have sutured it closed in layers, making sure no dead space was left for blood to accumulate. We would have used fine sutures on the skin to get a good cosmetic effect. The Spanish aid station merely threw in some sulfa powder and tacked the skin together with what looked like rope. Instead of healing, the wound fell apart, and we had to deal with the consequences.

Not only could you buy narcotics over the counter, but you could get prescription medications like injectable penicillin. If you had a cold and thought antibiotics might help, you could call in a "practicante" who would make a house call and give you an injection. These practicantes were something like a glorified nurse and weren't under any kind of supervision.

After some of the things I saw, I wouldn't have sent my *dog* to a Spanish hospital. Fortunately I didn't have a dog.

Spain had free socialized medicine for all. A Spanish friend went to a "Social Security" physician and barely got out the words, "I have a sore throat" when he handed her a prescription for penicillin and called the next patient. No exam, no nothing. Some of the doctors tried to get through 40 patients in a couple of hours. There was also private medical care, which was the obvious choice of anyone who could afford it.

They told a joke about a man who died and found himself at the Pearly Gates. St. Peter looked him up in his book and said, "I don't understand it. You weren't supposed to die for another 10 years." St. Peter called God. God asked the man how he died. The man described an illness and told how he had been treated by a Social Security doctor and had died. God shook his head in perplexity and told St. Peter, "I guess you'll have to let him in; those Social Security doctors have outsmarted me again!"

Under the Franco regime, Spain was a definitively Catholic country, and no divorce, birth control, or abortions were allowed. Condoms were sold in drug stores, but I heard of one pharmacist who assuaged his conscience by poking holes in them first. The Spanish obstetrician who worked with me at Morón had some way of obtaining birth control pills for his Spanish patients, but it wasn't legal.

He seemed to be quite competent, but another Spanish doctor I worked with at Torrejón was not. Even though he had been trained in the US, his medical care was far below standard. He diagnosed anemia in a woman without making any attempt to find out why she was anemic, and just suggested that she go buy some multivitamins with iron at the BX. He diagnosed one kind of vaginal infection without doing the appropriate tests, then treated it with the remedy for a different kind of infection. His errors were picked up by chart reviews, and we tried to get the hospital commander to take action, but he refused. I think he was afraid to stir up ill will with the Spanish community. He excused the physician's mistakes, saying "He's a fine, upstanding young man. He's a good father to his sons. I'm sure he means well."

This commander himself was incompetent and senile, and was an embarrassment to us all. He liked to touch people inappropriately, and one medical corpsman actually got a legal injunction against him saying he must not touch him. He sort of got the idea that touching was frowned on, but he would still do things like coming up to a woman, peering into her eyes, stroking the side of her face and asking, "Are those contact lenses you're wearing?" On a radio fund-raising program, someone challenged the commander to pull a shift in the ER as MOD; he respectfully declined and said he was flattered that anyone thought he was still capable of doing that (no one did think that—that was the whole point of the challenge). At one staff meeting he was supposed to brief us on what he had learned at a conference, and instead he rambled on about his experiences as a tourist. He was reportedly the oldest colonel on active duty and was about to (finally!) retire.

TDYs TO ZARAGOZA, THE NETHERLANDS, AND LISBON

I spent a month TDY (temporary duty) at Zaragoza Air Base because they were temporarily short of doctors. The hospital commander there was an administrator rather than an MD, and he was a real comedian. He greeted a new nurse with the question, "Do you fool around?" When he saw me in civilian clothes after hours in the hospital lobby he yelled out for all to hear: "Oh, it's you! I almost didn't recognize you with your clothes on!" Another embarrassing moment in the hospital lobby was when a visiting obstetrician was accosted by a patient's husband who shouted, "You're the one who got my wife pregnant!" (He was referring to infertility treatment, not adultery; he wanted to say thanks, not challenge him to a duel.)

The first day I worked in the clinic there, I thought I was working slowly, because I had to stop and ask things like, "Does your pharmacy carry Flexeril?" and "Is there a physical therapist I can refer this patient to?" and "Where do you keep the fluorescein strips?" The other doctor was an older man who liked to chat with his patients, and I guess they'd become used to his pace. At the end of my first day, the medical technicians asked me in awe, "How do you do it? You've seen more patients in a day than any doctor in this clinic ever did!" What can I say—I'm a fast woman.

They didn't have a room for me on base, so they put me up at a hotel in downtown Zaragoza. When I was on call, I had to stay in a room in the hospital overnight. There were seldom any patients at night, and we would get quite bored. One night one of the technicians figured out how to open the glass case with the hospital signboard and did some creative editing. He moved the letters around so that "Dental Clinic" became "Rental Clinic" and "Well Baby Clinic" became "Dead Baby Clinic."

Around 11 PM one night, one of the corpsmen noticed an unusual-looking spider on a branch outside the window and he captured it in a urine container. We brought it inside, examined it, and one thing led to another. We pretended it was an ER patient, admitted it to the hospital, made up a chart, wrote up a physical exam, made up a family history ("106 children, 104 of which died of being stepped on"), ordered lab tests ("silk spinning time" and "venom level"). We got sillier and sillier as the night progressed. We scheduled the spider for the air-evac, and even ordered a consultation from internal medicine for the next morning. We put the urine cup with spider in the middle of an unused patient bed in an empty room. In the morning, when the internist arrived, I told him we had admitted an unusual case during the night and I would like for him to examine the patient before we put her on the air-evac flight. She might have an endocrine or genetic disorder, and had the most marked arachnodactyly I'd ever seen. (That means long, skinny, spider-like fingers). He walked into the patient's room, asked, "Where is she?" and when I pointed out the cup of spider he cracked up.

I also spent a month TDY to Camp New Amsterdam in the Netherlands. One of their doctors was out of commission while he was being investigated. It seems he had a chronic pain problem and had been ordering narcotics for patients and appropriating them for his own use. They gave me a whole family-sized suite to myself over the Officer's Club. I had a delightful month there, got invited to people's homes, and had time to do some sightseeing. It was near Christmas, and I got to ride on a canal boat with Sinter Klass (the Dutch version of Santa) in Utrecht. I spent a weekend in Amsterdam, ate at a Rijstafel Indonesian restaurant, attended the Concertgebouw, bought wooden shoes, went on a canal boat tour, went to a sex shop, a Van Gogh museum, a Pannekocken house, and a music box museum. I went on a trip to Ghent and Bruges and a trip to the Christmas market in Cologne. I saw the Amersfoort market, saw workmen turning bricks in the pavement and washing street signs (apparently they give people work like that instead of just handing out unemployment checks), cows with blankets, a drive-thru windmill, uncurtained windows, prostitutes, open air markets and flowers, bicycles everywhere, marzipan, spice cookies. If global warming raises the sea level, the Dutch set an encouraging example that solutions can be found. Even their major airport, Schipol, is below sea level.

While doing a Pap smear on a patient I saw a string hanging out of her cervix. I asked how long she had had the IUD. She said she had had one years ago but they told her it had fallen out. I said nope it's still there, and removed it at her request, since her husband had had a vasectomy by then. Afterwards she said, "You mean I could have been fooling around all these years and didn't even know it?"

We had a disaster exercise where we had to wear gas masks around the clinic, which made it rather difficult to work. One day we had to make an ambulance run to pick up a patient who had fallen out of a tree while trying to retrieve a kite. We transferred him to a Dutch hospital, and all the way en route he kept asking over and over again where he was, what had happened, and what he was doing up a tree. He had a concussion and couldn't retain any memories.

I was sent TDY to Lisbon for 5 days with one of our nurse practitioners. We saw a few patients and did a few Pap smears at the US Embassy there, and got to meet the ambassador and the admiral who commanded IBERLANT (The Iberian Atlantic Command of NATO). Ours was sort of a courtesy visit; they didn't have any American medical services, but they did have a British flight surgeon assigned. We had plenty of time to enjoy Lisbon's fado music, shopping, and food. I had my first lobster there: it was selected from a tank, presented live at the table for approval, and then taken to the kitchen.

AEROBICS TESTING

We were supposed to exercise regularly to make sure we stayed in good physical condition; once a year we had aerobics testing to ensure compliance. I wasn't compliant. I've always hated to spend time exercising just for the sake of exercising—there are too many other things I'd rather be doing. My only exercise was walking from the parking lot to the building and walking up stairs when I had to. Yet I never failed an aerobics test.

For years I slipped through the cracks. There were different tests for men and women; the men had to run and the women had to do a set of exercises. When they scheduled the doctors for the men's test, I would say, "That test is for men only; you'll have to catch me when you test the women." And by the time they got around to testing the nurses they would have forgotten all about me. After years of this they finally caught up with me, but by then all that was required was to either run or walk 3 miles in a given time that varied according to one's age and sex. My walking speed has always been set on "high"—once I'm started going somewhere, I want to get there. So I had no trouble at all.

The last time I took the test, at age 43, I started out walking with some young men who worked with me. We were chatting, and I thought I'd keep up with them for a while for the sake of conversation and then drop back to old woman speed while they forged ahead at young man speed. I ended up keeping up with them for the whole walk without getting tired or even breathing hard. I could have done it twice in a row with no problem. Either the test was a poor measure of fitness or I had inherited "no exercise needed" genes. Once I heard Marvin Minsky of the MIT Media Lab speak at a conference; he said the need for exercise was an evolutionary defect that we would outgrow some day. Maybe I'm a mutant?

DERMATOLOGY AND OTHER SPECIALTIES

I managed to get some further education by spending time with the specialists in our hospital. I spent two weeks working with the dermatologist. One day he had a patient with crab lice; he caught one on a glass slide, and we looked at it under the microscope. The next patient was a little boy, and he let him look through the microscope just for fun. He said, "What do you see?" and the boy answered, "It looks like a crab." So its name was definitely appropriate. The little crab louse was still moving under the cover slip, and the dermatologist wondered how long it would live. He left it there overnight. When we came back the next morning, the cleaning lady had disturbed things and the glass slide had fallen on the floor, dislodging the cover slip. We looked at it: no louse. We spent the rest of the day wondering if it was still alive somewhere on the carpet getting ready to jump on us. We found ourselves scratching imaginary itches.

One definition of a specialist is a doctor who has his patients trained to only get sick during office hours. Dermatology was mostly an outpatient specialty; the dermatologist hardly ever had any inpatients. One day we had a patient with a severe sunburn. The dermatologist admitted him to the hospital on a Friday, gave him steroids to suppress the inflammation, wrapped him in a wet sheet and blew a fan on him. On Monday, I asked the dermatologist how the sunburned patient had done over the weekend. He said, "Oh my God! I forgot all about him! I forgot to make rounds." The patient was fine and apparently hadn't missed the doctor.

I went with the dermatologist when he was asked to consult on a Navy enlisted man who was in for a medical problem. They had noticed a funny looking lesion next to his belly button. It was just a benign nevus—a common mole. The dermatologist asked me what we should write on the consult sheet. I said, "Well, he's a Navy man, and it's by his navel, and it's a nevus, and it's unusual in appearance, so why not call it a 'novel Naval navel nevus'?" Sure enough, that's exactly how he wrote it down.

Warts are a common problem in a dermatologist's practice. Most will eventually go away on their own if not treated, and sometimes simple suggestion seems to work. The dermatologist had a plastic laminated card with a brightly colored picture of a frog, and he would stroke a child's wart with the magic card and tell them it would make the wart disappear. Sometimes it did!

Most kinds of skin cancer are relatively harmless, but malignant melanomas can be rapidly fatal. I saw an older man one day for some other problem, and as he was leaving my office, he said, "By the way, my wife wanted me to have you look at this." He had an ugly black irregular excrescence on his forearm. I'd never seen anything more suspicious of malignant melanoma, so I immediately trotted him down the hall to the dermatologist. The dermatologist wasn't worried; he told me it was undoubtedly just a large benign seborrheic keratosis, but he would biopsy it just to be sure. He did. The biopsy showed malignant melanoma.

That "by the way" ploy is a famous pet peeve of doctors. Patients pull it on you as they are leaving the office, and it almost always turns out to be either (1) the real reason they came to see you or (2) far more serious than the real reason they came to see you. Just as you think you're finishing the appointment, you have to switch gears, start all over, and be late for the next patient.

The dermatologist was my immediate supervisor and wrote my evaluations. One day I got called in for required counseling because I had gotten a speeding ticket. I was shocked when I got it, because it was for going over 15 mph out the gate of the air base, and I thought the limit was 30 there. I went to the site and looked: there was indeed a 15 mph sign right before the gate house, but it was off to the side and partly obscured by a tree. I had simply never seen it. The dermatologist said he was supposed to admonish me, but he couldn't say much because he'd gotten a ticket for the same thing only the week before. He said, "That sign really is hard to see, isn't it?"

I also got to work with the internists and make rounds with them. We had a flu epidemic and we opened an empty ward for the flu patients and had a regular assembly line system for treating them. The internists taught me to read EKGs and for a while I read all the EKGs for the hospital with them checking to make sure I didn't miss anything.

The internists admitted a pregnant woman with meningitis. I had just gotten through saying I hoped the infection wouldn't make her go into premature labor when I heard she had had a miscarriage in her hospital bed. A man dying of colon cancer was suffering through the terminal phase of his illness; the internists couldn't ethically do anything to put an end to his suffering, but they were delighted when he developed diarrhea, because that gave them an excuse to treat him with anti-diarrheal medication that might have a side effect of suppressing his respiratory drive. He died peacefully that night.

One of the internists was famous for his illegible handwriting. He gave a talk to the medical staff one day where he printed something on the blackboard, and the commander commented that if we hadn't learned anything else from the talk, we had learned one thing: the internist *could* write legibly if he really tried. The other internist nearly killed his wife. He had purchased a super-expensive bottle of vintage wine in France and was saving it for a very special occasion. He looked for it one day and couldn't find it. His wife told him she had cooked dinner with a recipe that called for wine and she didn't have any cooking wine, but she had found that bottle in the cupboard and used it.

I also got an education in neurology. We had a Spanish neurologist come to our hospital one afternoon a week to see patients, and he wanted them worked up ahead of time and presented to him. I volunteered for the job, got to see all the interesting cases, and learned a lot.

We had one of the rare psychiatrists who was not crazy himself and who had a sense of humor. I got in the elevator with him one day and said, "Good morning. How are you?" He looked at me quizzically and said, "Why do you ask?" I asked him why he always answered a question with another question, and he said, "Do I?" He had a Far Side cartoon on the door of his office of "imprinting gone awry" showing a flock of white-coated scientists following a duck.

One of his psych patients escaped one night when I was MOD. He got out the back door of the ward, went down the emergency exit stairs, and walked over to base housing. He walked right into someone's kitchen through an unlocked door. The woman of the house thought she was going to be attacked with a knife, but the patient left peacefully and the psychiatrist said he was really harmless.

I admitted quite a few inpatients, with a variety of complaints. One day alone I admitted a labyrinthine concussion, a diabetic leg ulcer, a case of splenomegaly with thrombocytopenia, and a patient with a pulmonary infiltrate. I had as many as 11 inpatients at a time, and had to make rounds before and after clinic hours.

The hospital administration wasn't entirely happy with my inpatient load. They thought GMOs were "here to see outpatients." On the other hand, they made me re-admit a patient I had discharged (he had back pain but I thought he was able to work). And I admitted patients who really needed to be in the hospital but who no one else wanted to accept. One of the internists referred to my inpatients as "Harriet's zoo."

I was concerned about preventive medicine, and I organized a Women's Health Days project where we invited dependent wives to come in for a comprehensive health survey, Pap smear, immunization update, and whatever else they needed. I visited the legal office about the privacy act. I was interviewed on the radio. We set up an efficient assembly line and were all set to go. Just as we got started, we were cancelled due to an alert that lasted four days. We finally resumed a month later. We got a lot done in a short time, seeing over 600 patients. I kept statistics and presented the information and lessons learned at a staff meeting. If a man had done this, it would have most likely earned him some kind of commendation or meritorious service medal. I received no recognition for my efforts—except for a couple of nice letters from grateful patients.

I gradually developed a reputation as a doctor who could deal with difficult patients, and I found that the specialists were actually referring patients to little ol' unspecialized me. For instance, a woman saw the internist for headaches. He evaluated her and found nothing wrong, but sent her to the neurologist just in case. The neurologist told her she didn't have any neurologic problem like a brain tumor so there was nothing he could do to help her. He sent her to the psychiatrist. The psychiatrist said he couldn't do anything for her because she wasn't crazy. She went back to the internist in desperation, saying no one could find anything wrong, but she still had her headaches. He referred her to me, and I explained that she had what we call a functional problem—where there was no tumor or anything visibly wrong, but where the way her body functioned was causing symptoms. I told her that I would work with her on a regular basis to help her cope with her condition so that the symptoms interfered as little as possible in her life. Just knowing someone cared did a lot, and talking about her life and her personal problems helped identify issues that influenced the pain. It was experiences like these that made me decide to specialize in family medicine.

Mrs. Kerfuffle was an unforgettable patient. She was an unhappy overweight woman who had grown up in Belgium, had been in a concentration camp as a teenager, and had been experimented on by Nazi doctors. She didn't know exactly what they had done to her, but she had never had periods and was unable to have children. She had a long list of complaints and spent much of her time bouncing from doctor to doctor; they all dreaded seeing her. The psychiatrist said she had something called concentration camp syndrome and there was nothing to be done; her condition was permanent. I worked with her for a long time, and I came to the same conclusion, but I didn't give up on her. I had her make regular appointments for followup, I talked with her about her dog and the few things that she enjoyed in life, and I tried to keep her consumption of medications to a minimum. I couldn't cure her, but I think I did help keep her out of trouble to some extent. She seemed to really appreciate my attention, and used to bring me little gifts.

And then there was Claudio Poltrone, an elderly Italian retired NCO with severe gout. He had so much uric acid in his system that it kept forming tophi, big lumps on his elbows and elsewhere. I would put him on medication and the lumps would shrink, but after a while he would decide he was doing so well he didn't need the pills any more. Soon he would come back in complaining, "I don't understand it—the lumps have come back!" I would patiently explain, but he never really seemed to understand.

A patient came in complaining of a bad-smelling vaginal discharge. I examined her and found a putrid tampon that she had forgotten to remove eons ago. The exam room stunk to high heaven for a couple of days afterwards. The exam room stunk another time when a corpsman found an old bottle of wine left over from some party and tried to open it. It had fermented and built up pressure, and it sort of exploded all over the room, decorating the walls, ceiling, and furniture and imbuing the room with the scent of a bad mistake in a wine cellar.

One poor chap came in three times in a row with gonorrhea and admitted to me that he'd caught it from the same girl each time. Some people just can't learn. He was so shamefaced and apologetic the third time that he brought me a box of candy. Another grateful patient brought me candy and a stuffed bear because I had let him out of the hospital for a weekend pass and he had won $2000 playing poker.

A man told me he had had a hysterectomy. I think he meant appendectomy. I HOPE he meant appendectomy! A woman was talking about avoiding pregnancy and she said, "Once a baby starts growing, it's too late; you can't just unscrew it."

I had an exhibitionist on sick call. I tried to be brisk and efficient and ignore the wares he displayed. I got out of the room as quickly as I could. I saw a man with prostatitis and told him that frequent ejaculation would help empty the gland and diminish his symptoms; he took the good news home to his wife, and she showed up the next day to ask if I had really given him a prescription to go home and have lots of sex.

I diagnosed tapeworms and granuloma inguinale. I did bone marrows, spinal taps, and sigmoidoscopies. On one sigmoidoscopy I found a cancer and later got to scrub in on the surgery to resect it (a hemicolectomy). I had to testify at a rape trial. A female airman with lesbian tendencies developed a crush on me, and insisted I administer her oath of re-enlistment in the back of a military cargo plane parked on the flightline.

I worked hard. One Friday I came home totally exhausted by the week's stresses, ready to crash and go to bed early. On the spur of the moment, my husband said, "Let's drive to Miranda de Ebro and spend the weekend with my brother." We went. I ended up doing all the driving myself. It was nearly midnight when we arrived, but I felt fine. My fatigue had vanished. I learned something from that.

THE END OF AN ERA

On November 20, 1975, Franco died; on the 22nd we watched King Juan Carlos' coronation on TV, and on the 23rd we watched Franco's televised funeral. It was the end of a 36 year Fascist dictatorship and the beginning of Spain's gradual return to a position of respect among the other Western democracies.

I was happy in Spain. From Madrid I could visit almost any part of Spain on a weekend. I used my 30 days' leave per year to visit the Canary Islands, France, Great Britain, Belgium, the Netherlands, Germany, Morocco, Portugal, Andorra, the Pyrenees, Italy, Monaco, Greece, Turkey and Egypt. I would gladly have stayed indefinitely, but the Air Force had a rule that no one could stay overseas more than six years in a row. I had reached that limit.

It was not only time to go back to the US, it was time to do a residency. I had chosen family practice, which was a bit ironic, because at that time I had never actually met a family practice specialist. My medical school at the University of Washington now has a highly respected department of family practice, but when I went there, it didn't exist yet. We met only specialists and subspecialists, and they continually made fun of the dumb primary care doctors out in Podunksville who had missed the diagnosis and had to send their patients to the Great Mecca to be cured. It was my experiences as a general medical officer that taught me the value of the family practice approach. Someone needed to take responsibility for the whole patient so he didn't fall through the cracks in the system. I told some of my patients that I was going to do a residency, and one of them couldn't remember what it was called. She asked, "What do you call that thing you're going to be where you refer patients to other doctors?" I hoped it was going to be a bit more than that!

On my last day at Torrejón I worked all night and assisted at two emergency C-sections. I flew back to the States the next day, just in time for my brother's wedding. He wore a white tuxedo, white shoes, and looked very elegant. It wasn't until he knelt at the altar that those of us in the front row could see he was wearing bright red socks. It was so typical of him; my sisters and I laughed so hard we almost fell out of our seats. After visiting with my family, I headed for Florida to go back to school.

7

Family Practice Residency/ Learning to Fly

○ ○

That this tiny two-seater box of metal managed to rise into the air at all felt unbelievable. Once we broke ground, it seemed as if I were floating on a magic carpet. The lightness and height made me tingle in somewhat the same way I feel aroused before making love. When I took over the controls, I felt as if I were at the center of my universe instead of orbiting someone else's. I felt then, and still believe now, that piloting a small aircraft is about as good as it gets.

—*Barbara Cushman Rowell,*
Flying South: A Pilot's Inner Journey

Eglin Air Force Base was in the Florida Panhandle, near miles of white sand Gulf Coast beach. I quickly found a house to rent in Fort Walton Beach. The area was all cut up by bayous, so to get around from my house to the rest of Fort Walton Beach where the downtown was, you had to go through parts of two other towns. The real estate man who rented me the house was ex-military, and he invited me to stay overnight at his house, fed me dinner, and lent me his daughter's Cadillac until my car came in. That's one of the perks of being in the service: you instantly belong to one big family of like-minded people who help each other out.

I had pre-ordered a new Volvo from a local dealer who was also ex-military. He'd been medically retired on 100% disability for a head injury, but was still functioning well enough to be the top Volvo dealer in the US. He gave me a really good price on my car but made me promise not to tell anyone how little it had cost.

My new home had one disadvantage: cockroaches. BIG ones that kept migrating in from the woods no matter how often the exterminators sprayed. They weren't too smart, though—they never managed to find the food in my kitchen! They did find a glass of champagne I was drinking in the bedroom. I set it down on the dresser for a few minutes and came back to find a cockroach using it as a swimming pool.

My husband came for a visit during the summer, but had to return to Spain to finish his PhD, so I was on my own again.

The Air Force was just starting a new family practice residency program at Eglin. As usual, I was the only woman in the program. But for the first time, I was in a hospital that actually had two other women doctors on the staff—a pathologist and an orthopedic surgeon. The pathologist was from India and the orthopedic surgeon was a petite blonde woman from Puerto Rico; it was impressive to see her manhandling limbs and bones and saws and instruments in the operating room. Orthopedics didn't want women: she had had to trick her way into a residency. Her first name was ambiguous, she deliberately wrote her application with no reference to her sex, and she omitted the requested picture. They hired her thinking she was a man. When she showed up, they were horrified, but it was too late to get rid of her.[1]

I worried that I would be behind the curve, since I'd been working as a general medical officer in Spain for six years and had had time to forget a lot, while the other residents were fresh out of medical school. I needn't have worried. I had accumulated enough experience and judgment to compensate for what I'd forgotten, and I'd kept up with reading the medical journals so there were no surprises. With my background, I may not have known as much about pediatrics as the pediatricians, but I knew more about internal medicine than they did. When we had a young patient with a familial tremor (which usually only shows up in adults), I was able to educate *them* about an effective new medication.

In one sense residency was a step backwards, because I could no longer work independently: now all my charts had to be co-signed by a staff doctor. In another sense it was a relief. Rather than bearing all the responsibility for my patients, I could rely on someone smarter to double-check everything I did. That relieved some of the pressure I'd felt when I was on my lonesome in Spain.

---

1.   This was a civilian residency, before she joined the military.

The family practice residency is a 3-year program. The rotating internship I had already done counted as the first year, so I started as a second-year resident at Eglin. We residents rotated through all the specialties, all the hospital wards and clinics, but we were also responsible for our own patients in the Family Practice Clinic. We were on call, usually every 3rd night. We had pet names for some of the specialists: dermatology was dummytology, the psychiatrists were sickiatrists, the pediatricians were "Peter Rabbits," ophthalmology was awful-mology, and internal medicine was infernal medicine. We also decided gynecology sounded like "guy" and should be re-named galnecology.

PLAYING STORK

We delivered a lot of babies. One day I added up all the pieces of paper I had to fill out and sign for each delivery: it came to 22. Although I had been taught to use forceps in my internship, Eglin did not allow residents to use them at all. OK, no problem. Less work for me. If a patient needed forceps, I could just call a staff obstetrician to take over.

I had duty one weekend continuously from 8 AM Saturday morning through until 5 PM Monday afternoon, and that weekend we had one emergency and complication after another. I got to lie down a total of maybe 20 minutes the whole time. By Monday afternoon I was in a fog, and didn't dare sit down for fear I might not be able to get up again. One of the staff obstetricians teased me, "What were you trying to do, pack a whole obstetrics residency into one weekend?"

One of the staff obstetricians was a foreigner. I can't remember from what country. But I distinctly remember him yelling at a patient in labor, "You want to have baby, you have to have pain!"

One father-to-be was adamant that he wanted the baby delivered NOW, not whenever his wife went into labor. He had decided they had waited long enough. We had great difficulty explaining to him why that was not a good idea for either mother or baby.

Sometimes deliveries are slow and difficult, and sometimes the baby decides not to wait for the doctor. We call these "precipitous" deliveries, and someone came up with a classification system:

    Class I. Jet Propelled Pipsnorter
       a. Patient must be unattended

b. In bed in labor room.

c. Scream of baby brings doctors, nurses and attendants on the double.

Class II. Complete or Total

a. Patient on stretcher on way to delivery room.

b. No gloves

c. Use emergency set *after* delivery only.

Class III. Incomplete or Subtotal

a. Stretcher in delivery room

b. Patient half on bed half on delivery table with or without one leg in stirrups

c. One of both gloves on with or without towel on hand

d. No anesthesia

e. Baby delivered in gap between stretcher and table

Class IV. Marginal or Borderline

A. Open Top

a. Routine patient on delivery table not draped

b. Anesthesia mask on face

c. Gown on with or without gloves and with or without a towel

d. Patient has both legs in stirrups and is pushing

e. Six hours later baby delivers himself because everyone else is asleep

B. Flat Top

a. Patient sitting up

b. Being fitted for spinal

c. Patient rises off table

d. Baby does hand stand as it comes out

C. Sims or Left Lateral

a. Patient on side for caudal

b. Both gloves on, no anesthesia

c. Baby lies comfortably between mother's legs.

Class V. Frustrated Type

A. Classic

a. Patient prepped, draped and catheterized

b. Operator gowned and gloved

c. Nobody watching perineum while doctor drapes patient

d. Baby hangs by cord

B. Breech

a. Baby slides down cord like fireman sliding down pole

b. Kick way out

c. Claws at placenta trying desperately to hold on

d. Fingers give way and baby hangs by chin

e. Tooth marks found on cervix and vaginal wall

C. Ambassador Presection

a. Patient on table in OR, prepped and draped for C-section

b. Lower uterine segment opened; baby missing

c. Baby found between legs playing with catheter.

I added one to the list from a true case I knew about:

Class VI. The Fumble
    a. Doctor gowned, gloved and ready
    b. Mother *really* pushes
    c. Slippery baby ejected so forcefully that it slips right through the doctor's
hands and falls on the floor.

This actually happened to an obstetrician at Torrejón while I was there. The doctor was scared that the baby might suffer permanent brain damage and that he himself might suffer a costly lawsuit, but baby was fine.

An overweight patient came into the family practice clinic for a routine checkup. I felt a firm mass in her abdomen. I asked if there was any chance she might be pregnant. She said no, she was infertile; she and her husband had tried for a baby for 15 years and given up. Besides which, she was still having regular periods. Was it a tumor? I consulted the staff doctor, who listened to her mass with a stethoscope and heard a heartbeat. I asked her again when she had last had a period. She said, "Well, I really don't keep track … come to think of it, it may have been a while." When we told her she was pregnant, she ran out into the waiting room, fell on her knees in front of her husband, laughing, sobbing, and babbling "Oh, a baby! We have to buy a crib! I can't believe it!" They were both practically in hysterics.

MY FIRST VASECTOMY AND OTHER MEMORABLE PATIENTS

My first vasectomy was unforgettable. The urologist was teaching me to do a vasectomy by talking me through the procedure step by step. The patient asked me, somewhat apprehensively, if this was the first one I had done. I could not tell a lie; I said yes. He reflected for a moment, and then said, "Well, that's O.K., Doc. It's my first one too!"

A friend who had had the surgery referred to it as "my conversion to a sports model."

I admitted a 6 year old for asthma and pneumonia. He kept crying "Shoot me!" and "Let me die!" as we started his IV. Another 6 year old was admitted for head injuries after being thrown 15 feet by a car; he had amnesia for the event and told us, "I fell down." I was called out at 5 AM to admit a 14 year old with diabetic ketoacidosis; the day before was the first day of school and in the excitement she forgot to take her insulin.

A woman brought her husband into the exam room with her, and when I asked her what the problem was, she jerked her thumb in his direction and said, "He is." She said she wanted marital counseling. What she really wanted was for us to make him do what she said.

We occasionally had to attend a formal "Dining In" or a "Dining Out." The "In" was for military only; the "Out" included spouses. We had to wear a special mess dress uniform that was horrendously expensive, especially considering the rare use we got out of it. Mine was a long dark-blue/almost-black skirt and short jacket, fancy white blouse and cummerbund. We looked like a bunch of penguins. One evening we had barely sat down to the formal dinner when our beepers beeped and two of us finished the evening hovering over a sick newborn in an incubator, wearing paper gowns over our penguin outfits. One of our staff doctors ended the evening even more unpleasantly, sitting on the curb outside the Officer's Club miserably ridding his stomach of the fruit of too many toasts.

A colonel came into the ER one night with a vibrator stuck up his ass. They retrieved it, but couldn't understand why he hadn't gone to a civilian hospital and paid whatever it cost to keep his mishap private. There is no way you can keep news like that from spreading on a military base.

My most memorable patient in the Eglin ER was a child complaining of rectal discomfort. When I examined her, I saw a white lump protruding from her anus. As I looked more closely, I realized it was moving: it was a mass of writhing, intertwined pinworms! I had to send her home pinworms and all, because the ER didn't carry pinworm medicine; all I could do was give her a prescription for when the pharmacy opened in the morning.

WHO'S NUTS?

I asked for an elective in psychiatry. Not only was I interested in it, but I knew it was a big part of family medicine, and I liked the psychiatrist, Roy Clemmons. He was a real character. I was eating lunch at his table in the cafeteria one day, and I asked, "Would you like a cup of coffee?" He said yes. I said, "Good. While you're getting yourself one, you can bring me one too." He thought it was so funny that he did bring me one, and it became a regular routine. He had a lot of colorful sayings like "Whatever blows your skirt up" and "Slipperier than greased owl shit." One innocent asked if greased owl shit was particularly slippery, and Roy went into a big fabrication about the multiple uses of owl shit as a lubricant.

He was a down-to-earth psychiatrist. He figured the best way to treat anxiety neurosis was to give the patient something to REALLY worry about. And the best way to conquer depression was to make the patient angry, because you couldn't be angry and depressed at the same time. One woman came in with suicidal thoughts and her head bowed down. He started saying she really *was* worthless, and we probably couldn't do anything to help her, and she would probably end up in the loony bin at Chatahoochee where degenerate types wallowed in filth and ate their own excrement. I observed as her head gradually lifted and she started to retort that she wasn't *that* worthless. Her depression lifted as we watched.

An enlisted man was sent in for a mandatory inpatient psych evaluation, and he did *not* want to be there. He started protesting about his rights. Roy sat him down and pointed to a water tower outside his window. He said, "You see that water tower? That belongs to the Air Force. If the Air Force wants to tear it down, it tears it down. If the Air Force wants to move it, it moves it. If the Air Force wants to paint it, it paints it. YOU have EXACTLY the same rights as that water tower!" The patient got the message and decided to cooperate.

A schizophrenic patient told us his number was 6, the mark of the beast. He asked if Dr. Clemmons was God or Satan.

We admitted a whiner who was feeling really sorry for himself; Dr. Clemmons decided his problem was that his second Mommy (his wife) had left him and all the red got licked off his candy.

Roy told another depressed patient that he had his head so far up his own ass, all he could see was black and all he could smell was shit.

Part way through my psych elective I was assigned a PA (Physician's Assistant) to do workups on my patients as if he were my intern. Dr. Clemmons informed me that I now had a slave and I could kick him.

Roy was a fount of practical wisdom. Someone asked him "What's the purpose of life?" and he said it was simple:

(1) Develop your abilities, reach your potential.
(2) Do something to leave the world a little bit better than you found it, even if it's just by planting a tree or making a baby smile.
(3) Enjoy yourself in the process.

He told us about his own training. On an internal medicine rotation he had been assigned to a ward of dying patients, and he told them "You're not dying. You're living ... until you're dead." He opened windows and a sun porch, got them involved in activities, sent them out on passes, and soon had them all enjoying life again. His boss complained that patients weren't dying on schedule and were out doing their dying all over the county in fishing boats and motels instead of in their hospital beds. Roy didn't see that as a problem, and I don't either.

He told us about a memorable patient he had as a psychiatry resident: a young man named Lester, who lived on a farm. Roy spent a great deal of time with him but couldn't find a thing wrong. In desperation, he called Lester's mother in and asked why she had had him committed. She said, "Cuz he's quar." It took a while to establish that she meant "queer" as in "homosexual"—which to her equated to crazy. Roy had seen no signs of homosexuality, so he asked the mother why she thought that. She answered, "Cuz he's stopped fuckin' pigs." The light dawned. Roy went back to Lester and asked, "You got a girlfriend, Lester?" Lester blushed, hung his head and said, "Yep." Roy asked, "She better than pigs?" Lester grinned and said, "Yep." Problem solved.

Roy was not the chief of psychiatry. The chief was a strange, nervous, insecure little man who frowned constantly, even when smiling. He sought me out one day to tell me he'd read a consult I'd written using the words hypnagogic and hypnopompic, and he seemed so impressed that it made me suspect he hadn't known the words and had had to look them up. We used to wonder, half-seriously, if we could induce him to have a psychotic break if we all kept staring at him; I still think there was a pretty good chance we could have.

There's a psychiatric condition called Munchausen's syndrome where a patient fakes an illness to get attention, often enduring multiple hospitalizations and even surgeries. We were referred a patient who had air in the tissues under the skin of his neck and chest—subcutaneous emphysema. This can happen when the esophagus ruptures and leaks air into tissue planes, but we couldn't find anything wrong to explain it in this patient. We put him on the psych ward, and later pulled him out with no prior notice for an x-ray or something so we could search his room. Sure enough, there was a syringe taped on the underside of the wash basin in his room. He'd been injecting himself with air. He had lots of freckles, so the injection sites were hard to detect. We couldn't absolutely prove it, but we told him what we thought and sent him back to duty with a big sticker on his medical record so that if he ever had ANY kind of medical problems in the future he would be sent right back to Eglin for treatment. As far as I know, his problem resolved. Munchausen's is very difficult to treat, but the fact that the Air Force "owned" this patient may have afforded at least a temporary cure.

We held group therapy for the psychiatric inpatients. They helped treat each other. One schizophrenic man thought he was getting private messages from the TV and had a number of other problems, but the group could tell when he was over-reacting. They would tell him to stop certain of his behaviors, telling him they knew he was crazy but he wasn't *that* crazy! And he would stop.

Another resident and I co-led an outpatient group therapy program for patients with assorted psychological problems. The other resident had been a pilot in Viet Nam, and had attended medical school after surviving 6 years as a POW. When one patient complained that she felt like her life was out of control, he commiserated, "I know what that feels like; when they were torturing me I knew that no matter what I said or did, the pain was going to continue." You could see the patient's face change as she realized that maybe her problems weren't quite so bad after all.

WORKING CONDITIONS

There was a room on the wards for the residents to work in, with desks, chairs, a blackboard, and x-ray viewing boxes. It was a former patient room. One day the administration decided they needed it for patients. They evicted us and put two patient beds into the room. We watched for the next month as not a single patient was ever admitted to that room, and we eventually got it back. Meanwhile, we had a makeshift desk in the lobby in front of the elevators, and our x-ray box sat on the floor. I took a picture of our new "office" with residents kneeling on the floor to read x-rays and with a sketch of a resident with a big screw through his body on the portable blackboard. I also took a picture of a resident sitting on a stool inside a narrow clothes locker reading a chart in his "new office"! We used the pictures to good advantage in the skit we put on at the end of the residency.

We were unhappy with this treatment and with other things about the residency program. I took the initiative to organize the residents so we could present a united front and present our gripes to the powers that be. They unanimously elected me chief resident and spokesperson.

We dictated medical records using a telephone system that connected to a room in the bowels of the hospital where the stenographers and Dictaphones lurked. Sometimes we said things we probably wouldn't have phrased the same way if we were writing it down ourselves. Or fully awake. Or thinking. Alert stenographers collected gems like these:

> The left leg became numb at times and she walked it off.
> Patient has chest pain if she lies on her left side for over a year.
> Father died in his 90s of female trouble in his prostate and kidneys.
> Both the patient and the nurse herself reported passing flatus.
> Skin: somewhat pale but present.
> On the second day, the knee was better, and on the third day it had completely disappeared.
> The pelvic examination will be done later on the floor.
> Patient stated that if she would lie down within two or three minutes something would come across her abdomen and knock her up.
> By the time that she was admitted to the hospital her rapid heart had stopped and she was feeling much better.
> Patient had bilateral varicosities below the legs.
> If he squeezes the back of his neck for 4 or 5 years it comes and goes.
> Patient was seen by Dr. Blank who felt we should sit tight on the abdomen, and I agreed.
> Speculum was inserted between the eyes.
> Discharge status: Alive but without permission.
> Coming from Detroit, Michigan, this man has no children.
> At the onset of pregnancy the mother was undergoing bronchoscopy.
> She was treated with Mycostatin oral suppositories.
> Healthy appearing decrepit 69 year old white female mentally alert but forgetful.
> When you pin him down he has some slowing of the stream.

One day we heard that a doctor was coming from another base to be admitted for a psychiatric evaluation. It seems he had launched himself over the counter of the ER to assault the belligerent husband of a patient who had come in for some totally inappropriate and trivial reason. He was our hero. He had acted out what every single one of us had wanted to do to some patient at some point of our careers. We knew he wasn't crazy. We wanted to meet his air-evac flight with a brass band and a red carpet. OK, he didn't have good judgment, but damn! It felt good to fantasize about doing what he'd done.

We had to carry cumbersome "bricks" on call—two way radios the size and shape of a brick. A little boy who noticed mine asked me if I was a policeman. Finally some of us chipped in and shared the cost of a smaller civilian pager.

MISUNDERSTANDINGS

I did a psychiatric consultation on an active duty woman who was still on crutches weeks after a simple ankle sprain. The orthopedic surgeon thought she must be either malingering or crazy. The ankle had long since healed, but she complained of pain and refused to put weight on it. I talked to her for a while, and found out that she had somehow gotten the idea that she was not supposed to put any weight on it until it was totally pain-free. I explained that the ankle was fine, and she couldn't hurt it by using it, but she would have to expect some pain as she started using it again. The muscles were going to be stiff and sore at first. She was delighted, threw away the crutches, walked across the room, and thanked me for explaining things to her. All she needed was permission to try walking on it. She didn't mind the pain; she had just been under the misconception that she would damage the ankle further if she walked on it while it still hurt.

I met a patient in occupational therapy who was doing exercises to try to get some of the function back in her arm. She had severe nerve damage. She told me her story, which I would not have believed if I had heard it second-hand. She had a broken arm, and the doctor put it in a cast. He warned her that the arm might swell and make the cast too tight, in which case the cast would have to be split to relieve the pressure. He even drew a line on the cast and wrote on it, "Split here if tight."

That evening, the arm began to hurt, and the patient and her husband looked at the instructions and decided they didn't need to do anything because she hadn't had anything to drink—she wasn't "tight"! She told the story like it was a good joke on her. I wondered if perhaps she and her husband *had both* been "tight."

An old man on the medical ward was by far the angriest person I have ever met. He swore and complained constantly about every little thing. "I ordered THREE God damn pieces of bacon for breakfast, and they only brought me TWO lousy fuckin' pieces. And they were BURNT, God damn it!" He was impossible to deal with, and the whole staff came to hate him. One day I sat with him quietly for a while and then said, "It must be hard to be so angry all the time." His eyes teared up. Later we learned that he had organic brain syndrome. The poor guy was trying to cope with a frightening, incomprehensible world the only way he knew how.

LEARNING TO FLY

The psychiatrist, Roy, had an airplane. Actually he had two: a Cessna 210 and an old bright yellow open-cockpit no-radio biplane named "Dog" because it flew like a dog. He took me for a ride in the Cessna one day and let me take the controls. I was enchanted. I had some vague idea that you had to go to school for years to learn to fly; I found out all it took was a short ground school class and 40 hours of instruction and practice. I decided I wanted to learn to fly.

I sort of went at things backwards. I decided I would buy a plane first and then learn to fly it. An old single engine Tri-Pacer was for sale at our local airport. A pilot friend agreed to take it for a test drive as a means of delivering my visiting sister back to Kentucky where she lived. The whole day was a comedy of errors.

Kelly left his charts and carefully prepared flight plan at home on the kitchen table, but he managed to break into a friend's airplane and borrow his charts. We got somewhat confused en route because we were missing one chart, but we arrived safely.

Then we went to take off for the flight home. First, something weird happened with the magnetos and there was a big flash of light as something sparked in the cockpit. The plane started anyway, and we took off. Then smoke filled the cockpit. I remember thinking, "I'm going to die, but at least I'm going to die doing something I loved." I remained calm and sort of detached. We declared an emergency and went right back to land with the fire engines standing by. After landing, it was quickly determined that the smoke was just some oil that had been spilled on the outside of the engine and that was burning off as the engine heated up. False alarm. We took off again.

We ran completely out of fuel in one tank and the engine tried to quit; we had to switch over to the other tank before we fell out of the air. We faced headwinds and were drastically slowed down. We had to land part-way home to refuel. We couldn't find the airport. And then we did. It was getting dark. The lights didn't work. Then they did. By then Kelly had developed a headache and was saying it was the worst day of flying he had ever experienced (this from a guy who had been shot down in Viet Nam!). By this time, we were rather behind schedule according to the flight plan we had filed. We updated our flight plan by radio, but somehow the flight service station failed to record it. As we were tootling homeward in the dark, we overheard the flight service station on the radio saying we were overdue and they were about to call out a search party. We tried to call and tell them we were all right, but we were out of radio range. Eventually we did make contact and landed safely. What a day! The wings didn't fall off, but everything else went wrong. People asked me if I wasn't afraid of flying after that experience. I said no, I figured I'd gotten a whole lot of bad luck out of the way in one day and should be due for a nice long streak of safe flying.

New LtCol with New Airplane

I decided not to buy the Tri-Pacer because a Cessna 172 Skyhawk appeared at our airport for sale: single engine, 4 passenger, shiny, and brand new. I fell in love with it. It was white with brown markings and sported the tail number N737FK ("November 7-3-7 Foxtrot Kilo" on the radio). I had recently read Richard Bach's book *Jonathan Livingston Seagull* so I named my plane Joanna Livingston Skyhawk. I took out a bank loan to finance it, and put it on lease-back with the airport so others could rent it to help pay expenses. The best part was that they threw in free flying lessons—as many as it took to get me qualified. The day I had my first flying lesson in my new plane was also the day I ate my first raw oyster, but I don't know what that has to do with anything.

About the same time, I was called into the commander's office with 3 men and we were told we had been selected for promotion. I couldn't pin on the new rank yet, but was told I could do so in a few months. The commander congratulated us and kept calling us "you guys" until I was about ready to spit. I wanted to invite him into the back room and take off my shirt and show him that I wasn't a guy.

I would be a LtCol. This is also known as "light colonel" and "telephone colonel" since when you are talking on the phone you can refer to yourself as "colonel" and they can't tell you aren't a full colonel. The insignia looks like a leaf—the same as a major's but silver instead of bronze. Later, when people noticed the new insignia and congratulated me on my promotion, I said I hadn't been promoted, I'd just been out in the rain and the color had washed out. I also told them that I hoped I never got to be a full colonel because I had heard what they were full of.

Anyway, I got my promotion and my airplane about the same time. While the others were out celebrating their promotions, I called a girlfriend and we went out to dinner to celebrate the purchase of the airplane, which I considered a far greater achievement.

I proceeded to take flying lessons and even with the rigors of the residency I managed to complete the course in two short months. I got another resident to cover for me one morning while I snuck out to the airport for my first solo flight. Most students solo after 8 or 10 hours, but I refused to consider it until I had 27 hours. I had to go around the airport three times, with 2 "touch-and-go" landings and a final full stop landing. On the first try, the airplane bounced a bit; the helpful air traffic controller commented, "Nice landingzzzz." I didn't care. I did it! I actually took off and landed a plane all by myself.

There is a tradition in the Air Force that after your first solo flight someone dumps a bucket of water on you or sprays you with a hose. Since I was in uniform and due back at work, and since no one was there but my instructor, I thought I had escaped. One of my fellow residents was a former Air Force navigator and his memory was part elephant. Five months later, at a residents' party at a house with a pool, I stepped out of the house onto the patio only to find myself flying through the air and landing in the middle of the pool fully dressed, with my watch and shoes and everything. They fished me out and the hostess found something dry for me to wear.

I took a ground school course on base that was also attended by a group of prisoners from the adjacent federal prison. Some of them had owned their own planes (and used them for smuggling?) before they got caught. They were just taking the course as an excuse to get out of jail for a while. Sort of like getting the little yellow card in Monopoly. Of course, I was the only woman in the class. That sort of goes without saying by now.

I recounted my first cross-country solo flight in the preface of this book. I went on to fulfill the rest of the requirements, then flew with my instructor to another airport to meet the flight examiner. He was an old guy who had been flying since the first pterodactyl soared. He scared me half to death. During part of the test, he asked me where I would land if the engine quit right then. I looked around for a grassy pasture or a straight stretch of road; but he yelled at me, "There's an old abandoned military runway right underneath you!" I didn't believe him and dipped a wing to look. Sure enough, there was a beautiful runway that I hadn't noticed. I really felt stupid. By the time I landed, I was so shook I made my flight instructor fly the plane home. But the examiner said, "She'll do." I got my license on the first try! I was a pilot! A real pilot!

I had a lot of fun flying with other local pilots. We took a weekend trip to Fort Lauderdale (we pronounced it Fart Louder, Dale!) to visit Kelly's elderly mother. When we got to her apartment, a beautiful young muscled blond surfer dude came to the door and said he was Mom's roommate and Mom was down at the dive shop. Kelly wandered around the parking lot of the apartment complex crying, "Mommy! I want my Mommy!" until she showed up.

We flew to an island, Cedar Key, walked into town for dinner, and got a ride back to the landing strip. The guy who drove us back was a trucker. He asked to see inside the plane, since he'd never had the chance before, and people were always telling him the instrument panel of his truck was like an airplane's. He took one look at all of the instruments on the panel and said, "Sheeee-it! I drove a truck for a hunerd and leventy leven years and I ain't *never* seen no bullshit like that!" I think that meant he was impressed.

On the way home from that trip, Roy was flying his plane and he must have been tired because he made a very hard landing, more like a controlled crash. Kelly told him, "I know what you were trying to do, Roy; you were trying to get me to pee my pants. But I fooled you. I didn't pee them, *I crapped in them!*"

There was an interesting pilot at our airport who seemed to have been everywhere and done everything. He had been a charter pilot for an airline, a test pilot, ran a construction business, had lived in Mexico, and I don't know what all. He flew with me to give me some pointers. When I tried a touch-and-go landing he said the runway was too long to waste on one touchdown, so he had me lift off and touch down over and over down the whole length of it. Then we pretended to be crop-dusters and skimmed the treetops in death-defying hairpin turns.

He told us about his experiences flying charters. He flew a drunken football team once, and said the stewardess came crying into the cockpit complaining that they'd torn her panties off. He claimed he had put the crew on oxygen, gone up to altitude without pressurization and let the passengers get hypoxic so they all fell asleep. Another time he stood by the gate in his airline captain's uniform as the passengers boarded the plane, puzzling over a book entitled HOW TO FLY in big letters.

He invited a group of us to go to the First International Air Show in Miami in his twin engine plane. He took off in a thunderstorm, and when we arrived he showed us how to do a perfect landing. He said the secret was to fly about six inches off the runway and then lower the left wheel half an inch, then the right wheel half an inch, etc. Which is exactly what he did. You couldn't even distinguish the moment of touchdown. We rented a car, and when we got to the parking area at the airshow, Roy pointed to us in the back seat and said, "Handicapped" and got priority parking. Under his breath he said, "mentally handicapped."

Pappy Boyington (of Black Sheep Squadron fame) was at the air show signing his book; across the field was the Japanese aviator who had supposedly shot him down, signing *his* book. We saw some fantastic stunt flying. I bought a souvenir plaque for my wall: "Women pilots know how to get it up."

For dinner, we chose a restaurant at random. As we walked in, Roy said in a loud voice, "This must be a good restaurant: other people are eating here and nobody is throwing up." He ordered oysters and instructed the waitress that he wanted them really fresh; he wanted them to be still saying "eeep" as they went in the pan. The waitress brought them and assured him, "They were eeping in the kitchen, sir."

Someone left an old DC3 parked at our airport with the understanding that the airport operator could use it whenever he wanted. I got to ride in the jump seat between the pilot and copilot for a low-level flight past the beach during the airplane fly-by parade for the Rocky Bayou Mullet Festival. Don't even ask!

I took Don up in my plane and let him fly. He was the resident who had been shot down over Viet Nam and had been a POW for 6 years. I think he said it was the first time he had touched the controls of a plane since Viet Nam. He was philosophical about his POW experience; he said it made him a better person, and he said he wasn't a hero, it was more like he'd made a mistake and lost an expensive piece of Air Force equipment. He also said he would be quite happy if he never tasted beans again. He and Roy got permission to fly the Air Force simulator on base. They managed to fly it into the ground and seriously crashed it.

My friend Kelly had been shot down over Viet Nam too, but in his case it didn't take. He described losing power over enemy territory and trying to glide the plane back as close to safe territory as possible. He asked his navigator how high the mountains in front of them were, and learned they were a couple of hundred feet higher than the airplane was, so they decided to bail out. Their parachutes drifted down, caught in the highest canopy of the jungle for a moment, and then pulled loose and fell down through the trees. They caught again in a lower level of the canopy, and Kelly was suspended a few feet off the ground. A helicopter rescued him before his feet ever touched the ground.

I hadn't told my parents what I was up to. When they came to visit, I met them at the airport in Pensacola and was going to surprise them by taking them the rest of the way in my new plane. Unbeknownst to me, a friend of a friend of theirs lived in the area and had read an article about me in the Fort Walton Beach newspaper and had clipped it and mailed it on. So they already knew about the plane. They said they weren't surprised that one of their daughters had learned to fly; they were just surprised *which* one. My sisters were the athletic and adventurous ones.

I had been in the newspaper because I had joined the 99's. This is a group of women pilots founded by Amelia Earhart and named 99's because that's the number of women who showed up for the first meeting. Some of us went to a 99's convention in North Carolina. As we approached for landing, the tower tried to turn up the runway lights. Something wasn't working, and he said over the radio, "I keep trying, but I can't get it up." I thought of the perfect comeback later: "Would you like for us ladies to come over after we land? We might be able to help you with your personal problem."

I hadn't done much instrument flying yet, but one of the 99's was an instrument instructor and let me fly through fluffy little clouds on the way home. It would be smooth until we approached a cloud, then it would get bumpy, then we'd come out the other side and it would be smooth again. I got the giggles every time we went into a cloud; I thought it was more fun than a roller coaster. On the way home, the air traffic controller warned us to look out for traffic—a Cessna at 8000 feet. Later he said "That 8000 foot Cessna is no longer a factor." I wanted to say, "Gee, that's a loooonnnggg Cessna!"

I heard some good stories about women learning to fly. One could never navigate, so she would just look for a runway and land, then she would ask to use the phone. She would know where she was when she saw the name of the town on the phone directory. Another was asked by the tower, "What are your intentions?" She didn't know what he wanted, so she said, "Well, after I land, I thought I would go home and fix dinner."

You are not supposed to use bad language on the radios. Once an airliner was told to go into a holding pattern, which he didn't think he should have to do. He said, "Bullshit!" without thinking. The controller heard him but wasn't sure which plane he was, so he asked, "Who said that?" Every pilot on the frequency answered, "United 234, negative on the bullshit." "American 35, negative on the bullshit." So they *all* got to say it with impunity.

I even joined the local chapter of the EAA—the Experimental Aircraft Association—just because they didn't have any women members and I thought they needed one. These guys built their own planes. One at our airport had built a Burt Rutan Varieze—a weird contraption that looked like its wings were sewed on backwards. The builder spent more time tinkering and polishing than flying, but he took me up in it once. I also got a ride in an open-cockpit WWII trainer; the pilot landed at our airport and Roy got into a conversation with him and had the chutzpah to ask him to take me up—and he did! It started with a crank on the side of the nose, sort of like those old automobiles.

DIVORCE AND A VACATION IN ALASKA

My husband was still in Spain pursuing his PhD, and I found that I was enjoying life more without him than I had with him. I enjoyed my independence and having my own friends, and it was a relief not to have to worry about doing something that might offend his macho Spanish pride—which might be offended by something as innocuous as my walking faster than he did or wearing slacks when he thought a skirt was appropriate. When he came to visit me in Florida, we decided on a divorce. We'd been married over 11 years, but we had no children, and he went back to Spain, so it was an easy, clean break. The director of my residency program was amazed when he heard the news—I guess he thought you had to have a nervous breakdown along with a divorce, and he hadn't noticed me acting any differently or seeming the least bit upset.

I took a vacation to visit my sister in Alaska. I met a pilot friend of hers and returned for a second, flying vacation with him. He was from Texas and loved Alaska because he would "never have to sweat again." We landed on the ice of a lake in a plane with fat tires: the trick is to fly low and see if the ice looks safe, then come around again and bounce the wheels on the ice, and if that doesn't crack the ice, you can land the third time around. We camped out by the plane on remote wilderness airstrips, we flew near Mt. McKinley's glaciers, we stayed overnight with friends who took us on a boat trip down a river, we flew over the Valley of 10,000 Smokes, we landed at Homer, the longest inhabited sandspit in the world, where we visited the Salty Dog Tavern; we followed the route of the Iditarod dogsled race part way by air, flew through mountain passes, spotted a herd of bison (yes, bison, in Alaska!), and often flew for 2 or 3 hours without seeing any sign of civilization except for a rare cabin. The pilot I flew with was killed a few months later when the plane his student was flying crashed.

There were lots of pilots in Alaska because there are hardly any roads there. One old-timer, we'll call him John Jones, lived in the wilderness and used a sandy beach for his airstrip. He became an expert in judging the state of the sand and could pick a firm place to land and take off. After many years, he married and went on a honeymoon down the coast of the United States. In California, he spotted a restaurant on the coast and proceeded to land on the beach nearby so he and his bride could have lunch. It never occurred to him that the flying customs in California might be different. When they returned to the plane after lunch, they were surprised to find police and a big crowd around the plane. He told them who he was, but they didn't believe him. They called the FAA in Alaska to check. They said, "John Jones? Oh, yes, we know him well. He's a great judge of sand conditions. He's perfectly safe on any beach—just don't let him near an airport!" They still weren't willing to let him take off; they insisted on calling in a soil expert. The expert took one look at the lightly-indented tracks the plane had made taxiing in on the firmly packed moist sand. He said, "You landed this way? Turn around and take off that way." End of story.

I met an enterprising gemologist in Anchorage who was trying to get an FHA housing loan for an airplane. He had found an old flying boat, a PBY Catalina. He planned to refurbish it and live in it. I never heard whether he succeeded.

In the airport restroom in Talkeetna, Alaska, there was a sign over the toilet: "Pilots with short props and low manifold pressure please taxi closer to the defueling pit—the next pilot may not be float-equipped."

When you are getting ready to take off, the tower tells you the current barometer reading so you can set your altimeter. In Anchorage one day, a pilot radioed back, "Tower, be advised, that altimeter setting puts me below runway elevation." The tower answered, "Up periscope, cleared for takeoff."

GRADUATION

Between my adventures in the air and in the hospital, the residency passed quickly. Since I had learned to fly, I decided to become a flight surgeon. What could be better than combining my two passions of medicine and aviation? I would have to attend a two month summer course after the residency: the Aerospace Medicine Primary Course at Brooks Air Force Base in San Antonio, Texas. First I had to pass a flight physical. I went to a flight surgeon who must have learned to do pelvic exams on cadavers. He was exceedingly rough, and it hurt. When I flinched, he said, "No wonder you're overdue for an exam; you don't seem to like them." I was accepted for the AMP course and the residency was nearly over.

We had a final dinner and put on a funny show with slides I had taken around the hospital and a script mimicking "60 Minutes" written by my fellow residents. Everyone got some kind of joke award. One resident who was a fanatical jogger was given a golden jock strap (a regular jock strap sprayed with gold spray paint). When they got to me, they said they had racked their brains for something appropriate, and had considered something to do with airplanes, but then they decided the most appropriate thing for a lone woman who had held her ground in a world of men would be another golden jock strap—so I got one too. I still didn't have those all-important dangly bits, but now I had something to put them in!

We had a 4th of July party with fireworks and frog races. I had tree frogs in the courtyard at my house, but I was afraid to touch one, so I got another resident to catch mine, and found a kid to let it out of its box to run the race. The suspense was ribbeting. One frog escaped into the swimming pool. Mine "frogot" to win.

I had put my furniture in storage and was staying at a former patient's house for the 2 or 3 days before I left. The patient was a general I had taken care of. When I was getting ready to go to the party I happened to show the general's wife my golden jock strap, and she suggested I wear it to the party over my clothes, complete with the two bright yellow tennis balls she loaned me. I did.

I went to New Orleans to take my Family Practice Board Exams. I passed, of course. I knew I would, because I had eaten at a Chinese restaurant and my fortune cookie promised "Success in all endeavors."

I met my sister in Asheville, North Carolina, went backpacking with her in the Smokies, and then headed to Texas.

8

Flight Surgeon Training

o o o o o o o o o o o o o o o o o o o o o o o o o o o o o o o o o

Before you can fly, you have to get laid.

—from a T-shirt with a picture of a confused baby bird just emerging from a cracked egg

At flight surgeon[1] school (the Aerospace Primary Course, or AMP), they no longer teach doctors to fly or even give them rides in airplanes; too expensive, I guess. They leave the introduction to actual flying to our first assignments. I didn't care; I brought my own plane and parked it at the civilian airport. I used it in my free time to start my instrument training, and to fly around for fun and sightseeing.

On my arrival at Brooks Air Force Base, I discovered that for once, I wasn't the only woman; there were 6 female and 68 male students. Not only that, but I was told I outranked everyone else. There were four other LtCols in the class, but

---

1. No, a flight surgeon is not a surgeon who operates on airplanes! A flight surgeon is a doctor (of any specialty or no specialty) who is knowledgeable about aviation medicine and who takes care of personnel who are on flying status, as well as their families (and by extension, missile officers and their families). He essentially functions as a family doctor for the flying squadrons. He is also responsible for environmental health, public health, and occupational health for the entire base; this involves making industrial shop visits and food service inspections and supervising the Bioenvironmental Engineer and Environmental Health Officer and their staffs. He supervises flight medical technicians, responds to the flight line with an ambulance for emergencies, and is in charge of the Physical Exam Section. He investigates aircraft accidents. He is required to log a minimum of 4 hours flight time a month in whatever aircraft his patients fly, to better understand their working environment. He earns flight pay.

apparently my date of rank preceded the others. I was therefore designated the class leader or commander or something—for whatever that was worth!

There were other classes going on at the same base. I met a female veterinarian who was training to be an environmental health officer and whose husband had given her a vanity license plate that said "DogDoc." I dated a German Air Force pilot who was there to re-train as a physiological training officer. Even those who were married were there sans spouse, so we got mixed groups together for restaurant dinners, line-dancing at the local bars, and other social activities.

DUCKS, OWLS AND CRISPY CRITTERS

We stayed in visiting officers' quarters and walked across a golf course to get to the building where our classes were. There were ducks on the grounds of the VOQ. I thought it was very insulting for us doctors to be greeted with "Quack! Quack!" every time we ventured outside. I would talk back, "I am not!"

We had two months of intensive classroom work in a variety of subjects, from the effects of altitude on human physiology to chemical warfare, from color vision to aircraft accident investigation, from hearing protection to global medicine, from motion sickness to flying safety.

In class one day they showed us a movie of an owl turning its head around in a complete 360 degree circle. We thought it was hilarious and throughout the rest of the course a group of us in the back would periodically start chanting, "We want the owl, we want the owl." Other favorite refrains were "Here come da judge!" and a high-pitched "Oh, no, Mr. Bill!" from a TV animation. We loved the lectures on aircraft accidents with all the gory pictures of burned corpses—we called them the crispy critters lectures.

We had quite a bit of out-of-classroom training too. We had to learn to do PLFs (parachute landing falls). First you stand on the ground and practice falling down in stages: you turn sideways and let your lower leg touch the ground first, then your hip, and then you sort of roll over on your back as you finish falling. The idea is to give way so as to minimize the impact on any one part of the body. One of the older students testified to the importance of learning this: he had actually had to bail out over Japan in WWII without this kind of training. He landed with stiff legs, broke a leg bone, spent months in a Japanese POW camp with no treatment, and lost half his body weight before he was rescued. He still had a slight limp.

After the ground-level training, we had to jump off a high platform to do a PLF. I was really scared, but forced myself to do it because I didn't want to be the only failure. Afterwards, in talking to the men, I learned that some of them had been every bit as scared as I had. That was an eye-opener for me. Men weren't braver than women; they were just culturally indoctrinated to ignore their fear and not admit to it.

Then we had to practice dropping out of a parachute harness into a swimming pool and swimming out from under a parachute canopy; also jumping out of a mock-up of an aircraft fuselage into a rubber raft. And riding an ejection seat up a rail to see what a real ejection would feel like. And running a radiation decontamination facility while wearing cumbersome protective gear. And then there was survival training.

SURVIVAL TRAINING

We had to go to a short survival course at a nearby Army facility, Camp Bullis. The idea was to pretend we had bailed out and had to live off the land until rescued. They gave us a piece of parachute and some nylon cord to rig up whatever shelter we could devise. We had canteens with water purification tablets that made the water taste like iodine, and a few other basic items. We did a lot of training with flares, setting out ground signals for helicopter search and rescue to see, and so on. They said we could try to catch fish or an armadillo, but the cows that were roaming around were off limits. There was an apocryphal story about a nurse who supposedly had shot a farmer's horse and insisted it was a cow; he finally gave in and told her she could keep the "cow" but she had to give the saddle back.

I had always loved camping and the outdoors, and I was in my element. I think I enjoyed it more than most of the men. The survival instructor was apprehensive at first, because he'd never had a woman doctor in one of his groups, but after he told a dirty story and I told one right back at him he decided I was one of the boys. One of the men didn't drink enough water (which *did* taste pretty putrid) and he got dehydrated, started vomiting, and had to be taken back to town. It was hot, but there were a few promising clouds. One doctor decided he would do a rain dance, and he started whooping and jumping around. After about 2 minutes of his antics, raindrops actually started falling. Moral of story: do rain dance only when rain clouds are present.

They made us think we had to subsist for 3 days on one meal's worth of rations, but the final night they brought us pizza. I had a wonderful time. The only problem I had was that a cow ate my camera strap. I had left it hanging on a tree and came back to find the strap all chewed up. At least the bovine glutton didn't try to taste the camera itself.

WEEKEND ADVENTURES

One weekend a group of us went on a float trip down a nearby river. A young woman was our guide, and the guys had fun telling her slightly inaccurate stories which she gullibly accepted. They told her I was their boss and they had to do anything I told them, then they said the Air Force never let them watch TV and a bunch of other nonsense.

Some of us were a little apprehensive about the rapids, and we asked if anyone ever fell overboard. She assured us she had never lost a passenger. Naturally, a few minutes later one of our number managed to break her perfect record by falling out; but he was quickly retrieved.

We had a great time and stopped at a famous cowboy bar on the way home. We were going to do it again the next weekend but our instructors spoiled our fun—they posted a notice on our class bulletin board that the water level in the river had changed and made the trip too dangerous. One weekend we went to Padre Island where an oil spill had gummed up the beach but the sunbathing was still fine. And another weekend four of us flew down to the border in my plane, spent a day in Mexico, and came back with a big piñata.

OFF TO WORK WE GO

We all had assignments waiting for us. I was to go to a missile base, F.E. Warren Air Force Base, in Cheyenne, Wyoming. I flew my plane up to Cheyenne one weekend and left it there for leaseback at the Cheyenne airport, looked at houses with a real estate agent, and took a commercial flight back to San Antonio.

About half way through the flight surgeon's course, I had received a phone call from the hospital commander at F.E. Warren. He said he had noticed that I was qualified in family practice, and he had a family practice doc there who also had flight surgeon wings and really would rather be a flight surgeon. He asked me if I would agree to take his job in the family practice clinic and let him have mine.

That would have meant that I forfeited the extra flight pay, plus I thought it was pretty obvious that I preferred to be a flight surgeon, or I wouldn't have been taking the flight surgeon's course. Plus, he kept calling me "dear." I was insulted. I said absolutely not, no way, and he backed off and told me the flying slot was still mine. But the conversation left a bad taste in my mouth, and it wasn't the end of that story.

When we graduated, they told us we had been one of the best, but one of the most irreverent classes they had ever had. There was a big ceremony, they pinned wings on us, and we were officially flight surgeons.

Before I could leave San Antonio, I had to visit a Western store with a fellow student who was from Oklahoma. He said Wyoming was cowboy country and I simply *had* to have a Stetson, a proper Western shirt, boot-cut Levis and cowboy boots. He and another friend took me shopping and saw that I was properly equipped, even to a leather belt with my name engraved on it and a belt buckle inscribed "OUR KITTIES CAT HOUSE—Massage Relieves Fatigue—Love, Sex—Reno Nevada—Pay and Play."

I had time to visit several national parks in the Southwest, do some camping and hiking, and try out my cowboy duds on a couple of trail rides before I had to report for duty at my new assignment.

9

Flight Surgeon at a Missile Base

○ ○
If it's a good idea, go ahead and do it. It is much easier to apologize than it is to get permission.

—Admiral Grace Hopper

When I arrived at F.E. Warren Air Force Base I had to report to the hospital commander—the one who had tried to give my job away. His first words to me confirmed my fears. He announced, "I've never worked with a woman before; I don't know how this is going to work out." He made it very clear that "No female is going to do *my* flight physical." He also made it clear that no female was ever going to be his Chief of Hospital Services even if I outranked all the other doctors in the hospital.

I had to fly a mission before I could be issued my own flight gear, and he loaned me a flight suit. He kept ogling my butt in the suit. Then he told everyone I'd only been there a week and already I had "gotten into his pants." I tried to ignore him.

I thought he was a sexist male chauvinist, but I hadn't seen nuthin' yet. He was reasonably fair to me and gave me a good Officer Effectiveness Report (OER). I ended up having far more trouble with my subsequent supervisors.

It could have been worse. My friend Gladys was assigned to another base as flight surgeon about this same time. When she first arrived, she was moved to the family practice clinic against her will because the other flight surgeon *refused to work with a woman!*[1] Later, when she was finally working in flight medicine, she found out two flight surgeons were coming in to fill one vacant slot. She asked

---

1.   This should have resulted in two courts-martial: for the flight surgeon for refusing, and for the commander for allowing him to refuse. But of course, nothing was done.

the commander why, and he told her he had no idea, but apparently SAC had just decided to do that. She called SAC and found out the commander had specifically *requested* two flight surgeons so he would have an excuse to move her back to family practice. When she confronted him, he had to admit that he had lied to her. Then he said, "Frankly, I feel uncomfortable having a woman in the flight surgeon's office."

My first commander was a surgeon, and when he left, another surgeon took his place. (Is there something about surgeons?) My new boss would rally us during exercises by having us chant, "BOY are WE enTHUsiAStic!!" while we did our best not to snigger. He got mad at the female pharmacy officer because she cried easily when she got upset. She tried to tell him to ignore the tears and continue the discussion, but he couldn't understand. He thought he should be able to order her not to cry. I don't think anyone particularly liked him, and I don't think he liked women.

F.E.Warren was the largest missile base in the Free World, with Minuteman missile silos and launch control facilities scattered over parts of three states. It was a former Army cavalry post, and many of its beautiful old historic red brick buildings were still in use; the commissary was in a former cavalry indoor riding arena. They still had one volunteer unit of cavalry that rode in parades.

The base was in Cheyenne, Wyoming, state capitol and home of the Frontier Days rodeo. Cheyenne was isolated: the sign on the Interstate three blocks from my house said, "Next services 42 miles." There were miles and miles of nothing but sagebrush, jackrabbits, and antelope.[2] They sometimes had to close the Interstate because of snow. The wind never stopped blowing; they used to joke about the guy from Cheyenne who flew to another city, got off the plane, and fell over. I would tell new arrivals that when it snowed, it snowed horizontally; they wouldn't believe me but eventually one day they would look out the window and say, "By golly, it *is* snowing horizontally."

The wind ensured that the snow was distributed unevenly. We had a Thanksgiving blizzard with 24 inches of snow the first year I was there. There weren't 24 inches anywhere: there were places where the ground was bare and others where there were four foot drifts. Nothing could move but snowmobiles, and even they had trouble. We couldn't leave the house for three days, and instead of a Thanksgiving turkey, we had to make do with an elk roast from the freezer. One new homeowner decided he would outsmart the wind: he built a snow fence to deflect

---

2.   Yes, I know they're technically called pronghorns, but everyone called them antelope so I will too.

the drifts off his driveway. Unfortunately he got it backwards and the fence made the snow pile up *on* his driveway.

HELICOPTERS

The base had no runway, only a helipad with 6 old UH-1H "Huey" helicopters. These were awkward aircraft. The design was cobbled together from a surplus jet engine they wanted to use up, and it involved putting parts in backwards and using gears to turn the action 180 degrees to where it was needed. They required several man-hours of maintenance for every hour they flew, and they were always breaking down. One day, when they actually managed to get all 6 helicopters in the air at once, they took lots of pictures because they didn't think it would ever happen again.

I loved flying in the helicopters. We flew out to the missile sites, we went on search and rescue missions, and we airlifted both military and civilian patients to Denver hospitals. We went on training flights to remote landing sites where we could see teepee circles: circles of stones left at Indian campsites where they had anchored the edges of teepees. I spotted them and pointed them out to the rest of the crew. I told them when the Indians got ready to break camp, they just got their rocks off.

Once I was left at a remote site in the mountains while the helicopter flew away and then came back so the crew could practice rescuing me. The chopper disappeared over the ridge and everything got really quiet. It was a lonely feeling standing there in the wilderness hoping they would be able to find me again. They did, of course.

The pilots liked to scour the mountains for elk so they would know where to go hunting. We flew over beaver dams, canyons, and herds of antelope. When the weather was good we flew with the doors open and tethered ourselves to rings in the floor for safety so we could lean out over the landscape.

The only time we ever found anyone on a search-and-rescue while I was there was when one of our medics spotted a lost hunter—who didn't want to be found and refused to get on the helicopter! We spent two full days with two helicopters scouring the area near Cheyenne for a mentally handicapped girl who had failed to come home; then we found out she was safe at a friend's house where she'd decided to go for a visit. Once we searched for a lost hiker high in the Rocky Mountains, right at the altitude limit of our helicopters; I'll never forget the sight of a bull elk standing on a bald mountaintop like a king surveying his domain.

It was easy to get lost in the mountains. One hunter from Germany was lost and rescued; the next year he went hunting in the same area, got lost again, and died before they could find him. It wasn't as tame as the Black Forest. Altitude and cold weather were killers.

I got to fly and make instrument approaches in the helicopters, although I never got to try hovering. The first time I took the controls was on a trip to take missile officers out to the sites. The helicopter was trimmed and flying level, so I didn't have to do much. I wondered what the missile officers thought about having a novice at the controls. When they got off, one of them commented, "You could really tell a difference when she took the controls.... it got a lot smoother!"

The helicopter pilots were all men, just like the missile officers. After I'd been there for over two years, a female helicopter pilot showed up at the flight surgeon's office for inprocessing. I was so delighted to see her I yelled, "A female pilot!!" and she was so delighted to see me she yelled, "A female doctor!!" This was in 1981, when a female pilot was still a rarity. It wasn't until 1976 that they had first allowed a few women into a pilot's training program as an experiment.

One day I was scheduled to fly with her. The air traffic controller that day was a woman, and the helicopter's crew chief was a woman. On the routine pre-flight check list a malfunction showed up and we never got off the ground. The squadron commander came out to see what was wrong, and he looked at us and said, "No wonder the bird won't fly; too many God-damned women!" He was joking.... I think.

The squadron commander was a smart cookie. When he flew, his copilot was always one of his subordinates, who were naturally hesitant to criticize anything the commander did. A safe flight involves copilot and pilot watching out for each other's mistakes. So before every flight, he would tell the lower-ranking copilot, "I want you to watch me carefully. I'm going to deliberately make a mistake on this flight, and I want to see if you can catch it." And then he would do his best *not* to make any mistakes.

He was also a bit profane. Once when he landed in Denver, one of the ground personnel did something unsafe, and he let him have it with both barrels. His copilot that day happened to be a young lieutenant who was very religious and proper and abhorred bad language. He felt obliged to remedy the situation by saying, "What the colonel *meant* to say was ... "

I got to fly a B-52, too! SAC had a Looking Glass airborne command post that could launch all our missiles and aircraft if WWIII started. They kept one of these planes in the air constantly for 30 years. The general from our base periodically flew up to Ellsworth to take his turn as Looking Glass Commander. Once he invited me along, and while he was flying his mission he arranged for me to go along on a B-52 Red Flag mission over the Nevada desert. The B-52 has 8 jet engines with enough power to potentially send it straight up like a rocket. I got to take the controls for a while. It was slow to respond, like driving a big heavy truck; but what a thrill! They had me make some of the radio calls to freak out everybody who was listening, because there were not supposed to be any women assigned to those planes. The general got teased for taking me to Ellsworth with him; his staff said, "Gee, are you so old and decrepit you have to take your doctor with you everywhere you go now?"

LAUNCH CONTROL FACILITY VISIT

All the missile officers were men. There were other missiles at other bases with four person crews that could include women, but the Minuteman missiles had two-man crews who were confined in a small underground capsule for 24 hours at a stretch. The powers that be considered that inappropriate for a woman.

Teams of two missile officers go out to the launch control facility (LCF) for a 24 hour tour of duty. They pick up side arms and secret codes, check out a government vehicle, and drive themselves to the site. At the site, they go underground by elevator and through a blast door into the launch control capsule. They can't leave for any reason until their 24 hours are up and their replacements have arrived. Meals are brought to them from the surface facility, which also has a dormitory for security police and maintenance personnel. The two missile officers must both turn a key at the same time to launch a missile; they sit at desks that are far enough apart that it would be impossible for one of them to turn both keys. There are beds for when things are slow, and at one end of the capsule there is a toilet behind a curtain.

Each LCF controls 10 missile silos, and each missile contains multiple warheads that can be programmed to hit different targets. Constantly changing secret codes verify that a launch command is real, and they determine which targets the missiles are programmed for. If one LCF is disabled, its missiles can be launched from another capsule.

One of the requirements of my job as a flight surgeon was to spend a 24 hour tour of duty at a launch control facility, 12 hours in the capsule itself and 12 hours upstairs with the security police and other personnel. As far as I know, I was the first woman whose duties involved Minuteman missile capsule duty.

I went with two young lieutenants. During the 12 hours I was underground with them, I used the toilet a couple of times, but *neither of them used it a single time!* I guess they were embarrassed, but I don't understand why. It was behind a curtain, and the background noise in the capsule was such that I don't think they could hear a tinkle. I worried that their bladders might burst before I left.

I wrote up a report of my visit and made suggestions about hearing protection, coping with the long hours of boredom, and decreasing muscle-strain headaches and backaches by ergonomic approaches. I concluded with a comment on sex discrimination; they didn't ask, but I told:

> As the first female to experience an alert in the all-male domain of the Minuteman capsule, I see no reason why female officers could not be assigned as missile crewmembers. There is adequate privacy for sleeping and using the restroom facilities, and I personally would have no objections to working in that kind of situation on a regular basis. I cannot imagine that two professional military officers of sufficient character and reliability to obtain a TOP SECRET clearance should have any difficulties performing their job just because one happens to be male and the other female.

Of course, we all realize the real reason they didn't allow women: the wives would have a hissy fit if we let their husbands spend time alone with another woman. Is this a valid military consideration? And gee, what if the two men were gay? What if any two people in the capsule decided to "Make love, not war"?

Along with those comments, I filed a formal query about the egress tunnels. I will explain. If the launch control facility is attacked or if for any other reason the crew can't get out via the usual blast door, there is an emergency provision. At the far end of the capsule, there is a hatch that can be opened. It leads to a tunnel to the surface, but the tunnel is full of sand. The sand is supposed to drain into the capsule, leaving the tunnel empty so the crew can use it to get out. As I remember, it was supposed to end just short of the surface; and I guess the officers were supposed to dig the rest of the way.

There were several rumors rampant among the officers:

> (1) The egress tunnels had never actually been tested to see if they would really work.
> (2) Some of the tunnels came out under the concrete pad for the garage, making it impossible to dig out.
> (3) All the sand would melt and fuse into a solid mass after a nuclear attack.
> (4) The time required to shovel out the sand would exceed the available air supply.

(5) The falling sand would engulf the individual who opened the hatch.

My formal letter of inquiry was answered by an official who explained, point by point:

(1) We don't know; we asked SAC headquarters but they haven't answered. [As far as I know, they never did.]

(2) "At no point should the egress tunnel opening protrude under the garage area. The opening at all sites, with the exceptions of "A" and "C", should be in the dirt area of the LCF complex. At "A" and "C" the openings will be under the asphalt, about one (1) foot in from the edge." [Note this says "should" and "will be" and does not verify that they "are."]

(3) Yes, if the fireball from a nuclear blast is in close proximity to the LCC, the sand will turn to glass and you can forget about escaping.

(4) Absolutely not. [But no numbers were supplied to substantiate this.]

(5) The falling sand should not harm the individual opening the hatch if he uses minimal caution and stands clear. The sand will only fill 1/3 of the capsule. [Which 1/3?]

I must say I didn't find these answers particularly reassuring.

Missile officers had a tough job. They had to worry about egress tunnels, they had to worry about starting World War III, they had to be highly trained to do something they fervently hoped they would never have to do, and they had to cope with long hours of doing nothing yet being instantly ready to respond with full efficiency. Sometimes snowstorms kept their replacements from arriving for two or three days. They were out of reach of their families.

I talked with a group of missile wives who were grousing about the long tours of duty (actually much longer than 24 hours when you count the briefings, travel time, etc.). One of them complained that everything happened when hubby was on duty—the toilet overflowed, the roof sprung a leak, the car quit, the kids got sick. Another woman said, "Honey, don't complain: you don't know how good you've got it. My husband used to fly all over the world. At least when your husband is in the missile capsule, you know *exactly* where he's at and who he's with!"

The launch control facilities were spread over a large area, sometimes two or more hours' drive from the base, often in another state. They didn't look like much from the surface, just a couple of low buildings inside a fenced perimeter, with a helipad outside. The missile sites themselves were even less noticeable: a fence, a flattish door over the underground missile silo, and not much else to see. They were guarded by motion detectors and alarms. When an alarm went off, the security police would rush out to the site from the LCF to see whether it was an intruder or just another jackrabbit.

We would occasionally have an incident at one of the sites. One New Year's Eve a maintenance man working in a silo inadvertently triggered a mechanism to release one of the missile supports, and it smashed him against the wall of the silo, killing him. I was out of town that night, and the hospital commander was on call for flight medicine. He had to go out in the middle of the night, climb down into the silo, and pronounce the man dead. I was glad I didn't have to do it.

In a lighter incident, a security policeman decided to take a pet home: he caught a rattlesnake in a pillowcase and set it beside him on the seat of the military vehicle. It proceeded to bite his leg through the fabric. He had to be sent to the nearest civilian medical facility for antivenin, but he was all right. About half of all snake bites don't even inject any venom.

FLIGHT PHYSICALS AND SHOP VISITS

Everyone on flying status or missile status had to have an annual flight physical. The medical corpsmen would tell the patients they had a choice of doctors for their physicals—male or female—but they recommended the female because her hands were smaller! My Dad told me if my male patients seemed embarrassed I should tell them that if I saw anything I hadn't seen before, it probably needed treating anyway. There was the young man, told to strip down to his shorts, who stripped *off* his shorts and was waiting for me dressed in nothing but a T-shirt. And there was an ROTC cadet whose first words to me were: "Oh, shit! A woman!" A couple of times I had to do a complete exam on a man with a very obvious erection; I just tried not to notice or comment. I even had trouble with the little guys: one 4 year old tyke was wearing a knit cap, and when I had to check his groin for hernia, he pulled the cap down to cover his face.

Many years later, I was at James Randi's Amaz!ng Meeting 2 in Las Vegas. The emcee was a LtCol who taught political science at the Air Force Academy. In his introductory remarks, he mentioned having been stationed at a missile base, so during the break I went up to talk to him. We compared notes, realized we had both been at F.E.Warren at the same time, and suddenly he pointed his finger at me and shouted, "YOU'RE the one!" After the break, he told the audience about his first flight physical as a young lieutenant missile officer—how intimidated and impressed he was by the high rank of the female LtCol who examined him, and how embarrassed he was when she did a COMPLETE physical. He introduced me to the audience and I held up the guilty finger for all to see. He went on to speculate that audience members might try to ask me about the details of his anatomy. On the next break, I reassured him that I couldn't remember doing his physical, and besides which, all assholes look alike. After that break, he told the entire audience exactly what I had said!

"EVERYTHING?"

My job included shop visits. I would go with the environmental health personnel to inspect the food service facilities. We got to prowl through the kitchens of the Officers' Club, the chow halls, and the snack bars, looking for lapses in sanitation or expired dates on stored food. We got to poke into the coolers and storerooms. We got to inspect the commissary and see behind the scenes in the back rooms and the butcher shop.

On the industrial shop visits with the bioenvironmental engineering personnel and safety inspectors, I got to go practically anywhere on base. We would poke our nose into everybody's business, looking for safety hazards, proper use of protective equipment, compliance with OSHA directives, hearing protection, noise levels, lighting levels, etc. We could walk right in and ask, "What do you do here and how do you do it?"

Once in the paint shop I was confronted by employees who were worried about working around asbestos. I tried to tell them asbestos was perfectly harmless as long as it remained encapsulated; the only danger was if people cut into it and spread particles in the air or tried to remove it without proper respiratory protection. I tried to tell them their cigarettes were a much greater danger to them. Don't know if I got through.

One thing took some getting used to. Most of the industrial shops were manned by enlisted men, and I outranked *everybody*. The minute I walked through the door, an NCO would spot me and call the entire shop to attention: "Ten-hut!" They would all stand there as if they had rods up their spine until I said, "Carry on."

BRINGING FAMILY PRACTICE TO THE FLIGHT SURGEON'S OFFICE

Before I arrived at F.E.Warren, the flight surgeon's office had mainly been seeing men. The exam tables in the flight surgeon's office were not even equipped with the stirrups necessary to do pelvic exams. I instituted real family practice for the first time. I got the necessary equipment and started doing everything from Pap smears to well baby exams to prenatal care. I took care of all the family members of everyone on flying status and missile duty. There was a family practice clinic, but they didn't have families assigned to specific doctors, so I was doing more authentic family practice than they were. I loved it.

A woman came in very embarrassed, saying she was afraid she had herpes. She didn't. She had syphilis. She wondered how she had contracted it, but it soon became painfully obvious. Her husband had had a flight physical several months before with a negative blood test for syphilis, and he now had a positive test, meaning that he had given it to his wife, and he had caught it *recently*. I wish I could have heard the conversations in that household after we broke the news to them.

Another patient was reported as a gonorrhea contact and tested positive but refused to accept the results. She claimed there was only one man who could have given it to her and she knew he would have told her himself if he had inadvertently exposed her. I tried to convince her that if there was even the slightest chance that she had gonorrhea, she should accept treatment to be on the safe side. She insisted she couldn't have caught it from anyone except the one man, and wouldn't take the treatment unless I confirmed that he had it. Of course, I couldn't do that because of patient confidentiality. I sort of cheated: I got his name from her, asked the public health people if he was the one, found out he was, and went back and told her, "I can't release any confidential information, but I can assure you that on the basis of the information known to me, I would strongly advise you to take the treatment." She did.

OB

All the doctors took turns covering the ER. When I was the MOD (medical officer of the day) I was responsible for seeing all the emergencies during a 24 hour shift. While covering the ER I was also simultaneously on first call for OB, internal medicine, and pediatrics, as well as being the flight surgeon on call. This meant if a woman came in in labor, I would have to leave the ER to do the delivery, both she and her newborn would become my inpatients for the next three days, and I would have to do the newborn exam and LOTS of paperwork. Sometimes things got a bit exciting, but I managed to juggle everything and I always had people I could call in for backup if I got a complicated case.

The OB scared me. I was well trained as far as doing normal deliveries, but I could not do a C-section if things suddenly went sour. It would take a while for an obstetrician to get there to bail me out, and I was worried that the delay might be disastrous. I would not have wanted to have my own baby without someone immediately available in case I needed an emergency C-section. One of the obstetricians was unreliable. When I tried to get in touch with him one day for advice, I found out that he was in another state parachute-jumping—while he was on call! I protested loudly to the hospital commander. I expected he would punish the obstetrician for dereliction of duty or being AWOL or something. Astoundingly, all he did was send the obstetrician a letter of counseling and arrange for a civilian obstetrician to provide backup if our obstetrician was not available! He also informed me that if the OB wasn't there when a C-section was needed, he himself was a surgeon and he could probably figure out how to do one. I was too shocked to even say anything. The point of having an expert available was not so much to know *how* to do a C-section as to know *when* to do one. And the point of having an obstetrician on call was that he should be on call!

That obstetrician should have been court-martialed, but he went scot-free. Later one of our obstetricians (I can't remember if it was the same one) did get into serious trouble. It seems he had liberated some Air Force hospital equipment, set it up in his basement, and was moonlighting, doing abortions.

A while later, another family physician was assigned to our family practice clinic and was also required to share first call for OB. He had had a year's extra training in OB beyond the residency—yet he also felt inadequate to deliver babies without having backup more readily available. He was braver than I was: he stood up for what he thought was his patients' best interests and he refused to take call.

The hospital commander had a conniption fit. He decided any doctor who refused to take orders must be crazy, so he had the doctor shipped off to a psych ward for evaluation. Much heartbreak and bad will, and of course the psychiatrists didn't find anything wrong with him. I felt guilty, because I had even more reason to stand up to the commander, but I had knuckled under.

I was fortunate enough not to kill anyone, but there was at least one close call. A patient began hemorrhaging after the placenta was delivered. An obstetrician happened to be passing through the ward making rounds, and he scrubbed in just in the nick of time to save the woman's uterus if not her life. She had a uterine inversion, something I had never seen, and it was only partial so I didn't recognize the signs. The obstetrician was able to force it back into place only with the greatest difficulty. If he hadn't been right there and we had had to wait for him to come in from home, I think the woman would have died.

I had a knack for getting blood all over my shoes and stockings when I delivered a baby. I delivered one that had the umbilical cord wrapped twice around its neck and also had a true knot in the cord. I kept delivering babies throughout my own pregnancy, and one time I was kicked simultaneously from within by my own baby and from without by the one I was delivering. Then I had my own baby in the same delivery room I'd been working in. I felt right at home.

The wife of one of my flyers went into labor and became hysterical. She was in the earliest stages, where the pain wasn't bad yet, but she kept screaming and moaning and overreacting. I wanted to slap her to bring her to her senses, but of course I couldn't do that. So I administered a verbal slapping, yelling at her, insulting her, and telling her I was ashamed to be a member of the same sex as someone who acted like that. Amazingly, she responded. She was an ideal patient from then on.

I'd never done anything like that before, and I was afraid my temper had gotten the best of me. I was fully expecting to be called on the carpet and punished. To my surprise, the patient came to my office afterwards and thanked me profusely for helping her get control of herself!

Besides the OB controversy, I had another run-in with the hospital commander over the emergency room. We had limited facilities at night, and some patients didn't understand that and would come in with routine problems that should have waited for appointments. One night I had a patient with a decidedly non-urgent problem and I politely explained to her that I could examine her that night but I couldn't do much more, and it would probably be better if she made an appointment with her regular doctor when the lab was open and appropriate tests could be done. She was very appreciative that I took the time to explain, understood that I had her best interests at heart, said she hadn't realized our night-time limitations, and gladly agreed to call in the morning for an appointment. I patted myself on the back for having resolved the problem without alienating the patient. But when I told the commander what I had done, he exploded. He informed me, "When YOU have your OWN ER, you can do whatever you want, but as long as you work in MY ER you WILL examine every patient!" Yeah, sure. I had to examine every patient and follow the commander's orders to the letter, but the other guy could leave the state and go parachute-jumping when he was on call.

SUPPLANTED BY DR. QUACK

After I had been Chief of Aerospace Medicine for a little over half a year, I got demoted. A new flight surgeon arrived who outranked me, so he became Chief of Aerospace Medicine and I became OIC (Officer in Charge) of Flight/Missile Medicine. His name was spelled (but not pronounced) the same as a crude Spanish word for sexual intercourse that is used as a swear word. That's how I always thought of him. Here, I will call him Dr. Quack, which is politer and sounds just ducky. I didn't invent that name: keep reading and you will learn where it came from.

He had been a pediatrician, and I think he resented the fact that I knew more about medicine than he did. Sometimes I wondered if he knew much about pediatrics: he apparently had never done a neonatal circumcision and refused when I offered to teach him how. He didn't treat me fairly; I didn't like him, I didn't particularly respect him, and I was glad when he finally left two years later and I resumed my old job as Chief.

When Dr. Quack left to take a position as hospital commander at another base, the flight techs presented him with a T-shirt that said "I Support Women's Lib" on the front and "Under Protest" on the back. I later talked to someone who was under his command at his new base. They said he worked out pretty well as a commander because he was always off playing golf and left them alone to do their jobs without his interference!

He demonstrated his lack of leadership abilities by failing to solve one of our problems and leaving it for me to deal with after his departure. Our new Bioenvironmental Engineer (BEE) was a former B-52 navigator. His degree was in electrical engineering, but when he tried to wire a timer for our coffee pot it short-circuited and blew up. He had his private pilot's license. He was always bragging about how he had guided B-52s all over the world. But when he rented a plane in Texas on vacation, he got lost. He looked at a map, decided all he had to do was follow the highway to the town he wanted to go to, and proceeded to follow the wrong highway to the wrong town. And then he came home and told everybody what he'd done! Some of us privately wondered if he was capable of navigating his way out of a broom closet. He was a loudmouth know-it-all who pretended to be an expert on things he knew nothing about. It got to where when someone said "Dipshit" we all knew who they were talking about.

We immediately suspected he was less than competent, and those suspicions soon coalesced into certainty. Several missile officers had complained of increased noise in the missile capsules after new equipment was installed, and I planned to visit an LCF with the BEE to measure the noise levels. I asked him to pull the folder for the LCF we were going to visit, because I wanted to check the last noise measurements. First he told me there were no folders; then he told me there were folders but he couldn't find them. Then he told me he'd looked at the noise levels and they were all OK, but he couldn't tell me where he'd seen them or what the numbers were. Finally, I asked his NCO, who immediately pulled the proper folder out of the file cabinet and handed it to me.

The folder did not show that he had ever visited that LCF, and I was unable to find any documentation that he had visited *any* LCF, much less one per quarter as required by SAC regulations. He told me he had made the required quarterly visits but "hadn't had time to document them." Other personnel in his section told me he had made no such visits. I reported him to Dr. Quack. Nothing was done.

Before the IG inspection, I reviewed all the LCF folders and there was no documentation of any LCF inspections since the departure of the previous BEE two years earlier. By the next day, when the IG team arrived, there was documentation in the files. I suspected the visits had been invented and the reports "pencil-whipped" at the last minute.

Later, when I resumed my job as Chief, I asked the BEE for the reports of the last three quarterly visits. He gave me three dates. I was able to verify from logs that no one visited the LCF on one of the dates. On the other two, I was able to verify that he was not on any helicopter flights nor any trips with Food Service or

Environmental Health, and he could not have gone alone, so he could only have gone out with maintenance teams which would have meant he stayed out of the office all day. No one in his office remembered him making any such visits. I documented all this and wrote a report, adding a few things like:

7. The SAC supplement requires the BEE to spend a 24 hour alert tour at an LCF, and Capt. D has not complied with this requirement.

8. I am also attaching a copy of a letter from Col B ... It is a sad state of affairs when a maintenance commander understands noise survey procedures and regulations better than the BEE. In reference to this matter, I have had to read the noise regulation to Capt. D word by word repeatedly, have had him argue with me and have had to order him to comply with the regulation.

9. I directed him to do noise dosimetry studies in the LCF's, and he argued with me about the need for it and the reliability of the procedure. Approximately 2 months after my initial request, dosimetry had not been done. When I asked his NCO, TSgt R. accomplished the survey promptly, finding a borderline noise level which resulted in a thorough evaluation by a team from Brooks AFB.

10. Capt. D has not completed the Air Pollution or R.F. Inventory, which he was asked to do prior to the Staff Assistance visit.

11. From numerous things I have observed over the last 3 years, I believe Capt. D has a lack of knowledge about his field, an unwillingness to admit it when he doesn't know something, a sloppy, careless approach to his duties and a "don't care" attitude which has adversely impacted on those working under him. I have had informed reports from other agencies on base to the effect that Capt. D talks a lot but doesn't know what he is talking about. I understand one individual who calls the Bio office frequently hangs up if Capt. D answers. I believe the only reason his office has performed well is that capable NCO's have gotten the job done in spite of Capt. D.

12. I therefore have reason to believe Capt. D is guilty of dereliction of duty, falsification of reports, lying to superiors and general incompetence.

13. I am bringing this to your attention for whatever action you feel is appropriate.

The hospital commander promptly called him into his office and told him to clean out his desk, get a haircut, report to the base commander for reassignment, and never set foot in the hospital again. He was lucky he didn't get court-martialed.

DR MUSHROOM

On disaster exercises, we wore big white helmets. One day a fireman told me I looked like an ambulatory mushroom. The flight techs thought that was pretty funny, so they made me a label for my helmet that said "Dr. Mushroom." Then they decided the other flight surgeon needed a nickname too. They made him a label that said "Dr. Quack." (They made it sound like an affectionate joke, but I suspect the name represented their true feelings for him.) Then all the flight techs wanted labels too. They became "Med MushQuack I" "Med MushQuack II" etc. Incredibly, no one ever told us to take the labels off.

We never faced an actual disaster, but we had a lot of exercises with patients moulaged to simulate wounds and broken bones. We had a great disaster response team. Everyone knew his job and we worked well together. We would set up a triage area, provide immediate treatment in the field, get the most serious injuries on the ambulance, and adapt to changing conditions. It got to the point that when I was supposed to give the team their periodic training I would just say, "Keep doing exactly what you're doing." We worked out a system where the other flight surgeon would do most of the actual triage and I would work the radios; this left me above the fray where I had time to think, make good decisions, coordinate things and keep count of the patients. When the IG team observed us they were very impressed, and characterized us as "the best they'd seen."

On one exercise at night, they waited until I had sent the ambulance back with a load of patients and then they informed me that there was another disaster at another location, expecting that I would panic, flounder, or fail to respond. Instead, I commandeered a cop car and proceeded to the second site.

Another time we needed to transport one more patient than the ambulance could hold; I directed them to load the stretcher into the back of a military pickup that happened to be handy. Then I stopped them and said if it were a real disaster we would do it that way, but since it was only an exercise it would not be safe to move a person that way and we would "simulate." The inspectors liked that.

On a chemical spill exercise, they directed us to go down a certain road, but they had announced the wind direction and I realized in time that that route would put us directly in the (imaginary) plume of toxic smoke, so I directed our driver another way. They were expecting to be able to declare our entire ambulance crew dead, but I outsmarted them. Another time we had to be "decontaminated" by fire hoses and learned the hard way that the back doors of the ambulance leaked! We learned how to handle an out-of-control patient by making him into a human sandwich between two stretchers.

MUSHING, MASHING, AND MISCELLANEOUS MEMORIES

We had a veterinarian who was a dog musher and went to Alaska every year to compete in the Iditarod dogsled race. He would come back from the Iditarod all crippled up, limping, and telling how he fell through the ice, but he couldn't wait to go back again. In the summer, he would put wheels on the dogsled and run the dogs around his pasture for training.

After one big snowstorm, our nurse anesthetist was stranded in the country; the roads were impassable and they couldn't even land a helicopter near her house because of the terrain. They needed her for surgery, so the vet hitched up his dogs and went to the rescue. There was a picture on the front page of the local newspaper of him mushing through the front gate of the base as he delivered her to work.

Part of his job was to do a census of the wildlife on base. He made a big joke of doing the "beaver count"—"What a job! I got to go out and spend all day looking at beavers!" We did have a lot of wildlife on base, from beaver to antelope. One night as I left the hospital late, I turned on my car's headlights and illuminated about 15 antelope grazing right beside the hospital parking lot.

Among other wildlife, there were bats living in the attics of base housing. The vet captured some of them, and about a third of them tested positive for rabies. One day a mother was sitting under a tree with her daughter when a bat dropped from a branch and bit the child. The mother knew the bat had to be tested, and she mistakenly thought it had to be captured alive. She managed to trap it in a towel and brought it in, still thrashing. Fortunately, that one tested negative.

The helicopter squadron's patch was worn on the sleeve of the flight uniform over the left biceps; it showed a beaver in a flight helmet. The helicopters were designated by the name Beaver followed by a number, and the radio base was called Beaver Dam. I think they chose that name so they could legally say Damn over the radio. "Beaver 29 calling Beaver … Dam."

Once we had a MASH party where we were supposed to wear something medical or something military. I wore a long slinky black T-shirt dress, with the squadron patch pinned right over my crotch. I told the guys that was the appropriate part of the anatomy for wearing a beaver patch, not the upper arm. I was a big hit. I also wore Plastibell earrings—small clear plastic devices used to circumcise infant boys. I had had a friend drill holes in the handles, and the bells dangled down. Unfortunately, no one knew what they were except the obstetricians and pediatricians. One of the nurses couldn't decide what to wear, and I suggested she wear a bath towel—like Hot Lips in the shower. She did! She was a big hit too!

The corpsmen put up a plaque in the front office that said:

OUR MOTTO:

WE SHALL STRIVE TO DO WHATS RIGHT
IT'S FOR YOUR HEALTH THAT WE SHALL FIGHT
WE DO OUR BEST, AND WITH GREAT EASE
TO STAMP OUT LIVES AND SAVE DISEASE.

There was a form called a Medical Recommendation for Flying or Special Operational Duty, AF form 1042. When a pilot or missile officer was unable to perform his normal duties due to illness, we would fill out this form and mark "Medically disqualified for flying or special operational duty." There were also blocks to check for "Medically qualified" and for clearance following periodic medical exams, aircraft mishaps, etc. For the flyers, we referred to this as putting them DNIF—for Duties Not Including Flying. We altered one of the forms with my name on it to make me DNIG—Duties Not Including Ground—so I could fly all the time. It said, "medically disqualified for duty on the ground; cleared for flying duty at all times; diagnosis: allergic reaction to terra firma." It was signed by Leonard "Bones" McCoy.

One of my flight techs was up for re-enlistment and he wanted me to do the honors. We did it in style. An American flag was required for the re-enlistment ceremony; we found a little one and attached it to the roof of the helicopter. We flew out to a local landmark, the Cowboy Bar, and had the pilot circle over it while we did the oath.

For a while I had a male physician's assistant (PA) working with me in the flight surgeon's office. We would get ready to make "rounds" and we would link arms and dance around in a circle as a joke. We noticed an interesting phenomenon. When he and I would make rounds on our hospitalized patients, I would ask the patients the questions and they would look at the PA when they answered. I had the rank and the education, but he was the man so he got the respect. We were both amused.

Re-enlisting a medical corpsman in a helicopter over the Cowboy Bar.
That's me in the front seat, on the right.
Note the American flag on the ceiling.

We were also amused when I got an invitation to the wing commander's annual Christmas Open House addressed to me and my wife. We were tempted to have the PA put on a dress and go with me as my "wife;" but I decided if they didn't care enough to remember I was a woman, I didn't need to socialize with them, so I didn't attend.

One of the family practice docs did a vasectomy one day. The medical corpsman held the bottle of anesthetic up for him as usual; the doc withdrew the usual dose, infiltrated the scrotum, and tested to make sure it had taken effect before he made the incision. The patient said he could still feel everything as usual. The doctor kept injecting more lidocaine and testing, and the patient kept saying he could still feel pain. The doctor finally said he couldn't safely give any more anesthetic and would have to go ahead with the procedure; he thought the patient was just anxious and was imagining things. After the whole thing was finished, he took a second look at the bottle of "lidocaine" and discovered it was actually a bottle of normal saline. He'd done the whole operation with nothing but a little salt water! Instead of being angry, the patient was proud of being macho enough to endure surgery with no anesthesia. He decided to make the best of it and brag instead of complain.

I didn't feel confident doing vasectomies on my own yet,[3] so I did one with the hospital commander who was a surgeon—he did one side while I did the other. *His* side kept bleeding; mine was complication-free. (Hee, hee!)

The guys who worked in the Mental Health Clinic thought that name carried an unfortunate stigma, so they put up a new sign that read: "Human Growth Center." We had a good laugh—one of the male doctors said he'd like to grow a couple of inches taller, and I said I could go for a couple more inches around the bust. All too soon, they discovered that Air Force regulations prohibited the name change, and the old sign went back up.

There was a sign in the x-ray department that I loved: "No x-rays taken during pregnancy without authorization." I wondered who got to authorize the pregnancies, and if there was any punishment for getting pregnant without that authorization.

My secretary mis-typed a letter once, and I caught the mistake just in time. We were requesting some breast exam pamphlets, and she left out an "r." I often wondered what they would have sent us if we'd requested beast exam pamphlets—it might have been interesting. I learned to be careful what I signed. My predecessor had once been tricked into signing a letter to some Wyoming state agency warning them that he had been seeing a lot of shepherds with gonorrhea and suggesting they start checking the sheep for VD.

FLYING HIGH

I continued to fly in my spare time, and eventually got my instrument rating. My first instructor in Cheyenne was a man who made me try landing at night without any lights; he said it would make hair grow on my chest. I had to remind him that a hairy chest might be desirable for men, but was not an attractive prospect for women pilots. My next instrument instructor was a woman, Vivian. With her, I flew "under the hood" all the way from Cheyenne to San Diego without ever looking out the window. She trained me well. One of the things she emphasized was "First, fly the airplane." On my check-ride, they tried every which way

---

3. I had been taught to do vasectomies, but had only done 2 or 3. Vasectomy did not appear on the credentials list of procedures I was supposedly qualified to perform. My residency program director sent this list to the hospital at F.E. Warren. The list included forceps deliveries, which my residency program did not allow residents to perform, and it included hemorrhoid banding, a procedure that I had never even *seen* done, nor had I even seen the instruments used in the procedure.

to distract me; but I had become bulletproof. The check-ride was easier than Vivian's training.

Vivian ran into the same attitude I had run into: women aren't supposed to fly. Preparing for a flight one day, she called the weather service as usual for a weather briefing. The briefer, hearing a young female voice, just told her, "Ma'am, the weather is too bad to fly today." She said, "OK, but would you please give me a standard weather briefing anyway?" He wouldn't give her the briefing and kept insisting that it was not a good day to fly, but wouldn't give her any specific reasons. Finally she said, "Look, I'm a single and multi-engine CFII[4] with a seaplane rating and an ATP,[5] and I'm type-certified in the Citation;[6] now please give me a standard weather briefing as your job requires you to do, and please explain to me exactly why you are advising me not to fly today." He back-pedaled, gave her a proper weather briefing, and told her the weather wasn't that bad and there was no reason not to go.

One of my best experiences flying was with Vivian in Washington State. The sky was clouded over, but we broke through to brilliant sunshine above and we could see all the mountain peaks poking up through the clouds: Mount Baker, Mount Rainier, Mount St. Helens, Mount Adams, and Mount Hood. One of my worst experiences flying was with her too. Coming home from Albuquerque, we hit turbulence the briefers had neglected to warn us about, and we were tossed around so much we couldn't maintain our assigned altitude. Air Traffic Control finally had to assign us a block of altitudes to bounce around in. It was like riding a bucking bronco. I was frightened, but Vivian wasn't. She said you couldn't really call it rough until your head started hitting the ceiling.

She had learned to fly in Cheyenne where the wind never stopped blowing. The first time she heard a report of "winds calm" at another airport, she almost panicked. She'd never landed without wind before, and wasn't sure how the plane was going to react!

At 6200 feet, Cheyenne was higher than mile-high Denver. Pilots from the lowlands would think something was wrong with their plane because they didn't know they needed to adjust the fuel mixture before takeoff to compensate for the lack of oxygen, and their plane wouldn't climb as fast as they expected. One poor soul on a night instrument flight filed a flight plan to cruise at 6000 feet; Air

---

4.   CFII = Certified Flight Instrument Instructor. She could teach instrument flying in both single and multiengine aircraft.
5.   ATP = Air Transport Pilot, the PhD of flying, which qualifies you to fly for the big airlines.
6.   Cessna Citation, a private jet

Traffic Control didn't pick up his error and approved his flight plan, and he flew right into the ground before he reached the Cheyenne airport.

Preconceptions struck again when my boyfriend Kirk and I took a trip in my Cessna. We visited my friend Roy in North Carolina; he took us to meet his sister and mentioned to her that we had flown there in a single engine plane. She turned to me and asked, "Are you a pilot too?" It was my plane and Kirk had not even started taking flying lessons at that point, but she automatically assumed the man was the pilot.

MARRIAGE—BETTER THE SECOND TIME AROUND

After two years at F.E.Warren, I re-married. When I first arrived at F.E.Warren, I had briefly been Kirk's boss. Two years later, we married quietly without telling anyone until afterwards. The judge who married us had the first name of Yogi, and Kirk said he looked more like a shoe salesman than a judge. He kept wondering if we were really married. After the ceremony, we headed towards Denver for a weekend honeymoon, and en route I asked Kirk if he felt any different now that he was married. He said, "Yes, I feel hungry; let's stop and get something to eat." I called my mother that night and told her I didn't have a boyfriend any more. I let her worry for a bit and then told her I had a husband instead.

A side benefit of marrying Kirk Hall was that I got a spellable and pronounceable last name. First I'd been Hoag (HO-ig, not HOGUE, HOWG, or HO-AG), then Celdrán (sell-DRAHN), then I'd reverted to Hoag again after my divorce. Celdrán got variously rendered as Celdron, Celdren, Selden, Sullivan, and just about anything else you can imagine. Hall was reassuringly normal. Now my only problem is convincing people that Harriet has only one T. They seem to really *want* me to be Harriett or Harriette. It would seem to me that when in doubt, less is better, but that's not the way it works.

After we had been married for about a month, Kirk was talking on the phone to a friend in another state and casually mentioned something about "my wife." The friend was flabbergasted: Kirk had been a bachelor for 41 years and had shown no signs of getting married. Kirk told him, "Well, it seemed like a good idea at the time...."

Another time he told a friend on the phone that he had married a nice enough woman, but that his wife didn't have the potential to progress any further with her education. He made it sound like I was a dummy, until his friend started to protest that I might be more educable than he thought, and he should at least give me the benefit of the doubt. Kirk finally told him the reason I couldn't go any further was that a doctorate was already about as far as you could go.

He was always joking. When he first met my sister Stephanie, she asked, "What do you do, Kirk?" and he answered with a perfectly straight face, "I run a whorehouse in Cheyenne." Stephanie wasn't sure how to react, but she didn't want to seem judgmental, so she just said something like "That's interesting." and quickly changed the subject.

He liked to show people pictures of a little "girl" with long curls and tell them it was his sister. Then he would make up some story about how she'd been trampled to death by a herd of bison or something equally improbable, and finally he would confess that it was his own picture taken just before he got his first haircut. One day when his father took him out for a walk he overheard a woman say, "That is a darling little girl, but why do they always dress her like a boy?" His father brought him home and told his mother, "He gets a haircut *today*." He did make a pretty cute little girl, and our daughter Kristin looked a lot like him at the same age.

Kirk could fix anything. Once an old washing machine broke down in a house he was renting out. He had never even looked inside a washing machine before, but he took it apart and determined which part needed replacing. It was so old that the part was no longer available. No problem—he took the old part to a friend who had a machine shop in his garage, they fabricated a new one from scratch, and he installed it. A day's work and a little ingenuity saved the cost of a new machine.

Another time, he was using a handheld calculator for a class, and got tired of replacing batteries. I saw him taking the back off it, and a while later I saw that he had connected something in its innards to the wall socket. He was always taking things apart and putting them back together again and never had any parts left over. He sort of communed with mechanical and electrical devices. They would work for him when they wouldn't work for me. I told him I thought they obeyed him better because they were scared he'd take them apart if they didn't cooperate. He was handy to have around, but I kidded him that I really married him for his Noritake—he had a set of china he'd picked up when he was stationed in Korea that he had never even taken out of the box.

My first husband and I had frequent conflicts about money. I would buy a new pair of shoes and he would say, "But you already *had* a pair of shoes!" Kirk and I never argued about money. Kirk had been investing in the stock market for years, and that was "capital," which you don't spend. I had a good salary, which was "money," which you do spend. If we ever had a conflict, it was along the lines of "I'll write a check for that." "No, let me write a check for that."

When I first met Kirk, he was a BioEnvironmental Engineer (BEE) who technically worked for me. He knew far more about his job than I did, and I recognized his competence and let him run his own shop. Unfortunately, he was passed over for promotion and reassigned.

I will explain about promotion gamesmanship and OERs in the next chapter. Kirk had had unfortunate run-ins and just plain bad luck with some of his reporting officials. My predecessor had told him, "Kirk, you're a good officer and a good engineer, but you don't know how to dance." He was meticulous and uncompromising but was more concerned with getting the job done right than with diplomacy and politics; this rubbed some of his less competent bosses the wrong way. So he missed out on promotion and we lost a competent BEE and got an incompetent one, Captain Dipshit (see above).

Kirk had the option of quitting and losing his investment in his career or of serving 4 1/2 more years as an NCO to finish out his twenty years and get full retirement as a Major. He had the courage and self-esteem to do the latter without feeling inferior. He went to Lowry Air Force Base in Denver for further training and was reassigned back to F.E. Warren as a technician in the Precision Measurement Equipment Lab. He no longer worked for me, and his job was way across the base from the hospital, so there was no chance that our relationship or our difference in rank would influence our job performance. Nevertheless, this put us in an awkward position, because while we had both been officers when we met, I was now considered to be "fraternizing" with an enlisted man. Enlisted and officers were two separate species and were not supposed to socialize with each other off duty.

Once during an investigation, an enlisted friend who had gone hunting with Kirk and me referred to me as Harriet and we both got in trouble—him for calling me by my first name, and me for allowing it. I remembered a story my father told from his days in the Army in WWII. He was a young lieutenant, and one day a friend from home, who happened to be an enlisted man, called to say he was passing through and did Dad want to meet him at the train station to have a beer. Dad went, they chatted, and he thought nothing of it. The next day his commander called him on the carpet: "You were fraternizing. That is not allowed." Dad asked, "Do you mean if my own brother, who is also an enlisted man, asked me to have a beer with him I would have to refuse?" The commander said, technically, yes, that's what those lieutenant's bars mean. Dad took them off and said, "If these bars mean I can't associate with my own brother, you can have them back, Sir." The commander refused to accept his resignation.

Many men would be threatened by having a high-powered professional for a wife, or would resent that their wife made more money. Kirk wasn't threatened; he was simply proud of me. He had the maturity that some men never achieve at any age.

GUNS

We used to joke that we people in the military were "trained killers" which was pretty funny because the biggest thing I ever killed was a spider. The Air Force didn't let me near their guns until I'd been on active duty for 17 years; then they finally decided for some obscure reason that I should go to a one-day class. They taught me to take a gun apart, put it back together and shoot. It didn't seem too difficult; I was only one point shy of earning a marksmanship ribbon.

I had never met a gun until I met Kirk. He liked to hunt. He did his own reloading and used a chronograph to measure the velocity of his loads. He took me out to a local gravel pit and taught me to shoot a pistol and a rifle.

We went hunting several times in Wyoming, camping out with friends. He managed to drop every animal with a single shot, so it didn't seem cruel. One year Kirk had an antelope license in addition to his usual deer license, and I went antelope hunting with him the first day of the season, planning to meet our friends at a campground in a deer hunting area the second day. We walked over the prairie, found a nice antelope standing still and posing, and Kirk shot it. He gutted it, took it home, hung it in the garage, and we headed out to meet our friends for deer hunting. We arrived at the campground mid-morning; our friends weren't there—they were out hunting. So we went too. We drove down a road, parked, and walked out into the woods. Within a very short time, Kirk had shot his buck. We brought it back to the campground and had it hanging from a tree by the tent by the time our friends returned. We met them at the camp-ground entrance, and they told us there were no bucks out there—in fact they hadn't seen a single deer all day long. As they approached the tent and saw the hanging carcass, they asked, "What's that? Is that your antelope?" We told them if they couldn't tell the difference between an antelope and a deer, no wonder their hunt was unsuccessful. They never did get a deer on that trip; Kirk was the only one.

We let the two carcasses hang for a while in our cool garage. The little boy next door was intrigued; he thought meat came from the supermarket. I decided our garage was "home on the range, where the deer and the antelope play." Kirk butchered them and I wrapped the pieces for the freezer, writing labels that would help me remember what was inside: "Little pieces of deer back," "large piece of antelope arm," "big chunk of deer leg," etc. We had some of the antelope made into sausage. We invented venison recipes. We used some of the little pieces to make sweet-and-sour-deer-un-shishkabobs (you don't want to know!).

Kirk was lucky at hunting but my aunt was even luckier. She welcomed her husband home from an unsuccessful day of deer hunting by saying "Never mind, I shot one in the back yard this morning. It was trying to eat my garden." To top even that, my sister went hunting in Alaska with a hunter whose luck belongs in the Guinness Book of Records. He had a Dall sheep permit and they hiked into the mountains to camp overnight before the season started the next morning. At dawn, the instant the season officially opened, he awakened in his sleeping bag, looked out the flap of the tent, saw a Dall sheep standing right there, and shot it before he even got out of his sleeping bag.

PREGNANT!

I was 36 and had just about decided to have my tubes tied, but Kirk said his mother was older than that when she had him, and it might be nice to have children. I thought about it for a while, and I began to like the idea. I went off my birth control pills, and two months later I was pregnant.

That's when the shit really hit the fan. You see, when a woman is pregnant, she can't stay on flying status. No matter that under FAA regulations I could pilot my own plane right up until I went into labor; Air Force regulations wouldn't even let me ride along on a helicopter flight. I waited as long as I could to tell them, but then I had to put on the maternity uniform and admit I was knocked up. Dr. Quack's immediate reaction was a shocked "Don't you know how to prevent that?!" I wasn't going to get a bit of sympathy or understanding from that source.

This was just the excuse Dr. Quack and the hospital commander and the family physician/would-be-flight surgeon had been waiting for. They thought that since I couldn't fly, I should have to leave the flight surgeon's office and let the other guy have my job; especially since it was really a *man's* job in the first place. I thought that was nonsense. I had a temporary medical condition, and when a male flight surgeon had a temporary medical condition, like a broken leg, he simply stayed in his job until he could go back on flying status. And I had a condition that was darn well *guaranteed* to be temporary, with a precise end in sight. I had worked hard to establish a good family practice and good relations with the squadrons, and I thought continuity was the best thing for the office.

Oh, boy! First the commander tried to get permission from headquarters to have me keep flying despite the pregnancy. They told him, "Not only no but hell no and you should have grounded her 2 months ago." Then he asked about removing me from my job. They didn't know *what* to do, because there was no precedent. There had never been a pregnant flight surgeon in the Strategic Air Command before. I told them there was plenty of precedent for a flight surgeon being temporarily grounded for a medical diagnosis and staying in the job. I cried. I protested. I ranted. I got to keep my job. No one was happy about it.

Next crisis: the obstetricians automatically put all pregnant women on a limited duty profile where they were not required to work long hours overtime. I was scheduled for 24 hour ER shifts. The commander said, "But she's a *doctor*! She has to take her turn as MOD." The obstetrician pointed out that I was also a 36 year old woman pregnant for the first time and deserved at least the same consideration as a younger woman in a less stressful job. He also pointed out that I probably would have been glad to let my husband have the baby if I'd had any choice in the matter.

We reached a compromise: I had to pull a few more MOD shifts but could have a PA work with me to do most of the work at night so I could get some sleep. That didn't exactly work as planned: I had to sleep on the floor of my office, and the first night I ended up staying up all night with premature twins and a screwed-up air evac. When my friend Gladys was pregnant at another base, she didn't even get the concession of a PA—they made her keep pulling regular 24 hour MOD shifts throughout her pregnancy. But even that represented a gain: until just a few years earlier, women had not been allowed to remain on active duty once they were pregnant.

The games continued. Dr. Quack came up with another plan. He announced that the flight surgeon wannabe was going to do my industrial shop and food service inspection visits and I would have to cover his family practice patients for him while he was out of the office. This was just harassment. There was no earthly reason I couldn't continue to do my own shop visits. All it involved was driving to a building and walking around inside the building. And I could even sit down whenever I wanted. I protested loudly. I prevailed, but it just created more ill will.

At age 36, I was an "elderly primigravida."[7] One of my patients got pregnant about the same time and was about my age. She was in a second marriage, and was sort of embarrassed because her daughter from the first marriage was also having a baby. She was worried that her age would be a problem, but I reassured her that she was healthy and at no increased risk for complications. As it turned out, she and I had uneventful deliveries, and her daughter was the one who had complications. We joked that she should have waited until she was our age and old enough to do it right.

I got tired of people asking me when the baby was due. I wanted to say, "Oh, I'm not pregnant; I have an abdominal tumor and I only have 6 months to live." People would ask my husband if he was hoping for a boy or a girl and he would say, "Actually, I was kind of hoping for a pony." One day in the public library, a lady I hadn't seen for a while came up to me and congratulated me on being pregnant. Kirk exclaimed loud enough for everyone to hear in the hush of the library, "PREGNANT! I thought you were just getting FAT!"

I ended up working full time right up to the day before I had the baby. Then four weeks maternity leave and an arrangement with a good babysitter and I was back on flying status and everything was back to normal.

She was Kristin Ann Hall, 8 pounds and 3 ounces of cuddly miracle. Her Dad was an only child, had never been around babies, and had never changed a diaper, but he was a fast learner. By the time the baby was 6 weeks old he was such an accomplished parent that I could go TDY for altitude chamber training while he just carried on smoothly. When the pediatrician asked if he wanted her to grow up to be a doctor like her mother, he said, "Absolutely not! I want her to grow up to be the madam of the biggest and best whorehouse in Washington D.C. so she can influence kings and presidents." He also solemnly informed people that children were no trouble as long as you had them modified at birth: he claimed to have drilled a hole in each foot so you could fasten the baby's foot to the floor and let her walk around one way in a circle, and then change feet and have her walk the other way.

Having my own baby was a good chance to find out if all that advice I'd been giving my patients for years was good advice. It was. There were no surprises or alarms. The first month was hard on both of us because of lost sleep, but when she was a month old we did what I always advised new parents to do at that age: we trained her to sleep through the night. We fed her at our bedtime, and didn't

---

7.   A primigravida is someone who is pregnant for the first time. I was 37 by the time the baby was born.

feed her again until time for us to get up, no matter how much she cried. All it took was two nights. If you wait until a baby is much older, it doesn't work as well. And it isn't a good idea to do it before a month of age because you want to make sure the baby is healthy and growing well and can tolerate 8 hours without eating. It sure makes life easier all around.

COMBAT CASUALTY CARE COURSE

I was one of the first doctors selected to attend a newly required C4—Combat Casualty Care Course. It was held at near San Antonio at Camp Bullis, where I'd been to Survival Training. I didn't know what to expect. It was designed to prepare us to work in battlefield conditions in a field hospital. We had classes, learned emergency medicine skills, had field exercises and mass casualty drills, and lived in a tent. It was sort of like playing MASH for a week.

As usual, I was the sole female in a large tent of men. There was no need for privacy, but the guys insisted on hanging up some blankets to make a screen for my corner of the tent, despite my loud protests. We slept in our uniforms. We had to wear a helmet and carry a gas mask everywhere we went, even when we got up in the middle of the night to go to the bathroom. We ate field rations.

We got to go on night patrols with the Marines. They showed up at our campfire with their faces painted in camouflage, and we followed them out into the night. The object was to creep silently through the woods and find, sneak up on, and "capture" an "enemy" patrol without being detected and captured yourselves. It was like kids playing hide and seek. Or like paintball without the paint. The biggest challenge was trying to avoid stepping on the ubiquitous fresh cow pies in the dark!

The best part of working with the Marines was that I finally learned why they are known as "grunts." They would jog by in formation every morning to the cadence, "Hunh! Hoo! Hreep! Ho!" or something like that. It sounded much more like grunting than counting.

We had to traipse through the woods carrying stretchers and do various other exercises. For one, they took us one at a time to where a rope was strung across a ravine. We were told to hang from it by hands and crossed legs and inch our way to the other side. We were secured with a safety line so if we fell we would hopefully be caught before we fell to our deaths on the rocks far below. They told me everyone else had made it all the way across, so I tried really hard. I got most of the way, but as I worked my way up the upslope of the rope on the far side, the grip strength in my hands gave out, and I had to let go. I was saved by the safety line. THEN they told me no one had made it all the way and I had gotten as far as most of the men did!

We learned Advanced Cardiac Life Support. Then we had goat lab. They anesthetized goats, shot them with rifles, and then let us remove the bullets, repair the wounds, and do various other surgical procedures on them for practice. Goats drool copiously when they are anesthetized—there were buckets under their heads to catch the overflow. It was messy and smelly and gory. When we had exhausted the learning opportunities of our goats, a technician came around with some kind of bright green liquid in a syringe and put them out of their misery permanently. When asked what I had learned, I said "I learned if anyone comes toward me with a syringe full of green liquid I should run the other way."

When we broke up camp, we had to collapse the cots and deliver them to a collection point. I organized my tent mates and we marched over there in formation, carrying the cots and singing "M, I, C, K, E, Y, M-O-U-S-E!"[8] I was told that the song was inappropriate and we must stop. Some people just don't have a sense of humor.

ER PATIENTS

The security police brought a patient to the ER one night—he was crazy drunk and had managed to kick out a window in the cop car on the way in. When I got to the exam room, he was on the floor with three cops sitting on him. I couldn't get near him. He was thrashing violently and called me a "Fucking bitch" and told me not to come near him. The cops couldn't put him in jail unless he had been medically cleared and sobered up. I couldn't very well medically clear him when I couldn't get near him, but he looked pretty healthy. I told the cops we could observe him in a hospital bed, but we didn't have any secure facilities, so they'd have to guard him and protect us from him; they wouldn't do that. I called the psychiatrist on call at Fitzsimmons Army Hospital in Denver and explained the situation. They had a secure, locked ward, and agreed to accept him—but only if I medically cleared him first. I couldn't figure out how I was supposed to accomplish that, so I ended up just sending him down there for admission anyway. I don't know what happened, but he didn't come back.

---

8.   In case younger readers don't recognize this ditty, it is "The Mickey Mouse Club March," the theme song of the after-school TV show dinosaurs of my vintage used to watch faithfully.

Another drunken airman was confronted in our ER by his commander, who had been called away from a party to take responsibility for him. The commander was not happy to be there in the first place, and he was even less happy when the drunk started cursing him. He said, "Do you know who I am?" The drunk wasn't too clear on that. I bet he was REALLY clear about it the next morning after he sobered up.

I often wished we had a video camera to tape the behavior of drunks in the ER. Most of them had no memory of what they had done. I thought watching themselves on videotape might be a good deterrent.

A woman came in complaining of abdominal pain. She had a large belly, regular contractions, and was obviously in labor. I said, "You're having a baby." She said, "No, I'm not." She insisted she wasn't pregnant. She said she'd thought she was pregnant and had gone in for prenatal care and the OB clinic had asked when her last period was. She was still bleeding every month, so they told her she couldn't possibly be pregnant. She said, "OK, you're the experts." and went home. She continued to have a period every month throughout her otherwise normal pregnancy. I'd never seen this before, but it can happen rarely. She was one of the rare ones. Two hours later I delivered a healthy baby boy.

A father brought his teenage son in with a severe sunburn—he'd fallen asleep at the lake. I was standing there when the corpsman asked what the problem was and I took one look at him and blurted out "Stupidity" without thinking. I could have been in big trouble if they had complained. Fortunately, the father agreed with me and seconded my impromptu diagnosis.

At Christmas, a group of colonels from other units came to sing Christmas carols in the hospital wards and ER. One of them was Japanese; as they left the ER he came up to me and whispered, "Strange customs you Christians have!"

One evening we heard a loud rumble like a freight train, and one of the corpsmen was picked up and bodily thrown through the double doors into the ER by a freak windstorm—sort of a mini-tornado. His back was never right after that.

A security policeman came in one winter evening with an injury sustained by falling down the icy steps at police headquarters while carrying a heavy ammo can. He'd been walking down the steps in the dark wearing sunglasses, which I couldn't exactly understand and which just might have contributed to his accident.

Another security policeman shot himself in the chest with his own gun while on duty, while sitting alone in his patrol car brooding about a failed love affair. I'd never actually treated a gunshot wound before, but luckily the surgeon on call arrived at the same time as the patient.

One of the obstetricians had recently married a very attractive young woman. When he was MOD, she would join him in the on-call room. The corpsmen were intrigued by the noises that would ensue.

A man dislocated his shoulder. I had him lie face down with a weight attached to the arm to stretch the muscles before I attempted to reduce the dislocation. As he lay there, he suddenly said, "It's fixed!" It had spontaneously popped back into place!

A patient was struck by lightning while playing golf. On discharge from the hospital, he was advised that in the future he should pick golf partners who were taller than he was.

We got a phone call from a desperate mother, "My husband was chopping wood and he just cut my daughter's arm off with the ax!" They arrived shortly; the girl had a small laceration that probably could have been fixed with a steri-strip, but we put a couple of stitches in to make everyone feel better. I learned that lesson over and over in the ER: don't be too quick to panic, because things are usually not as bad as your imagination represents them. Or as someone once instructed interns, "In case of cardiac arrest, stop and take your own pulse first."

An Unwelcome Transfer

I had been at F.E.Warren for over four years when the Air Force offered me a transfer. The hospital at Plattsburgh Air Force Base in New York desperately needed a flight surgeon, and they had an opening there for my husband too. I agreed to take the job.

Unfortunately, the commander at Plattsburgh was expecting a man, and when he learned that his new flight surgeon had no dangly bits, he was taken aback. He quickly discovered that I was also qualified in family practice, and he finagled a switcheroo. There was a psychiatrist at Plattsburgh who was also qualified as a flight surgeon, so he decided to give my job to the psychiatrist and to utilize me in the family practice clinic instead. He "desperately needed" a flight surgeon until the instant I was assigned to the job, and then all of a sudden he didn't need a flight surgeon at all. He called to tell me this. I let him know I was unhappy.

I still have the standard welcome letter he sent me: on the bottom, he had hand-written, "I know you will enjoy the area and could later be worked into aerospace medicine depending on performance at a later date." At the time, I had been a flight surgeon for 4 ½ years, I was the Chief of Aerospace Medicine at the largest missile base in the Free World, I was an instrument-rated pilot with my own airplane, I was providing comprehensive family medical care in the flight surgeon's office including delivering babies, I was seeing more patients than any other flight surgeon in SAC, I had good Officer Effectiveness Reports, I had excellent ratings and even personal kudos from IG inspection teams, and I had been nominated for SAC flight surgeon of the year.[9] And this idiot expected me to start from scratch again and prove to him that I was good enough to be a flight surgeon?

I suspected perhaps there was an iota of discrimination against women involved in his decision. I suggested as much to the base IG (inspector general). He agreed with me, and thought I had a clear case against the commander for sexual discrimination, but he advised me not to make a formal complaint. He said the commander would be able to weasel out of it and all it would do is hurt my career. I fumed and fretted. I knuckled under, but I was so bitter I didn't even feel like putting up a Christmas tree that year.

I have proof that I was not just being paranoid about this commander. He really was prejudiced against women. He gave a public speech on base where he said things like, "Women are not as dedicated to their jobs as men." And "Women are not motivated towards a career." I hope there is reincarnation and poetic justice and he is reborn as a woman. And I wish I could choose what kind of woman and what he looked like. Of course, I don't believe in reincarnation; I used to, but that was in a previous lifetime. (Joke. Not original.)

---

9.   Nominated, but of course not selected. What did you expect?

10

Plattsburgh, New York

Peace is our profession.

—SAC motto

By the time we were ready to move, I was pregnant with number two daughter. If the commander had known that, he would have had one more reason for not wanting me as a flight surgeon, but he had made his decision before I got pregnant. Before we moved, Kirk and I flew my plane to New York to find a house and to leave the plane there. Kirk had his pilot's license by then but was not instrument rated. He was flying over Pennsylvania when the weather deteriorated; we managed to switch seats in mid-air (not easy in a Cessna) and I called to pick up an instrument flight plan en route and proceeded into the clouds. All went well until it started snowing, and I realized we were picking up ice on the wings. Ice is not a good thing to have decorating a single engine plane. It interferes with airfoil surfaces and makes planes fall out of the sky. I immediately got on the radio, declared an emergency, and requested vectors to the nearest airport. We were safely on the ground a few minutes later, but I was too busy flying to look at the charts, and I didn't even know which airport they had guided us to until we went into the terminal and read the signs. We had to leave the plane there and rent a car for the rest of the trip. Kirk eventually went back to get it after we were settled in New York, and he found a bird's nest established inside the cowling, on top of the oil cooler. He had to perform an eviction and baby-birdicide before he could fly.

LIVING IN PERU

Kristin was 19 months old, and we started across the US in a caravan of two cars and a utility trailer, with a portable crib and with CB radios to keep in contact. We visited relatives en route, and introduced Kristin to her first pig (at least the first of the non-male-chauvinist kind). We told her it went "Oink, oink!" and she repeated "Wink, wink!" We had purchased a house in Peru, New York, a short drive from the base; we moved in, found a good babysitter, and reported for duty.

We could see a local cemetery from our back yard. When my father, who had grown up in New York State, came to visit, he asked if we knew that it was against the law in that state for anyone who lived within a mile of a cemetery to be buried in that cemetery. I said no, that seemed strange, why? And he explained that you couldn't be buried if you were still living anywhere; you had to die first.

The climate was as snowy as Wyoming but not as windy. The first time it snowed, we saw neighbors on cross-country skis in the street in front of our house. I explained to Kristin that they were skiing and told her she could try that when she got bigger. Twenty minutes later, she announced, "I bigger now; go ski?" She was also impressed by her first sight of huge Lake Champlain ("Water pool!") and when Kirk retrieved our plane from Pennsylvania, she danced around it in delight singing, "MY airpwane!"

Instead of Chief of Aeromedical Services, I was the Chief of the Family Practice Clinic. I continued to get angrier and angrier at the hospital commander as I got pregnanter and pregnanter. Not only did I not get the flying job, but they became short-handed in flight medicine again and they pulled a reservist to come in and cover. He learned that someone in family practice had wings, and he came to find me. He started to chew me out, saying just because I was pregnant was no reason I couldn't work in the flight surgeon's office temporarily, and then they wouldn't have had to inconvenience him. I informed him that there was nothing I would like better, and I told him my story. He apologized, saying, "I guess you're not the one I should be mad at."

There was no OB service at the base hospital, so I went to a civilian obstetrician. Kimberly Alexandra Hall, 9 pounds 2 ½ ounces, arrived one September night after a surprisingly easy delivery—I think I had to push a total of about three times! They asked me if I wanted to have the baby in a delivery room or in a birthing room; I told them I'd never even *seen* a birthing room but had spent many hours in delivery rooms delivering 200 or so babies and felt quite comfortable there. They asked if I wanted natural childbirth; I said HELL NO, I want everything you can give me for the pain. Our next door neighbor asked Kirk if he wanted her to help with the laundry or anything while I was in the hospital; he informed her he did all the laundry when I *wasn't* in the hospital and could manage just fine. That's one of the perks of marrying a long-time bachelor.

PROMOTION TO COLONEL

While I was on my one month of maternity leave, I got a call from my nemesis the woman-hating hospital commander. He had told me a while back that I was on the list to be promoted to full colonel, and I had asked him when it would take effect. He said he didn't know. He did know, but didn't bother to tell me. He let me assume it would be on the anniversary of my previous promotion, in June. Now, in October, he was calling to tell me the day had arrived. Usually when someone is promoted, especially to the rank of full colonel, there is a big to-do, an announcement is made over the intercom, the commander comes to the workplace to pin on the new insignia, and there is a party to celebrate. In my case, instead of congratulating me, he mumbled something about since I was on maternity leave did I want to bother to come in, and I decided if he was going to be that way about it, no I didn't. I got a phone call from the Surgeon General of SAC congratulating me; he was *much* nicer about it than my own boss! Even though I wasn't promoted the first year I was eligible, I was promoted the second year and I was a full colonel after only 15 years on active duty.

I had to get a new official photograph taken as a "bird" colonel in my uniform with the shiny new silver eagle insignia on the epaulets. I went to the Base Photo Lab as instructed. I had two ribbons: a National Defense ribbon, which everyone got during Viet Nam, and the longevity ribbon which you got automatically after five years' active duty, with a little metal ditzel added for every subsequent 5 years. The photographer took one look and said I needed to go back and put on the rest of my ribbons for the photo. I told him those 2 were all I had.

He said, "You must have a training ribbon. Everyone has a training ribbon." I said no, I didn't go through the usual training; I went straight into an Air Force internship. He asked if I'd been overseas; I must have an overseas ribbon for my time in Spain. At that time I was not authorized an overseas ribbon—I can't remember exactly why; I did eventually get one later. He said I must have commendation or meritorious service ribbons, because no one ever got promoted to full colonel without them. I told him I'd never received one. Most of the doctors I knew who had been awarded commendations had either written themselves up for the awards or had been good politicians whose bosses were looking out for their careers. I had never planned to make the Air Force a career, and had not "played the game"—and even if I had, they probably wouldn't have been generous to a woman. I once saw a cartoon of a general with a chest full of medals, showing them off to a woman and pointing to one medal. He says, "I got that one for keeping my mouth shut." The only kind of commendation I ever got was a misguided certificate thanking me for helping with the victims of the Rocky Bayou fire during my residency. If I did any such thing I sure don't remember it; in fact, I didn't even know there had been any such fire. The photographer went through a list of every medal he could think of, and I kept saying, nope. Don't have that one either.

Official Photograph of New Full Colonel with only 2 ribbons—National Defense and Longevity

The photographer was adamant: no one could possibly be promoted to full colonel with only 2 ribbons. He called Personnel and had them look up my records. After a long session on the phone he came back scratching his head. "It looks like you're right; you do only have 2 ribbons. I'll have to take your picture like that." He couldn't understand it. He wasn't happy.

OERs

Since promotions depend on OER's more than anything else, this might be a good place to explain them. The Officer Effectiveness Report is an annual report card for officers. (There is also an APR, or Airman's Performance Report, for enlisted personnel.) The front side of the report has a job description and 10 areas of evaluation (job knowledge, judgment, leadership, etc.) each rated on a scale of 1 to 5 with specific comments to justify the rating. The back has an overall rating of 1 to 10 and narratives by the rater, additional rater and endorsing officer.

Sounds pretty straightforward—but in reality it is an example of military gamesmanship at its worst/best.

If you want to be promoted, your OER must indicate that you are a super-perfect paragon of military everything, able to leap piles of buildings at a single bound and capable of walking on water without getting your shoes wet. It has to say you're wonderful in every way and has to give specific examples. ALL your ratings must be top ratings. The rater must over-inflate you like a balloon that is near bursting. Now, I'm not saying that raters exactly lie, but they do put on the rosiest colored glasses and exaggerate a bit here and there!

At one point during my career, someone at the Pentagon realized that something was wrong with this system. It somehow didn't make sense that 99% of their officers had the highest potential and were "well above standard." It sounded like the raters lived in Lake Wobegon, where all the children are above average.

The military mind has difficulty with the concepts of average and percentile. There is an apocryphal story about an Army general who asked to see a list of the weights of all his personnel. He saw that 10% of them were over the 90th percentile for the group. He instituted a weight control program to get those 10% down to the 90th percentile level, and a year later, asked for the results. Although the original 10% had lost weight as instructed, Lo and Behold!—10% of his personnel were still over the 90th percentile! So he insisted that they lose weight too. If allowed to continue, the general's program would have resulted in everyone weighing nothing.

Anyway, they realized something was wrong and ordered a quota system. Only the top people could get the top ratings. You were allowed to give them to a specified percentage of the OERs in each wing. So if you happened to have the best 10 officers in the entire Air Force working for you, you would have to downgrade 9 of their OERs. The quota system wasn't any fairer than the over-rating system, so eventually they went back to the over-rating system. But because of the quota years, an officer's record might have a very uneven showing.

This confusion was bad enough in the regular Air Force, but in the Medical Corps it was worse. Most doctors who wrote OERs for other doctors had no idea what the conventions were and didn't care. Often they didn't have any idea how the ratee had been doing his job, so the easiest thing was to ask him to write his own report. I stayed late one day to help an MD from India write his own report—I kept suggesting he write things like "the best surgeon I have ever seen" and he kept protesting that wasn't true and he couldn't say that about himself, and I kept explaining that he was expected to say those things and wouldn't get promoted unless he did. He was fighting both cultural and military conventions.

Your supervisor is supposed to give you career counseling to help you with issues like this. Good career counseling can help an officer plan the best route to promotion and job success. The only career counseling I ever received consisted of two words: "Get out."

When I finished my internship, I was given a "training report" in lieu of an OER. I didn't see it until years later. It said lots of good things about me, and ended "Her pioneering efforts have convinced us to ask for lady interns at our hospital." I guess I should be flattered that I influenced their opinion of women, but I was annoyed that they had to make a point of my sex. The report had recommended me for "career retention and specialty training," which they had blithely ignored by turning me down for the radiology residency as "not retainable."

My first OER as a general medical officer at Morón was written by a newcomer to the Air Force. He rated me 7 out of 10 overall, and 3 out of 4 for promotion potential, and the endorsing official, the base commander, commented, "Secondary to her sex she has been forced to overcome a number of handicaps to her acceptance as a physician and as an Air Force officer. She has successfully done so and in addition established good rapport with a great number of her patients and those working under her supervision." He, too, couldn't help but comment on my sex.

When I became DBMS at Morón, the base commander wrote my OER. He criticized me for not attending and supporting special activities on base; he thought my example had resulted in dwindling attendance from my personnel. I cracked up when I read the endorsement, by a major general whom I had never met, "Concur. I am not personally familiar with the daily performance of this officer, but have confidence in the commander's evaluation." Not only was that faint praise, but the commander himself was not familiar with my daily performance and had no basis for judging how good a doctor I was.

At Torrejón, my ratings varied. The first year, my supervisor was a career military man, who praised me effusively. The next year, my supervisor was Dr. Muddle, who rated me as a mediocrity, checking only the "meets standard" boxes and leaving all the comments sections entirely blank. An OER like that is the kiss of death. It was such a bad OER that the endorsing official, the hospital commander, checked the "nonconcur" block.

In my residency, I got training reports with cryptic comments like, "If her ability to relate to her colleagues improves, she will be a valuable asset …" and "Although she did not seek out opportunities for education and patient care beyond that which was expected for her, she did a commendable job while on duty." The reason for these comments is a mystery to me. I thought I related very well with my colleagues, at least the ones I respected. (Hmm … maybe that was the problem!). I had taken the initiative to organize the residents and they had unanimously elected me chief resident. We were busy enough during residency training that I can't imagine what other opportunities I was supposed to be seeking out, and I couldn't see that any of the other residents did so. Come to think of it, he could have mentioned that I had "sought out" extra training in psychiatry and liaison psychiatry, had participated in a voluntary after-hours journal club, had applied to become a flight surgeon after residency, and had obtained my private pilot's license and started working on my instrument rating during the residency in furtherance of that goal.

At F.E.Warren I started out with an excellent rating from the prejudiced hospital commander. Then Dr. Quack arrived and replaced me as Chief. He gave me ratings that were not so excellent. He said I had "worked hard in my field to become accepted," and was "learning flight surgeon duties and obligations rapidly." Which would seem to imply that I didn't already know them and hadn't performed them properly in my previous position as Chief. He also said I "needed to participate more in administrative duties commensurate with my rank." Which was pretty ironic considering that he had precluded me from doing administrative duties by replacing me as Chief of Aerospace Medicine. He said, "She wishes to remain a flight surgeon throughout the remainder of her career. She does not want to be Chief of Hospital and/or Clinical Services. Her desires should be honored and maintain [sic] the rank commensurate with the position she wants." So in essence, he was saying, "don't promote her." And his grammar was lousy.

Looking back at some of these OERs, I wonder how I ever got promoted.

When Dr. Quack finally left and I resumed my position as Chief of Aerospace Medicine, my next OER, from the hospital commander, said:

> When Dr. Hall became Chief of Aerospace Medicine, she immediately began an aggressive reorganization of the programs for which she was responsible. The Aerospace Medicine service has vastly improved under her direction. With an understaffed office, she managed to provide immediately accessible, high quality medical care to over twice as many patients as in previous years. She increased rapport with the line by assigning flight surgeons to each squadron and instituting regular squadron visits and briefings. Recognizing a potentially hazardous noise situation in the missile capsules, she initiated actions resulting in an extensive reevaluation of the capsule environment and a planned revision of Air Force noise regulations to cover a duty day of greater than 24 hours. She led the disaster response team to an "outstanding" rating on the ORI, and was commended for her command and control and the efficient teamwork of her crew. The ORI team characterized her to me as "the best we have ever seen." She organizes her time to accomplish far more than most physicians in the office, while enthusiastically pursuing out of office duties both during and after duty hours. Promote to Colonel immediately.

Apparently my pregnancy, 4 weeks maternity leave, new motherhood, and Dr. Quack's departure had magically improved my performance. At Plattsburgh my reporting official, a psychiatrist, made an astute comment:

> She does not tolerate fools gladly, an attribute that personally secure colleagues find constructive and positive; yet she is always polite and always observes the finest details of officership, professionally courteous behavior, and ethical conduct.

This implies that insecure and foolish colleagues found me irritating, but that it was *their* problem, not mine. He also stressed that I was "clearly ready for increased responsibility"—which may have helped influence the Powers That Be to allow me to finally take the flight surgeon job I'd been sent there to do—but not until the following year.

What really disgusted me was that an additional flying slot had been authorized for our hospital. It could have been filled by any doctor with wings and the doctor could have continued to do his regular job while flying 4 hours a month and earning flight pay. There were only two of us with wings, both of us full colonels. The commander offered the flying slot to the male colonel, who turned it down. He never offered it to me. The slot went vacant for several months, until the day the commander left. I could have flown on weekends with no impact on my job, and it would have meant another $370 a month in my paycheck. He was willing to *let the slot go to waste* rather than let *me* fill it. If that isn't just plain willfully malicious, I don't know what is. It still raises my blood pressure just to think about it.

The good news is that after the prejudiced commander left, my troubles were over. I don't know whether it was because as a full colonel I was too high to mess with, or because people in the Air Force were finally learning to accept women, or because the luck of the draw finally chanced to favor me. Whatever the reason, I was consistently treated fairly from that point on.

BABY STUFF

We told Kristin (now age 2 years and 2 months) that the new baby was "her" baby sister. When she came home from the babysitter's, she ran in and asked, "Where my baby? Where my baby go?" and located Kimberly before she even bothered to notice me. We told her when Kimberly got bigger, she could play with her; she bent down to look in the baby's face and ordered her, "Get big, baby!" No sibling rivalry for her! She protected her baby sister, kept her pacifier plugged in, and even learned to change her diapers (while sitting on her to hold her steady).

One night Kirk asked if he could give the new baby some Tylenol because she was running a fever. I had to tell Kirk that no, you didn't give newborns Tylenol, you treated their fever as a medical emergency. We were off to the hospital in a flash. She had a complete workup including spinal tap and was sent by ambulance to the pediatric ward of a civilian hospital across the lake in Burlington, Vermont for 3 days of IV antibiotics and close observation. It turned out to be only a virus, and she was soon back home with multiple puncture marks in her arms and scalp from IVs and blood tests. 18 holes in all; we called her the Golf Course Kid.

She did the same thing again a few weeks later, but that time she was enough older that she stayed at our hospital. The highlight of that visit was when she managed to annoint a nurse's uniform with the diarrhea that leaked out of her diaper. Again, nothing but a virus. After that, she stayed healthy.

Life was hectic with two kids in diapers. Kirk and I were both on mobility, which meant theoretically we could be called anywhere in the world at a moment's notice. We had to have powers of attorney, money on hand, and arrangements in place so that someone could instantly take over our kids if needed.

Kids could be a pain in the neck sometimes, but they were sure entertaining. Kirk learned to watch his language. One day he hurt himself and said, "Shit!" without thinking. Kristin picked right up on it and said, "S'it? … S'it? … Sit DOWN!" We learned new words like "poof tace" for toothpaste, "mirfcake" for earthquake, "mazageen" for magazine, and "ut-SUNT" for elephant. Also "bankel" for blanket—no, I take that back, Dad was the one who invented that one. We watched them learn to count "one, two, three, three, three, three." When Kim noticed the new moon she informed us the moon was broken. When we dressed for a party, Kristin was surprised at Dad's tie: she said Daddy had a ribbon on and he looked "pretty;" Mommy, on the other hand, looked "silly" in her long dress. Thanks a lot. After watching a Shirley Temple movie, Kristin wanted to see "Pimple" again. One day she solemnly asked me if I had licked the blood off her when she was born. She had seen a mother deer licking a newborn fawn on TV. I explained that no, the nurse had wiped off the blood with a towel. The babysitter toilet trained her, but one day she had an unexpected accident in the bathroom; the babysitter found out she'd been trying to pee standing up like the boys.

One day we found Kristin in her crib playing with a tiny object. She proudly showed it to us, saying, "Look, Mommy, I found a green fing!" We asked where she had found it. She said, "In my nose."

And then there was the day we overheard her talking to herself, trying to get boys and girls straight in her own mind, "Let's see now. I'm a girl. And Kimberly's a girl. And Mommy's a girl. But Daddy's not a girl. He's a boy." Short hesitation and a sigh, "Cause he doesn't know any better." Poor Kirk; he was outnumbered. When we got a cat, even the cat was female.

We weren't churchgoers, but when the babysitter kept the kids over the weekend, she would take them along to Sunday school. One morning we heard Kristin singing to herself in her crib,

> The B-L-B-I-B.
> That's the book for me.
> I stand alone on the word of God,
> The B-L-B-I-B.

She spells better now.

Like all good parents, we kissed minor scrapes and bruises to make them better. One day Kristin slipped on the kitchen floor and sat down really hard. She got up, presented her posterior to Kirk, and commanded, "Kiss my butt, Daddy!" Kirk thought quickly, kissed her on the top of the head, and told her kisses there were good for ALL OVER.

We took the kids to the base child care center while their regular babysitter was on vacation. They told me Kristin should have her eyes checked because she complained she couldn't see the TV; I asked Kristin and she explained that was because a boy's head was in the way. She came home disgusted one day because the little boy she was playing house with wouldn't let her be the father. When I picked Kim up, she came running to me yelling, "Daddy, Daddy!" The teacher looked at her very strangely and said, "That's not your Daddy." I reassured her that I took it as a compliment if she confused me with her Daddy because I knew what her Daddy meant to her.

One day I had picked the kids up at the babysitter's and was driving home, still in my uniform. Kristin, in the back seat, looked at me admiringly and said, "Mommy, when I grow up I want to be just like you." I was flattered, and was about to ask her whether she meant a doctor like me or an Air Force officer like me, when she continued, "I want to have long hair and big teeth and wear glasses."

I had to do something for recreation, and I found I could work on my worldwide stamp collection with a child in my lap and let them look at the stamps and lick the stamp hinges. One day Kristin recognized a British stamp with a picture of Queen Elizabeth and exclaimed, "Gracious socks! It's Quizzibizzibus, the King!"

The two kids next door kept us entertained too. The little girl explained that her younger brother had table manners but he didn't use them.

BACK ON FLYING STATUS

All good things come to those who wait. Finally the prejudiced hospital commander was gone and I was reassigned to the flight surgeon's office as the new Chief of Aeromedical Services. I was in my element again. It was a SAC base with an alert facility where the flight crews had to spend days and nights on alert, ready to run out to their planes and deliver nuclear bombs to the Soviet Union if the President pushed the red button. Sometimes they had to go sit in the airplanes ready to go instantly, and the flight surgeon had to drive around to the planes to check on them. Instead of house calls, I made "airplane calls" to deliver aspirin for headaches.

There was a helicopter search and rescue squadron at Plattsburgh with the same UH-1 Hueys I knew and loved from F.E.Warren. They had a hoist for picking patients up in places where they couldn't land. One day they decided to let me ride the hoist for fun. The helicopter hovered over a grassy spot, and they pointed out a flower in the grass and lowered me down so I could pick it without ever touching the ground. On the way back up, the hoist got stuck. I dangled in mid-air for a while and had visions of flying all the way back to the base like that, but they managed to fix it before I could get too worried. Another day we flew low over Lake Champlain while the rescue personnel practiced jumping out into the water; I didn't volunteer to try that!

We also had a small group of T-37 jet trainers so the copilots could stay in practice and log some pilot-in-command time. There was a parachute and a five-point harness that was supposed to be tightened up so the strap between your legs made you hunch forward when you walked. The first time I went up, we had smoke in the cockpit and had to declare an in-flight emergency and turn back to land with an ambulance and fire trucks standing by. Another time I got to do some of the flying myself, and actually landed the plane myself at the nearby civilian airport—which was really neat because my husband happened to be flying my airplane at the same time, landing at the same airport, and I heard him on the radio. I went home and told him I knew what he'd been doing at 11:03 that morning and he thought I either had spies out or was psychic. He really got paranoid when I visited the radar facility one day and tracked him on radar!

The helicopters and the trainers were just sidelines. The main aircraft assigned to Plattsburgh were the SAC alert aircraft: FB-111 fighter-bombers carrying nuclear weapons and KC135 tankers to refuel them in mid-air. The tanker was the military version of a Boeing 707 and was like a barn inside—mostly empty, and we could walk around. At the back, there was a small compartment with a sort of mattress where the boom operator could lie face down and use controls to "fly" the refueling boom into the receptacle on the receiving plane. It was fun to look out through the windows in the floor of the tanker and watch the pilots in the other plane. On one flight the boom operator was a woman and she let me try operating the controls. I told her hers was only the second job I had learned of that a woman could do lying down! I loved to lie there looking down at the scenery; we flew right over Niagara Falls one day.

The FB-111 was a swing-wing jet whose wings folded in closer to the body after takeoff to reach higher speeds. It was capable of breaking the sound barrier, but we weren't supposed to do that because it annoyed the civilian community and was hazardous to window glass. The cockpit accommodated two, side by side. The ejection mechanism ejected the entire cockpit capsule as a unit. There was a navigation computer on my side that was amazing. I could punch in the code "99" and it would figure out where we were, which direction our home base was, and would turn the plane and take us straight home automagically.

It was the only plane in the Air Force arsenal that was approved for low-level terrain-following at night. It could fly 200 feet off the ground to stay under enemy radar, and it had its own terrain-following, forward-looking radar that could see a hill ahead and pull the nose up just enough to clear it. There were 3 computers in the navigation system that all had to "vote" on what to do next, and if they couldn't agree, the plane would "fail upwards"—the nose would pull up so you'd be sure not to hit anything. Sometimes the computers would argue as we were flying along straight and level, and the pilot would have to keep forcing the nose back down.

I got to try flying formation with other planes, which was really tricky. We did midair refueling and watched the boom from the tanker come right over our heads into the receptacle. One day we flew low over the Maine woods looking for moose, and then "buzzed" a sailboat out in the Atlantic. There was no one visible on deck. I can imagine what they must have thought when they heard the roar of jet engines that close overhead. We were going so fast we were probably out of sight by the time they got up on deck. I wonder if they reported a UFO.

It cost the Air Force $10,000 in maintenance and fuel for every hour the FB-111s flew. One day we flew for 3 ½ hours. I got to taxi, fly formation, fly a PAR[1] approach, and do a touch and go landing. I realized, "They just gave me a $35,000 present that money couldn't buy, and they're even paying me extra flight pay to do it!" As far as I know, I was the only woman whose duties had ever required her to spend flight time in this particular aircraft. The pilots loved the plane dearly. One was about to retire, and he wondered aloud what he could ever find to do as a civilian that could compare with that kind of flying.

Some of the flights were long and there was no place to pee. The men carried little plastic packs with absorbent material, so all they had to do was open their zipper and point their appendage into the bag. I tried using a gadget called a Jill's

---

1. Precision Approach Radar. This is a really fun way to land, but is only available at a few military airfields. You don't have to navigate, watch your instruments, look for the airport, or do anything but follow sequential instructions. The radar operator guides you in as you descend, telling you that you are "slightly above glidepath" or "slightly to the right of glidepath" so you can make corrections.

John, a funnel device adapted to female anatomy. It leaked. I hoped no one would notice the wet spot on the seat.

There was a lot of paperwork involved with flying. They used to joke that the plane wouldn't fly until the weight of the paper equaled the weight of the aircraft.

The new B-1 bomber was a hot topic of conversation. Apparently the flight surgeons had to sit on a jump-seat where there was no way they could survive an emergency ejection; at least one flight surgeon refused to fly in it. Planes were getting so complicated and automated—there was a rumor that the next Air Force plane was being designed for a crew of one pilot and one dog; the dog's job was to bite the pilot if he tried to touch the controls.

It was cold in the winter. We were issued parkas and mukluks. Snow removal from the runways was the first priority: by the end of the winter there would be a huge mountain of snow piled up at the side of the runway, and we would make wagers on how long it would last. Sometimes even though the planes could fly, the roads on base would be too bad for cars, and they would close the base and let us stay home. After Wyoming, snow didn't bother us much. One morning Kirk had shoveled out the driveway and I was on my way to the babysitter's with the kids when they called to say I didn't have to come in. The only time I ever got stuck in the snow was when I had borrowed another doctor's car to go to the alert facility to give a briefing to the crews on alert; I spun the wheels in the alert facility parking lot and had to get help.

Once during a big exercise it got so cold we decided to close the flight line. It was 40 below with the wind chill, and we had had three flight line personnel in a row come in to the ER with frostbite. They did NOT want to interrupt the exercise, but had to bow to medical opinion. When the flight line re-opened, I spent all of one day driving from place to place in a staff car with a safety officer, checking to make sure everybody was staying warm.

MALE STRIPPERS AND ALL-FEMALE AMBULANCES

The nurse practitioner who worked for me was retiring. The nurses held a big retirement dinner for her at a local restaurant and invited me. No other doctors were invited—I guess I was considered an honorary nurse. As we were eating dinner, a good-looking young man pranced in, announced he was our stripper for the evening, and proceeded to dance, remove items of clothing, flaunt his assets (yes, *all* of them), and he even sat on the honoree's lap and French kissed her.

The chief nurse was sitting there turning fourteen shades of red and saying, "I don't believe this! I'm not seeing this! I can't believe I'm here!"

One day we got a call for an in-flight emergency. These were common and routine; we would drive a field ambulance out to the flight line, stand by while the plane landed safely, and head back to the hospital. We were rolling along, running our siren, when it suddenly struck me that there were no men on board. The two enlisted medics with me were both women and they were talking about boyfriends while I fiddled with the siren controls to make different sounds. I felt like I had entered an alternate reality. What a delightful new experience!

It occurred to me to wonder what it would be like if all the world's military were women. Would things be different? Would we be less authoritarian and more conciliatory? Would we still have wars? Oh, yeah—I guess we would; I forgot about Maggie Thatcher and the Falklands. Some women have more balls than some men.

ER

I kind of enjoyed being MOD. You never knew what was going to come through the door next, and it was a challenge. There were long stretches of boredom when the corpsmen watched MTV in the back room, and there were rushes when we were overwhelmed by too much to do at once. The dining hall closed at 6 PM and didn't reopen until breakfast, so we had no way to get food. Sometimes the techs would use a credit card to trip the lock and break into the kitchens to see if there might be something left out like peanut butter and bread. Other than that, we either had to bring food from home or order in pizza. Domino's got a lot of business from us.

Most of the doctors hated MOD but I had a good attitude about it. I didn't plan on getting any sleep, so I could be pleasantly surprised when I did. There was a call room on the medical ward, but every morning about 6 AM the cleaning staff would come on duty and would start making so much noise it would wake me up. I finally found a solution: I brought a sleeping bag and air mattress from home and slept on the floor of my office in the flight surgeon's wing. My secretary wrote the following bit of doggerel for me:

Ode to a Good Night's Sleep

Since you cannot be sung to sleep on your new tooshie cushie, this talking lullaby will have to do:

Rock-a-bye Col
On the floor sight
When the phone rings
The Doc will arise.

Up you will go
To save another body,
And down you will go
For more "hyped-up" coffee.

Now nitey nite Doc
Don't think of interruptions,
Just close your eyes and
Dream away those disruptions.

—Your Sandwoman,
Jenni

One night we were standing around the front desk of the emergency room when a bat flew in through the open door. It floundered around the hallways and finally clung to a wall. We had to call Animal Control to come and remove it.

A woman patient had all the signs of being an alcoholic, but she insisted she only had one drink a night. I finally thought to ask her how she prepared that drink. She said she got a 16 oz tumbler and filled it almost to the rim with gin and sipped on it throughout the evening.

A woman who was working in a hangar made the mistake of sticking her head out the hangar door after the power mechanism had been activated to close the immensely heavy door. It caught her head and crushed it like a watermelon. Another woman was admitted to the hospital for suicidal thoughts; she managed to convince the staff she was all right, but when they discharged her she went straight to the highest bridge in the area and jumped off. There was an investigation, but the psychologists hadn't done anything wrong. She had deliberately deceived them and they had no way of knowing her actual thoughts.

One of our most interesting patients was admitted by a colleague of mine on Christmas Eve. I made a copy of his Narrative Summary (Clinical Resume):

Kringle, K. AD/Arctic AF 0-7 000-00-0000
D & T: ELF
USAF Hospital Plattsburgh, Plattsburgh AFB, NY 12903
Register number: classified.
Date of admission: 24 December 1986
Date of discharge: AMA 0100 25 December 1986

CHIEF COMPLAINT: Frostbitten tallywhacker.

HISTORY OF THE PRESENT ILLNESS: The patient is a three hundred and eight year old supernatural being employed as a stealth sleigh driver, powered by reindeer, who comes in on Christmas Eve stating that he was coming over the northern part of the Yukon Territory and, unfortunately, the fly of his pants came open, and his member was exposed to some rather cold air flowing by at rather high velocity. Unfortunately, he did not notice right at first and attempted to slide down a chimney at which point, he then scraped his member on the edge of the bricks. He now comes in appearing quite uncomfortable, and complaining of pain in his genital area. He also noted some mild abdominal discomfort, and admits to drinking large amounts of ethylene glycol earlier this evening, prior to his trip. The patient is rather vague about his trip but indicates that he really needs to be on his way, and really just wants something for his pain.

PAST AND FAMILY HISTORY: The patient gives a remarkable lack of much past family history despite his age. He notes that about this time every year he does get rather anxious and occasionally requires some sedatives to calm him down. He also has occasional bouts with hemorrhoids, and was recently seen at this hospital for the same complaint while on a supply run. Family history is rather unremarkable, in fact, he doesn't recall that he has any family other than his wife, twenty-two elves, and eight reindeer—one who seems to be constantly bothered by a red and runny nose. He is employed as a sleigh driver for the Arctic Air Force, but fails to reveal much other detail, saying he is on a "Super-Duper Top Clearance Mission." He does claim to have recently recharged his batteries. Apparently, by that he means he had a nuclear-powered penile implant because he said even at 308 years old he still does enjoy his sexual activity, and that he just wasn't quite as potent as he used to be.

PHYSICAL EXAMINATION: The patient has a blood pressure of 168/90. Pulse is 72, and regular. Respiratory rate is 18. He is afebrile. The patient is a rather old, jolly fellow. He is dressed in fur from his head to his foot and his clothes are all tarnished with ashes and soot. His eyes have a twinkle, his dimples how merry. His cheeks are like roses, his nose like a cherry. The stump of a pipe he clenches in his teeth, and the smoke encircles his head like a wreath. He is rather short, and has a little round belly that shakes when he laughs like a bowl full of jelly. The rest of the examination is remarkable for a rather large member. It appears to have some external abrasions, and some very mild frostbite at the tip. An eerie glow seems to emanate from his left femoral region, this is apparently his nuclear-powered implant.

LABORATORY DATA: Is remarkable for an ethylene glycol level of 38.

DIAGNOSIS: 1. Frostbitten penis secondary to exposure with some external abrasions.

2. Ethylene glycol intoxication.

3. Obesity, and mild gastritis secondary to number 2 and to excessive intake of snacks tonight.

<u>COURSE IN THE HOSPITAL</u>: The patient was admitted to the Internal Medicine Service. Surgical consultation with Dr. Costanzo was obtained, who debrided some frostbitten area. Right after this, the patient became quite agitated and signed out against medical advice (AMA) stating that he had a trip which he must complete tonight.

<u>DISPOSITION</u>: The patient was advised to keep his member covered for the remainder of the trip, and that we will look forward to seeing him again next year.

Signature of Physician: William Osler, M.D.

WE CALL IT THE BOX OFFICE

For a Women's History Day luncheon I was asked to give a speech about the history of women in the Air Force, illustrated by incidents from my own career. The vice wing commander introduced me, saying there didn't use to be women in the military, but now women could be found everywhere: in the hospital, in the cockpit, and on the flight line. I stood up and announced, "Apparently no one has told Col. Goddard—when women fly, we don't call it the cockpit; we call it the box office." The audience erupted—not so much at the joke as at the fact that I had embarrassed the vice commander. I think my fear of public speaking vanished for good at that exact moment. They loved my talk. I heard later that an enlisted woman at one table had commented on my high rank and wondered out loud who I slept with to get promoted. I suppose I had been screwed, but not in the way she meant.

One day as I went through the gate and showed the security policeman my ID card, he said, "Have a good day, Sir." I wore my hair pulled back, and people frequently thought I was a man until they did a double take; besides, some people still went by the old rule that you addressed the rank rather than the individual, so I wasn't offended; in fact, I barely noticed. An hour later, he phoned me; he had figured out who I was (I was the only woman colonel on base, so it wasn't hard) tracked me down at the hospital and proceeded to apologize profusely for his mistake. A nurse I knew had been working at an induction facility when a smart aleck young recruit asked her, "Should we call you Sir or Ma'am?" She said, "Kid, if you can't tell the difference, we don't need you in the Air Force."

There weren't many women colonels at the time; I was never at a base where another one was assigned. Until 1967, the law had allowed only one female colonel in each branch of the service, and women could not be promoted to general. In 1971, Jeanne M. Holm became the first female general in the Air Force. The year I made colonel there were only 3 women generals in the entire Air Force, and only 13 in all the Armed Forces combined; most of them were nurses. I knew there were other women colonels who outranked me because their date of rank preceded mine, but I liked to think that there were only 3 women in the Air Force who held a higher rank than I did. I'd never imagined I would come that far.

People stared at me a lot. I'm sure not very many high-ranking women officers had children as young as mine. I took the kids in for a well baby checkup. I was walking down the hall in uniform with the baby in one arm and holding the toddler by the other hand; my husband was behind me carrying the diaper bag. He watched as people stared, and he stopped to tell one woman, "Yes, they're both hers."

I learned a new version of the Airborne Ranger running cadence:

> I saw an old lady running down the street
> With a pack on her back and jungle boots on her feet.
> I said, "Hey old lady where you running to?"
> She said, "I'm on my way to Airborne Ranger school."
>
> I said, "Hey old lady haven't you been told?
> Airborne Ranger School is for the young and the bold."
> She said, "Hey young punk who you talkin' to?
> Because I'm an instructor at the Ranger School!"

HOME SWEET TENT

We had a field exercise where we had to set up tents, live in them for 3 days, eat MREs (Meals Ready to Eat—the modern version of C-rations) and attend various kinds of training. Some of the personnel had never slept outdoors before in their entire life. I was the "participant commander." They set up a big tent for my group with a signboard inscribed "Hall Hall" over the door. They dug a little moat in front of the tent, with a piece of plywood for a drawbridge, and they dug up some wildflowers and planted them by the door. Home Sweet Home.

One of the training exercises involved a stretcher obstacle course. A team had to carry a patient on a collapsible canvas stretcher and negotiate fences, crawl spaces and other obstacles. At one point they would be surprised by pretend gunfire and would have to put the stretcher down and lie flat for protection. They had timed races. Someone suggested I would make a good patient, since I weighed less than practically anyone else. My team consisted of 4 very young, very athletic men. We went like the wind. They *dropped* the stretcher when the pretend attack occurred, and one of the stretcher supports collapsed. They picked it up without fixing it and kept running. I got bounced all over and was black and blue from bumping on the collapsed metal support, but my team won the race by a wide margin. Our winning time was 1:54; the next best time was 3:00.

On the last evening of the field exercise, they let us go back to the hospital long enough to take showers. We dispersed all over the building to all the available showers. I was getting tired of eating field rations, so as we entered the hospital through the ER entrance, I handed a $20 bill to the ER tech at the desk and told him to call Domino's and order me a pizza. By the time I finished my shower I had a nice hot pizza to eat on the way back to the tent. I shared.

Training was never over. I went TDY to an Aircraft Mishap Investigation course in California, a mini-residency in occupational medicine in New Jersey, and to re-take my Family Practice Boards in Boston. Becoming board-certified in Family Practice isn't enough; you have to re-qualify every 6 years. I passed with flying colors: 96th percentile.

11

Chief of Clinic Services

**Never tell people how to do things. Tell them what to do and
they will surprise you with their ingenuity**

—George Patton

I had been stationed at Strategic Air Command bases for eight years. SAC is
responsible for all our nukes and is famous for strict discipline. They told a story
about the father of SAC, General Curtis LeMay: he tried to drive a jeep past a
sentry without proper clearance and the sentry shot at him. He demoted the sentry … for missing! They say once you're in SAC you're never going to get out.
You've been "SACumcised." But fate intervened to get me out of SAC and into
MAC (Military Airlift Command).

I was transferred suddenly to McChord Air Force Base near Tacoma, Washington in 1987 on a humanitarian reassignment because my father had suffered a
severe stroke. He died within a few days, but we pursued the reassignment to be
near my mother who had also been ill with cancer and rheumatoid arthritis. That
was the end of my flight surgeoning, because McChord had an opening only for a
family practice physician. In fact, the commander had asked for someone he
could use as a Chief of Clinic Services to replace the current one, who was not
working out. Under the circumstances, the location was more important than the
job, so I accepted.

We trekked cross-country with two cars, a utility trailer, and CB radios. The
kids were 2 and 4. We packed a survival kit of toys and goodies to distract them
in their car seat confinement. When they got fussy, we used the CB radios to say,
"Pull over at the next rest stop and take your kids before I kill them!" We found a
nice house near the base in a town called Puyallup (pronounced pew-AL-up) and

settled in. We were an hour's drive from Seattle and had a view of Mt. Rainier from almost every room, and we liked it so well we are still there 20 years later.

My military flying career was over. I was in the same situation as the unhappy pilots who had been assigned to fly an LGD (Large Gray Desk). I had racked up a total of 307.5 hours in the following aircraft:

B052H	6.0 hrs
T039A	0.7 hrs
T037B	3.8 hrs
C130B	5.0 hrs
SFB111A	2.0 hrs
UH001N	9.7 hrs
UH001F	47.5 hrs
TH001F	154.5 hrs
KC135Q	50.9 hrs
KC135A	18.3 hrs
FB111A	11.1 hrs

I had also racked up quite a few civilian flying hours in my own plane and several others, including a seaplane.

Dr. Del Beccaro, the McChord clinic commander, was worried when he first met me. I wore my hair pulled back, no makeup, and I looked like a prudish schoolmarm. He wanted a new Chief of Clinic Services, but he wasn't sure if I was someone he could enjoy working with. He took me to lunch at the Officer's Club, and his first impression of me was quickly dispelled. He told a dirty joke; I told one back. That reminded him of another, which reminded me of another. Our tablemates sat back in awe as we outdid each other in telling stories of questionable taste. Sometimes we finished each other's jokes; they asked us if we'd gone to the same school or something. We were two peas in a pod. He decided I was going to be OK after all, and we became good friends.

He could have been accused of sexual harassment. He talked about sex. He told me the reason women are always patting their hair—because they don't have any balls to scratch. When I did something right he told me it was pretty good … for a woman! But I realized it's not what someone says, it's how they say it and how they act. With him it was good-natured fellowship and friendly teasing, and I gave as good as I got. He made it clear that he liked and respected me, that he appreciated my abilities and my good work. After all those years I finally had the boss I deserved. Things were looking up.

ADMINISTRATIVE DUTIES

Soon after I arrived, Dr. Del Beccaro gave me a document to read about some problem in the clinic and asked for my opinion. I read it and reported back to him promptly with a suggested course of action. He was impressed, and said his current Chief of Clinic Services, Dr. Bumble, would have dithered around for a week and still not have been able to decide what to say. Dr. Bumble was demoted to just plain doctor, and I got his administrative job.

I had never thought I would enjoy an administrative job or would be any good at it, but now that I had no option, I was pleasantly surprised. I spent half my time seeing patients, and the other half was occupied by committees, paperwork and other administrative duties. Surprisingly, I took to it like a duck to water. I discovered I had a knack for organization, could get along well with subordinates, and could actually accomplish things to improve patient care. I had an open-door policy; I could multi-task and switch gears to solve an administrative problem between patients. When someone came to me with a complaint, I saw it as an opportunity to fix something rather than as a problem to be upset about. I enlisted the rest of the staff as equals and allies, and asked them to brainstorm with me rather than ordering them what to do. I found that I truly loved my new job.

I found I could even get great cooperation from people who were not in my chain of command. I could go to the administrative clerks and they would bend over backwards to help me with whatever I asked. At one point, I asked the commander to appoint me to a health consumer panel so I could hear complaints and suggestions directly because I was the one who had the power to do something about them. He said, "That's funny. Your predecessor always said he didn't have any power." I reminded him that exercising power takes balls, which some of us had and some didn't.[1]

I began to realize how bad my predecessor really was. Subordinates would react with amazement when I made any decision. "Wow, I asked a question and I actually got an answer!" Then we realized a key to the credentials files was missing. It had been signed out to Dr. Bumble. We asked him for it repeatedly in person and in writing, and finally had to threaten him. At that point he informed me that he was "planning to make a concerted effort to look for the key next weekend." We eventually had to give up and change the locks.

---

1. There are balls and there are balls. Maggie Thatcher and I had real (psychological) balls; men like Dr. Bumble had only ineffective meat balls.

McChord had only a clinic, not a hospital. We had no inpatient beds and no emergency room. We did have ambulances for flight line response and to take patients to the ER at Madigan Army Medical Center at nearby Fort Lewis. The clinic building was an old brick dinosaur that was bursting at the seams. We needed a whole new facility, but the funds were not available. As a stop-gap, the commander arranged for a cluster of prefabricated units to be installed behind the existing building. It was fun watching the units come in by truck and be lifted onto the foundations with a crane. Soon I had a brand new office with two exam rooms and could run things my way.

I was in the unique position of having a general working for me. He was a Brigadier General in the reserves who had been hired as a civilian general practitioner. He was a bit overweight: he had been a child in the Netherlands during WWII, and had promised himself he would "never be hungry again."

Of course, I was the only woman doctor again. Women patients gravitated to me; I ended up doing a lot of Pap smears, but I enjoyed that. I saw a woman who had a small area of red rash on one side of her neck; it had been treated with steroid creams and anti-fungal remedies to no avail. I asked her if she wore perfume and where she applied it—her hand went right to the spot where the rash was, and the light dawned—she was allergic to her perfume. Even seeing patients half-time, I managed to keep my patient count around 20 patients a day. The average for full-time doctors in MAC was 19.2 at the time.

I was called to be expert witness at several courts-martial. The military justice system works under the UCMJ (Uniform Code of Military Justice) and is very different from the civilian system. Once when I was a prospective juror for a civilian trial, the lawyer asked me which I preferred. I told him it depended. If I were a defendant, I would much prefer the civilian system; if I were a prosecutor, I'd take the military system any day.

Sometimes it seemed like I spent my life in meetings. I was chairperson of seven committees: Professional Staff, Records Review/Utilization, Pharmacy and Therapeutics, Quality Assurance/Risk Management, Credentials, Infection Control, and Child Advocacy. I was a member of 9 other committees: Executive Staff, Aeromedical Council, Rabies, Library, ERAA, Key Staff, Medical Readiness, Child Development Center Advisory Committee, and Drug and Alcohol.

When I had been in my new job for seven months, we were treated to an HSMI (Health Services Management Inspection). This is like the final exam for a medical facility. A team comes in and studies every nook and cranny of your operation, and finds every little thing you are doing wrong. They are very critical and picky, but we passed with flying colors. They rated my management of clinic services as "excellent" and had some very nice things to say about me. "... performed exceptionally well in overseeing the responsibilities of SGH and the professional staff and was perceived by the entire staff as very supportive and responsive to individual situations ... regarded as a highly effective leader and a key member of the executive management team.... Instituted a number of initiatives to improve health care delivery and had improved committee organization and function markedly.... an extremely well motivated leader and manager ..." Unlike the effusive statements on OERs, praise from the HSMI really meant something; they were notoriously hard to please.

As a colonel, I got invitations to VIP community events like yacht club outings. I also got the unpleasant duty of going out on death notifications with a line officer and a chaplain. We had to drive several hours to Long Beach, Washington one Christmas eve to tell a mother her son had died in a car crash. He'd been driving the wrong way on the freeway at 2 AM. She took the news pretty well. Her first question was whether he'd been drinking (we didn't know, but it was probably a reasonable assumption) and her second question was whether the Christmas gifts she'd sent him could be given to some other young serviceman.

THE FAT BOY PROGRAM

We had a lot of patients on the "Fat Boy" program. The Air Force had strict weight requirements, and if you were found to be overweight you were monitored and required to lose at a steady rate until you reached your goal. When I was at Torrejón we used to admit problem patients to the hospital and put them on a medically supervised 200 calorie diet and exercise program, but that was no longer an option. Here's what I used to advise my patients:

(1) Keep a careful food diary of everything that goes in your mouth: food, drink, chewing gum, everything.
(2) Establish your baseline calorie intake by eating the way you normally do for a week.
(3) Cut down by 500 calories a day.
(4) If you are not losing a pound a week, keep cutting down until you are.

This method has several advantages:

(1) Keeping a diary makes people more aware of what they are eating.

(2) It self-corrects for mistakes like mis-estimation of portion size or self-deceptive under-reporting.

(3) It allows cheating. Since average calorie intake is the key, you could splurge on 1000 extra calories one day and make it up by eating 100 fewer calories a day for the next 10 days.

(4) It allows the patient to choose the kinds of foods he enjoys eating and to distribute the calories however he wants (five 200 calorie snacks a day = one 1000 calorie meal a day).

(5) It automatically self-adjusts for changes in physical activity, so if you prefer to exercise more and eat more, you can do that.

(6) It HAS to work, if the laws of physics haven't changed.

Of course, the basic plan is simplistic, and other things like adequate nutrition and psychological factors also need to be addressed. I would have the patient bring in his diary at each follow-up visit so I could see whether his food choices were healthy and so we could discuss any problems he was having. This method is simple, easy to understand, respects patient autonomy, and puts the responsibility where it belongs: on the one who is putting the food in the mouth.

Sometimes just keeping a calorie intake diary is all it takes. For instance, one of my patients had been eating a lot of yogurt because she assumed it was lo-cal diet food. She had never actually looked at the label, and was astounded to learn that each yogurt cup contained 240 calories. The neat thing was that I didn't have to "tell" her—she came in all excited to tell ME what she had discovered!

CHOLESTEROL, SMOKING, ALCOHOL, AND AIDS

The Air Force had developed a Healthy Heart program. I was appointed to give classes from their script, teaching high risk patients what they could do to lower their risk. I also ran my own Stop Smoking classes, using information I had researched myself and giving out prescriptions for nicotine gum. Among other things, I had discovered that the radioactive Polonium 210 in tobacco smoke exposes the lungs to 10,000 times the background level of radiation. Attendees would ask me if I had ever smoked and I would tell them, "No, I'm not as brave as you are. I'd be scared to death to run that risk." It seemed to get their attention.

We had to evaluate lots of people for alcohol rehab. It was Air Force policy to give everyone a second chance, and even an alcoholic pilot could be returned to the cockpit if he went through rehab and proved himself over a period of time. I saw lots of young men who were underage drinkers. They would complain that if they were old enough to serve their country and die for their country they should be old enough to drink. I would tell them that if they were old enough to serve their country they were old enough to obey its laws. The law said you had to be 21 to drink.

I liked to take an occasional drink, but I was almost paranoid about it. I would never drink if there was any chance of being called out, because someone might smell alcohol on my breath and not know whether it was from a sip of wine or a whole bottle of vodka. If the security police stopped you on base, they didn't have to do a blood test: if they smelled alcohol and thought you were acting belligerent, their judgment was enough to label it an alcohol-related incident and send you to rehab.

We started universal HIV testing and for the first time I had to tell a patient that he had tested positive for AIDS. At the time, it was practically a death sentence. All AIDS patients were sent to Wilford Hall in Texas to be evaluated and treated by the experts there; then they would return to our base to be monitored as long as they stayed healthy enough to work. We had one woman AIDS patient who had caught it from her husband; fortunately their child tested negative.

We all had to attend AIDS training classes. When I was in med school I never imagined I would hear anyone, much less a woman, stand up and talk about anal intercourse in public.

Someone came up with this list of possible slogans to promote National Condom Week:

1. Cover your stump, before you hump.
2. Before you attack her, wrap your whacker.
3. Don't be silly, protect your willy.
4. When in doubt, protect your spout.
5. Don't be a loner, cover your boner.
6. You can't go wrong, if you cover your dong.
7. If you're not going to sack it, go home and whack it.
8. If you think she's spunky, cover your monkey.
9. If you slip between her thighs, be sure to condomize.
10. It will be sweeter, if you wrap your Peter.
11. She won't get sick, if you wrap your Dick.
12. If you go into heat, wrap your meat.
13. While you're undressing Venus, dress up that penis.
14. When you take off her pants and blouse, suit up your trouser mouse.
15. Especially in December, gift wrap your member.

16. Never, never deck her, with an unwrapped pecker.
17. Don't be a fool, vulcanize your tool.
18. The right selection, will protect your erection.
19. Wrap it in foil, before checking her oil.
20. A crank with armor, will never harm her.
21. No glove, no love.

AN EAGLE WITH A WARPED SENSE OF HUMOR

I had to give the Winter Safety Briefing to the troops, and I started by saying I wanted them to be safe because if they got sick or injured it meant more work for me. And we all knew that colonels didn't like to work. I told the story of the colonel and the lieutenant who got into an argument in the Officer's Club bar. The colonel said he thought sex was highly over-rated and was about 90% work and only 10% pleasure. The lieutenant said he didn't agree; he thought it was more like 10% work and 90% pleasure. They appealed to the bartender, an enlisted man who was moonlighting there. He said, "I'm sorry to say this, but I think you're both wrong. It must be 100% pleasure, because if there were any work involved, you'd have the enlisted men doing it for you."

My jokes were not always in the best taste. I have never been afraid to call a spade a spade. I figured if anyone got embarrassed that was their problem and not mine. I didn't realize what a reputation I had until I was scheduled to speak to the Officers' Wives Club and the president asked me eagerly if I was going to tell one of my dirty jokes!

As the only woman colonel on the base, I stuck out like a giraffe in a herd of guinea pigs. I got so tired of being *noticed,* sometimes I wished I could fade into the woodwork. I hated shopping at the commissary because everyone remembered me and I couldn't remember them. A patient would come up and ask me about "those little white pills" while I was trying to pick out a ripe melon. One woman stopped me in the BX and told me all about her trip to Africa, and I still have no idea who she was. We had a club of all the full colonels on base, the Eagles, that met periodically in a club room over the Officers' Club. The names of all the members back to time immemorial were on a plaque on the wall. I was the only female member they had ever had.

I'M A MOMMY, TOO

People were always asking me if I wanted to be called Dr. or Col. I told them I had worked hard to become a doctor and had become a colonel only by virtue of putting in time, so I'd just as soon be addressed as Dr. I went to pick up the kids at day care one day and the lady at the desk called me Mrs. Hall. I was so surprised I almost kissed her. What a relief to deal with someone who didn't see me as Doctor or Colonel! I could relax and just be a mother among many.

The kids loved day care. I usually had to wait for them to tear themselves away from what they were doing before I could get them to go home with me. I never felt that they were deprived by having a working mother. In fact, I was not really cut out to be a mother; I probably would have been frustrated staying at home with them when they were little and would have made all our lives miserable. They got lots of affection and hugs from their daytime Mommies, and in the evening they got the old Mom who was just that much more able to enjoy them. Their Dad was a better mother than I was—he was patient, attentive, and he was the one who always fixed their hair.

When we first moved into our house in Puyallup, a neighbor told us there had been a black bear with a bear cub down the hill from us a couple of years before. Four year old Kristin must have overheard that, because one night she was afraid to go to sleep. She said she was afraid a bear would get into her room. I told her matter-of-factly that there were no bears around any more, and even if there were, her room was on the second story and there's no way a bear could get up there. I said if she saw a bear it would be an imaginary bear and she could zap it with her imaginary magic zapper and make it explode. We practiced pointing our index fingers like a gun and saying, "Zap! Go away, bear!" a couple of times and she went happily to sleep and never mentioned bears again.

My mother lived with us for a while, and one day she was walking in the backyard with three year old Kimberly when they spotted a dead bird. My mother didn't believe in confronting young children with harsh realities, so she told Kimberly the birdie was just resting and he would fly away soon. She told me what she had done. I despised that kind of deception. I went straight to Kim and asked, "Did you and Grandma see a bird today?" and she said disgustedly, "Yeah, him was dyin'." Grandma hadn't fooled her for a minute!

Death is a natural part of life. When their Grandpa died, we simply told the kids he had died and we would miss him, but his memory would always be a part of us. No platitudes or comforting myths about heaven. A few months later Kimberly, barely 3, reassured me, "He still lives in our hearts."

We never lied to the kids. We tried to answer even their most embarrassing questions in plain terms that they could understand. We did pretend there was a Santa Claus, but when they asked if he was real I just asked them what they thought. They figured it out pretty quickly, then demanded that we keep pretending!

Kids are so literal. One day Kirk found Kim merrily dancing around in the wading pool with her very best dress on, now sopping wet. Dad didn't want her to put it in the laundry hamper wet, so he told her to leave it out to dry. The next morning he opened the front door and there was the dress carefully laid out on the doormat beside its detachable pinafore, left "out to dry."

12

Retirement

I did that already.

—*Beverly Sills*

By 1989 I'd been in the Air Force for 20 long years, nearly half my life. It was a turning point. My commission was a reserve commission, which limited me to 20 years service. I could have traded it for a regular commission and stayed longer. I was "in the zone" for promotion to brigadier general, although I doubt if I ever would have been chosen, and I really didn't want to be. I was tired of being owned. Twenty years of the military was about all I could stand. I wanted my freedom. And I needed a vacation: my daughters were 6 and 4, and I hadn't had time to *breathe* for years. My husband had already retired when our daughters were 1 and 3. The 3 year-old had asked, "Daddy 'tired?" and we said yes, that too. Now Mommy was tired.

I left the clinic in good hands. By then, we had another woman doctor who was planning to become a flight surgeon. And a woman transferred in to take my place as Chief of Clinic Services.

I retired the day before my 44th birthday. I finally got a Meritorious Service Medal at my retirement ceremony. Instead of the 2 measly ribbons I had when I was promoted to colonel, I ended my career with a still not very impressive total of six.[1] I had decided long ago not to look for tokens of official recognition but to find my own rewards in the satisfactions of doing a good job. At my retirement ceremony, they presented me with a nice plaque but took it back again because it hadn't been engraved yet. I never saw it again. I'm actually rather glad I never saw it again, because that somehow made it a truly representative symbol of my Air Farce career.

The military has its own unique language. SNAFU is Situation Normal: All Fucked Up (or for the squeamish, Fouled Up). When someone is either retiring or getting ready to move to a new assignment, he is considered to be FIGMO, slang for Fuck It—Got My Orders (sort of like, "I don't have to care any more; screw you; I'm outa' here.") The cake at my retirement ceremony was inscribed "Dilligas—Good Luck—Col. Hall" DILLIGAS is military slang for "Do I Look Like I Give a Shit?" And I was now an ORF: Old Retired Fart. Or if you prefer, Old Retired Female.

The Cake at My Retirement Ceremony

---

1.   The Meritorious Service Medal was a reward for good performance; the other 5 weren't. They were:
     1) National Defense—for being in the military during the Viet Nam years
     2) Longevity—for being on active duty for more than 5 years
     3) Outstanding Unit—for being assigned to a unit that won an award before I arrived
     4) Overseas—for being stationed overseas
     5) Training—for basic training, which I never did. Someone had decided everyone should have this ribbon whether they had actually been through the training or not.

When a psychiatrist friend of mine retired, he said he considered his career a success because he'd never been sued for malpractice. That's a pretty sad comment on what lawyers have done to the medical profession. I considered my career a success because I'd proved those guys wrong who said women weren't retainable, I'd proved that a woman could do the job well and be accepted as an equal, and I'd had some unforgettable experiences both in the air and on the ground—and I hadn't been sued either.

When you retire from the military at 20 years, you immediately start getting retirement pay equal to half your base pay. We told the kids if anyone asked what their parents did, they could say we were both unemployed and living off checks from the government. I promised myself a year or two off, planning to go back to work at least part-time after that; but I never did. I kept so busy in retirement I wondered how I had ever found time to work.

When Beverly Sills retired from singing and became director of the New York Metropolitan Opera, people used to tell her she still had her voice and should go back to singing. She would show them a bracelet she wore, engraved with the letters I.D.T.A.—they stood for "I did that already." It was time to try something different.

Would I do it all over again? If I'd known what I was getting into back then, I might have run for the hills; it's probably a good thing my crystal ball wasn't working. My 20 years in military medicine were punishing, challenging, rewarding, discouraging, educational, and frustrating, but never dull. I wouldn't have missed it for anything, but I'd hate to be starting it all over again! On the other hand, I really wouldn't have to: the experience today would be a very different one. I ran across a woman who is currently stationed at David Grant where I did my internship and who recently graduated from the same residency I did at Eglin. I asked her if she had encountered any difficulties as a woman in medicine and in the military and she didn't even know what I was talking about.

Years after I retired, I discovered that one of my neighbors was a retired female Army LtCol helicopter pilot and former squadron commander. When I revisited F.E.Warren Air Force Base, there was a female flight surgeon in my old office. In 1970, only 7% of American doctors were women; today half the students in medical school are women. My husband's military urologist is a woman. The airlines are hiring women pilots. Women are fighting in Iraq and have been POWs and wounded amputees. Times have changed, and I like to think I played a small part in changing them. I like to think I helped win the Cold War, too. Delusions of grandeur.

We're not home free yet. In a study at Harvard, Asian American women took a math test after either being reminded that they were women or being reminded that they were Asian; those who were thinking about being women did worse on the test. It seems even women are still a bit prejudiced against women, even in the most advanced Western societies. And in some countries women still aren't allowed to drive and have to hide their face and wear a tent in public. Call me a cockeyed optimist, but I think the human race is slowly evolving in the right direction. I have hopes that things will continue to improve.

Remember the man at the flight service station who told me women aren't supposed to fly? He was wrong. Everyone can fly. Some people fly planes; some let their imagination soar; some rise high in a profession, a sport, or some other endeavor; some stand high in the estimation of their friends and family; some do the best they can to rise above a bad situation. We can all spread our wings and reach for the stars.

I have news for that man: women *are* supposed to fly. Only I would rephrase it: *people* are supposed to fly.

APPENDIX A

Little Old Lady's One-Liners

See chapter 4.

Two old maids opened a cat house. They sold 8 cats the first day.
The gigolo in the leper colony was doing real well until his business started falling off.
Cuddle up a little closer; it's shorter than you think.
All light headed gals are not blondes, by cracky!
Did you hear about the cannibal who passed his grandma in the woods?"
"I can't get over a girl like you, so reach up and answer the phone."
You can have your cousins—of all my relations I like sex the best.
The fastest 4 handed game in the world is when it slips out.
It's sure hard to be good—in fact, it's got to be hard to be good.
She was only a farmer's daughter, but she couldn't keep her calves together.
Height of passion—2 old maids playing squat tag in an asparagus patch.
She was an angel until she swapped her harp for an upright organ.
Where there's a wilt there's no way.
Speaking of thievery, what about those kisses that were snatched and vice versa?
There's a new washing powder called Fugg. If Rinso won't rinse it and Duz won't do it, Fugg it.
Did you hear about Tom, Dick and Harry? Tom's mother made him stop.
If sex is a pain in the rear to you, you're doing it wrong.
Said the fly as he walked on the mirror: that's a new way to look at it.
What causes so many divorces is the same old tale.
I used to go out with a perfect 36 till my wife came home with a loaded 45.
She believed that the way to a man's heart was through her stomach.
I drove my car with one hand and my girl friend wild with the other.
It was a typical country romance—started out with a pint of corn and ended up with a full crib.
How does a little mouse entertain his girl friend? With his mouth organ.
The over-eager bride came, walking down the hill.
She's a fine upstanding girl—and wonderful lying down too.
Many a tight nut has been loosened by a small wench.

Greater love hath no man than to lay down his wife for a friend.

No, little Audrey, a woodpecker is a bird not a Decoy.

New rule at a girl's school: Lights out at 10:00; candles at 11:00.

They fired the bus boy because they caught his finger in the dishwasher.

He bought his girl a bicycle; now she peddles it all over.

Did you know that a donut is a cookie that's had it?

She used peroxide in her bath water cause she knew that on the whole gentlemen prefer blondes.

And where do you think cousins come from? Ant holes.

Funny gal, Lady Marlboro—every time you touch her box she flips her lid.

The meanest man in the world is the one who didn't tell his wife he was sterile until after she got pregnant.

Then there was the lady who took a vinegar douche when she went to bed and woke up in the morning with a sour puss.

The young choir singer chased her boy friend all over the church and she finally caught him by the organ.

There is a new vitamin made from chicken blood. It makes men cocky and women lay better.

He took his little dream boat out in the fog and mist.

They got a half-assed tribe of Indians down in Florida called the Semiholes.

Mrs. Lovejoy named her first set of twins Adolf and Rudolf. Now she's naming her second set Getoff and Stayoff.

He spent the night with his sister-in-law—he had it in for his brother.

Why was the little boy expelled? He raised his hand to leave the room and the teacher told him to stick it out till lunch, so he did.

Have you heard about the new cereal called Snatch? You eat it right out of the box.

I'm not selling brushes, and that's not my foot in the door.

There's only one thing wrong with sex—it's so habit-forming.

She was a real estate man's wife, but she gave lots away.

What has 8 legs and a cherry? 4 barmaids and a Manhattan.

Witches don't have babies cause their husbands have holloweenies.

A WAC is a double breasted soldier with a built-in fox hole.

Definition of Predict: a month old bride who is 3 months pregnant.

Two old maids took a tramp through the woods—and nearly killed him.

If you deal in stocks, United Fruit is a good buy; they've just invented a banana that throbs.

The talkative bull—every time he saw a cow he wanted to jabber.

We've got a real muscular bull at our farm—put him on a diet so he can get into a tight Jersey.

He chased his girl friend up the tree and kissed her between the limbs.

The sexpot married a carpenter cause he was her tongue and groove man.

The way to tell if a girl is ticklish is to give her a couple of test tickles.

An old man who can still make love is a lucky stiff.

The window washer scared the boss right out of his secretary.

Meanwhile back at the oasis, the Arabs were eating their dates.

"To be bored stiff," says Ida the office idiot, "is the best way."

One of the twin beds could be called period furniture.

Song of the anxious swain: I wonder if I'll ever see my girl friend Flo again.

New book: "Sex after Death; or How to be Laid in a Coffin."

In golf, it's distance; in a cigarette, it's taste, in a Volkswagen it's impossible.

Hear about the drunk midget? He walked into the home for girls and kissed everybody in the joint.

Country breakfast: a roll in the hay with honey.

Was that musician frustrated! His flute went flat in "My Fair Lady."

The old maid found a tramp under her bed and her stomach was on the bum all the rest of the night.

Beatnik's definition of virginity: big issue over little tissue.

Do you know why an Indian wears a jock strap? Totem pole.

The farmer couldn't keep his hands off his wife, so he fired them both.

Get up off the table, Mabel; the $3 is for the waiter.

Girls, it's all right to listen to your boy friend's words of love, but don't let him fill you with baloney.

Then there was the little boy who was walking down the street with his teeny weeny waggin.

They caught him picking Miss Yale's lock and now he's doing the Jail House Rock.

Confucius say: Wife who keep hubby in dog house sometimes discover he has moved into cat house.

Have your heard about the thrifty tomcat that put everything he had into the kitty?

His family wasn't too pleased about our engagement—especially his wife.

I've got the most beautiful wife in the world—the trouble is, her husband wants her back.

The sultan had 10 wives—9 of them had it pretty soft.

She was really a smart girl. She could play post office all night without getting any mail in her box.

You know, you should never argue or fight with a lady; just dicker.

She was an atomic mama—blown up by a guided muscle.

Then there was Judy, the juvenile delinquent. She got kicked out of school for doing pushups in a cucumber patch.

She said she would do anything for a mink coat; now she has it and can't button it.

Rectal specialist: a super duper pooper snooper.

The latest love ballad: I used to kiss her on the lips but it's all over now.

He got 10 years for pumping Ethel behind the station.

Sex is bound to be popular—it's got such a central location.

It wasn't the hen or the egg that came first—it was the rooster.

The rooster got caught in a rain storm, so he made a duck under the barn.

This crazy mixed up Indian couldn't tell heads from tails; he kept bringing home scalps with holes.

I lost my girlfriend; I forgot where I laid her.

A basketball player makes a poor husband; he dribbles before he shoots.

Man who fishes in other man's pond may catch crabs.

The old maid got tired of using candles, so she called the electrician.

He goosed a ghost and all he got was a handful of sheet.

She was a pregnant skeleton; she didn't have the guts to say no.

The honeymooners wanted to fly United, but the stewardess said no.

He took me to a vacant house, and was I floored.

APPENDIX B

Captions without Cartoons

Over the years I collected medical cartoons from various sources. Here are a few of my favorites.

1. Two little girls looking into a trunk. "This is my hope chest. So far I have a stethoscope, a prescription pad and an appointment book."

2. Woman at reception desk in doctor's office. "I didn't call first, because whenever I do make an appointment, the symptoms disappear."

3. Woman doctor to anxious patient, "Take off your clothes and stop worrying. To me you're just a patient, not a man."

4. Two little boys see woman doctor leaving her office with a bag of golf clubs. "Wow! She IS a real doctor!"

5. Woman to clerk in pharmacy, "What do nine out of ten WOMEN doctors recommend?"

6. Doctor with double-headed stethoscope, "It's the new stereo model."

7. Woman to doctor who is listening to her chest with a stethoscope, "How can you hear me with that thing in your ears?"

8. Doctor to obviously pregnant patient, "You missed step no. 2 which says take the suppository out of the aluminum foil."

9. Child getting undressed for doctor, "Does this mean I have to assume the lithotomy position?"

10. Mother to small son, "Of course you have to go to college. You want to marry a professional woman, don't you?"

11. Cinderella to Fairy Godmother, "Would you mind sending me to medical school instead?"

12. Little girl to father, "I think it's time we had a talk about sex, too, Daddy. Shall we start with the heterosexual aspects first?"

13. Little girl to little boy, "Let's play doctor. I'll be the M.D. and you blush a lot and try to say things that will make you sound like an open-minded patient."

14. Woman doctor to male patient who is visible only from the back, "Very nice, but I said your *tongue*, Mr. Jones, stick out your *tongue*."

15. Tobacco company executive to graveyard full of headstones, "Thank you for smoking."

16. Woman to doctor, "One more question. If exercise kills germs, how do I get them to exercise?"

17. Patient tells doctor "I suffer from nagging aches and pains." There are balloons coming out of his joints saying "Stop eating junk" "Lose weight." "Sit up straight." "Get shoes that fit." "Learn to serve a tennis ball properly."

18. "The patient had been spilling sugar for some time." (Patient sitting up in hospital bed emptying sugar container onto tray and bed.)

19. Woman to doctor, "Thank goodness I'm sick. I'd hate to feel this bad if I were well."

20. Doctor hits patient's knee with hammer; patient's false teeth fly past doctor's head.

21. One doctor to another, looking at wall of framed diplomas, "That one's my lawn mower warranty. I put it up to see if anyone really notices."

22. Child to professional woman coming home, "Mom—what's a housewife?"

23. Man in bed with ice pack on head, talking on telephone, "What do you mean you don't make house calls—I'm your husband!"

24. Mother reading bedtime story to little girl, "Jack and Jill went up the hill to get a pail of water. Jack fell down and broke his crown—and Jill bandaged it up and later became a famous doctor."

25. Woman at cocktail party, "No, I'm not a WOMAN doctor ... I treat both sexes."

26. Fully clothed child with naked mother, doctor and nurse. "Remember dear, you promised. Now it's your turn."

27. One doctor to another, "Well, none of these tests gives an answer ... guess I'd better go examine the patient."

28. Woman clinging to chandelier above exam table. Doctor says, "Aha! It's a little tender there, isn't it?"

29. Doctor angrily pointing to his diploma where it says "therapist" and sign painter who has just painted "the rapist" on his office door.

30. Patient in hospital bed. Doctor tells nurse, "I've given him vitamins A, B, C, D, E, F, and G, and he still looks like H."

31. Doctor to nurse, "I had a dream last night that I was locked in solitary confinement on Devil's Island ... and Mrs. Popavich tunneled in for an examination."

32. Psychiatrist to patient, "Nonsense! You certainly don't have a split personality! Zero divided by two is still zero!"

33. Elderly woman to doctor, "I don't mind being a senior citizen. What worries me is graduation."

34. Nurse to 2 patients in waiting room, one of whom has an ax embedded in his head, "Who's next?"

35. Doctor reading from book in front of patient, "Here we go! Step one: take off your shirt."

36. Doctor examining patient with sunflower growing out of his anus, "You're eating too much fiber."

978-0-595-49958-8
0-595-49958-9

CPSIA information can be obtained
at www.ICGtesting.com
Printed in the USA
LVOW03s2325280118
564397LV00001B/58/P